MEZZA ITALIANA

Zoë Boccabella

MEZZA ITALIANA

An enchanting story about love,
family, *la dolce vita* and
finding your place in the world

ABC
Books

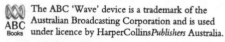
The ABC 'Wave' device is a trademark of the Australian Broadcasting Corporation and is used under licence by HarperCollins*Publishers* Australia.

First published in Australia in 2011
by HarperCollins*Publishers* Australia Pty Limited
ABN 36 009 913 517
harpercollins.com.au

HarperCollins*Publishers*
Level 13, 201 Elizabeth Street, Sydney NSW 2000, Australia
Unit D1, 63 Apollo Drive, Rosedale, Auckland 0632, New Zealand
A 53, Sector 57, Noida, UP, India
1 London Bridge Street, London, SE1 9GF, United Kingdom
2 Bloor Street East, 20th floor, Toronto, Ontario M4W 1A8, Canada
195 Broadway, New York NY 10007, USA

National Library of Australia Cataloguing-in-Publication entry:

Boccabella, Zoë.
 Mezza Italiana : an enchanting story about love, family,
 la dolce vita and finding your place in the world / Zoë Boccabella.
 ISBN: 978 0 7333 2954 8 (pbk.)
 Boccabella, Zoë.
 Italians – Australia – Biography.
 Immigrants – Australia – Biography.
 Australian Broadcasting Corporation.
305.851094

Cover design by Natalie Winter
Cover images of eucalyptus leaves, key, coffee beans, red beads, gold picture frames, Italian stamp, lemons, olive branch, wine cork and back bottom right photo of Italian street from Shutterstock. Remaining images courtesy Boccabella family.
Author photo on back flap and front top left by Roger McCarthy
Internal design by Natalie Winter and Zoë Boccabella
Typeset in 10.5/15.5pt Minion by Kirby Jones
Printed and bound in Australia by Griffin Press
The papers used by HarperCollins in the manufacture of this book are natural, recyclable products made from wood grown in sustainable plantation forests. The fibre source and manufacturing processes meet recognised international environmental standards, and carry certification.

For my mother, Sandy
1948–2008

To my ancestors who bravely emigrated

E al mio caro marito, Roger

CONTENTS

Recipes

'By what sweet charm I know not the native land
draws all men nor allows them to forget her.'

Ovid (Publio Ovidio Nasone) *Born in the Abruzzo, 43 BC*

Prologue —
The Earthquake — 3.32am, 6 April 2009

Nestled in a hollow on the side of *Monte Circolo*, the village sleeps. Centuries-old stone houses huddle up next to each other. Doors are closed tight. The bells in the turreted church tower are still. From the castle ruins on the mountain peak above, the cobblestoned village laneways glisten like a spidery web under the moonlight. Fossa's streets are deserted, its inhabitants tucked up inside. It is spring but it is still cold. An owl cries out, its wings flapping a muffled beat as it flies over the village and heads back to the nearby forest. Streetlights glow a dim orange, lighting up the wall of the church. A cat disappears through a hole cut out of the bottom corner of a stable doorway.

Inside one house, the wall clock ticks loudly in the kitchen. It is almost half past three. The buffet hutch is crammed with glasses, crockery, jars and some bottles of olive oil. One of the glasses trembles ... just for a moment, ever so slightly. In the living room framed photographs, books and collected treasures clutter a marble-topped chest of drawers. Next to it stands an armoire crammed with folded linen, the door creaking slightly ajar. The thick walls of stone and smooth white plaster enclosing centuries of my family's belongings and memories stand solid and protective.

Suddenly a thunderous jolt slams into the house. The foundations shudder and tilt, deep cracks scribble up the walls. Chunks of plaster dislodge and fall, breaking into dozens of pieces as they hit the tiles. The kitchen buffet hutch topples over. Jagged shards of glass and ceramic splay across the terrazzo floor. The stone walls groan and waver, threatening to topple. It is too much for the ceiling of one room; it detaches and smashes down onto beds below. A few lichen-splotched terracotta tiles follow, shattering, and opening the house to the elements.

On the peak of the mountain, the castle ruins rain down stone bricks on the village below. Part of the mountainside buckles and dislodges, gathering momentum as it slides towards the houses in its path. Mammoth boulders break away and tumble down, crushing small cars parked along the road above the village and hurtling through roofs. They leave a path of splintered trees and deep craters. The river flows backwards, and then the concrete bridge cracks and implodes. There is a sound like a blustery wind but there is no wind. It is the trees in the forest being brutally shaken; some crack and fall.

The deep, resounding thunder and violent thrusts of the earthquake last an eternity to those caught initially in the vulnerability of sleep. Arms are held over heads; some huddle underneath furniture, others cry out or are shocked into muteness, many take their last breath. Then the *terremoto* stops. For a moment there is an awful silence. Darkness is complete. And then, tiny sounds of tentative scrabbling, whimpers and calls for help.

In a moment when all feels lost, the strength of the human spirit can soar.

Antique Linens

'*Buon Natale*, Zoë.' A determined Nanna Francesca pulls me down to her height and kisses both my cheeks (she is four foot something and formidable).

I try to get away with kissing just one of hers, wishing she would say 'Merry Christmas' like, I presume, everyone else in Australia is. For a tiny woman she is strong and holds me firmly to her ample bosom for the second kiss.

Even at thirteen, I can be just as determined. 'Merry Christmas, Nanna.'

'I've told you! Call me Nonna!' she wails, as though mortally wounded.

'Nanna is more Australian.' This, I reason, is where we live after all.

'*Mamma mia!*' She throws up her hands and launches into a tirade of Italian directed at my father.

He nods and makes soothing noises, giving me a look over the top of his mother's head as if to say, 'Can't you just humour her?' But when she isn't looking, he gives me a wink.

On the outside, my grandparents' house looks like a traditional, if somewhat neglected, Queenslander: painted white with a rust-coloured corrugated iron roof. But when you step inside the hallway, you walk down plastic-covered carpet into a lounge room cluttered with reminders of Italy. Pressed copper plates from the Abruzzo region share wall space with framed wedding photos, maps of Italy and a picture of a mountain village covered in snow. In the sixties, my grandparents sheathed the original VJ walls in sheets of fibro painted with white high gloss for a 'fresh, clean look'. The lounge suite is not covered in plastic like the carpet. Nanna Francesca has hand-sewn floral cotton slips to protect the leather-look vinyl. She removes these only when very important guests come to visit, certainly never for family.

Nanna Francesca's glass-fronted cabinets are crammed with cocktail and hi-ball glasses, gold *espresso* cups, coffee pots, ceramic swans and heart-shaped trinkets. The swans and trinkets are *bomboniere*, each originally containing five sugared almonds, and are from the weddings of couples now celebrating milestone anniversaries. Framed photos fight for space on top of the glass cabinets; there are so many that several pictures are obscured from view including, thankfully, one of me in primary school with a gap between my two front teeth. (My father had a gap between his two front teeth at the same age prompting my grandfather to nickname him *zanna*, which means tusk or fang.) The only concessions to the frames are a chiming clock from the thirties and the *pièce de résistance* — a garish gold plastic miniature of the Vatican, which fascinated me when I was a child. It has tiny windows that glow red when Nanna Francesca plugs it in (only she is allowed to touch it). In one of the windows smiles the face of Pope John Paul II.

It is the mid eighties and my first teenage Christmas. I am hoping for the latest Madonna record or a frosted-pink lipstick. Nanna Francesca thrusts a present into my lap.

'For your glory box,' she says before I can begin to tear at the paper.

I pull out a tablecloth, which is to be the first of a burgeoning collection, and smile a rehearsed 'Thank you'. My voice sounds a cheerful octave higher than usual.

Decades later, the same tablecloths adorn my wooden kitchen tabletop. It is now me who places the settings and carries forth from stove or oven the dishes that my ancestors once cooked, creating a few of my own along the way. All my life my family has gathered around the table — faces young and old creased in laughter or strained in hot debate. The table was the stage for the dramatic ebbs and flows that made up decades of family life. Tablecloths varied according to hostess — Nanna Francesca's checked or floral cottons, my mother's purple cloth for Easter or my Australian grandmother's practical plastic at their beach house. Even the most beautifully starched and ironed white damask tablecloths would end up like a Pro Hart 'cannon' painting after one of our extended family meals.

Purple splotches where red wine had toppled when someone leant on the table to pull their chair in, the odd gravy smear, creamy flecks of Parmesan and crumbs, lots of crumbs ... we mostly ate crusty bread.

My mother came to use mainly white cloths after years of perpetual stain removal. 'You can toss it in the wash with bleach afterwards. White is easier,' she would say. Candle wax was best removed with a blunt butter knife after a stint in the freezer. And cloths that had become worn from years of use had holes lovingly darned.

It took me a while to appreciate the role of the tablecloth. For a long time they remained disappointing presents from Nanna Francesca 'for my glory box'. To me they represented the life of an 'Italian Mamma', a good little Italian girl who would marry and have children and spend the rest of her life cooking and caring for family — things that as a teenager I had no desire to get trapped into. I was as stubborn in resistance as Nanna Francesca was in inducement. As a little girl, I was the daughter my grandmother never had, but in my teens, we clashed.

Nanna Francesca was quite traditional, with a great love for the Italy she had left behind in 1934. She had curly hair which she brushed into thick waves and skin that turned deep mahogany under the Australian summer sun. Her dark brown eyes were the smaller almond shape that hints at the Arabian influence in southern Italy. She had a glare that could burn through steel, which we dubbed her 'Calabrese' look. An Italian dressmaker made all her dresses. Each one came to a length just below the knee. Nanna Francesca teamed them with

8

sensible low-heeled shoes, matching handbags and, in times past, matching gloves and hats. She despaired at my wearing jeans or *black* (for her, only for funerals or when in mourning). Even though by then it was the eighties, I could not get away with wearing black until I was over sixteen. And, as for when I dyed my dark hair blonde when I went to uni ... '*Santa Maria!*'

Even my grandmother's Christian name is an Italian custom, though Nanna Francesca's birth triggered some heated family debate. Her father wanted to follow the Italian tradition of naming the firstborn daughter after the paternal grandmother, his mother. However, Nanna Francesca's mother wanted to buck tradition (perhaps since her own name was Francesca) and name her daughter after her own mother, Soccorsa. This delayed the lodging of her birth certificate and consequently her date of birth was submitted as 19 February, though we always celebrated her birthday on the actual day she was born, the twelfth. In the end Nanna Francesca was named after his mother, Francesca.

Her father's protestations over the name must have been heroic to ultimately bring round the indomitable Carrozza women (short, stout and strong). From what my grandparents and my father have told me, I understand that in most other issues my great-grandfather Domenico was quite laid-back. He was a slim man who liked to play the guitar and chain-smoke roll-your-own tobacco. When he immigrated to Australia, Nanna Francesca initially remained in their Calabrian seaside town of Palmi and continued living in a small house with her mother and maternal grandmother, a time which she described to me as one of the happiest of her life. I smile to think of the three females living contentedly there together, two with the same name — Francesca — a name that, as the firstborn daughter of my generation, could have been mine.

Growing up, I was secretly glad that my parents had not called me Francesca (my mother was not Italian so perhaps she felt no obligation). Part of me now feels a little sad this naming tradition stopped with my generation. (That said, I love that my mother had had the name Zoë picked out since she was thirteen, eleven years before I was born.) For many years, I have been the only one in our Boccabella line without an Italian Christian name. However, the significance of the name Francesca became more apparent to me when I first saw my great-grandmother's monogrammed linens.

Nanna Francesca kept her precious family linens locked away in a cupboard in a darkened room of her Queenslander. I never saw her use them. She said that her mother brought them out to Australia in a *baule* — a huge glory box — along with blankets, kitchen utensils, crockery, and 32 litres of olive oil in tins. Tucked in this glory box, the linens travelled in the hull of a ship from Naples across oceans and seas, on a train from Sydney to Stanthorpe, by horse and cart to Applethorpe and later by ute to Brisbane.

To run my fingertips gently over the embroidered initials of my great-grandmother, Francesca Carrozza, fills me with wonder. The pillowcase they adorn has aged to the colour of tea-stain but to me it is infinitely precious. Did great-grandmother Carrozza embroider these initials herself, or had her mother or even her grandmother stitched them for her to add to her glory box? This question can never be answered. I become conscious of how precious family history is. The past of my ancestors has sculpted my present. But it takes me a long time and several significant journeys back to Italy for me to really comprehend this …

I grew up in the Brisbane people called 'a big country town'. The term is overused now and in reality it was a city, nothing like a rural town, but it was certainly quieter than it has become. Suburban life had an unpretentious naiveté and old-fashioned ambience. Shops shut for the weekend from midday on Saturday, the alcoholic drink of choice was mainly the local beer, and 'exotic' food pretty much meant Chinese, the Greek café or Italian, and many Anglo-Australians even looked at these askance. It was the notorious 'Joh' era, the nineteen-year reign of a dictatorial Queensland premier whose government and police force became embroiled in corruption. Outside observers often considered Queensland to be a police state and many of the locals to be 'rednecks' or unsophisticated in their thinking. This fostered a mindset where one strove not to stand out or be different. And yet, just as my grandfather was born under Mussolini's fascist regime, I grew up in this climate and adapted, knowing no other way.

I remember standing up in front of the class in primary school when it was my turn to present a project on an overseas

country. I had really wanted to do Egypt but my parents —
both high school teachers — convinced me to do Italy.

'We've got so much stuff on Italy at home,' Mum said.

'You'd be silly to do it on anything else,' chimed in Dad.

I didn't want to hurt their feelings but I had done my 'food'
project on Italian cuisine and, with reservations, my 'capital
city' project on Rome, but this time I had really wanted to
learn about those pyramids. Sniggers rippled through the
classroom as I unrolled the piece of cardboard and held up my
project revealing a map of Italy, the bottom of the cardboard
stubbornly trying to curl back up. The part that made me most
self-conscious was that my parents had insisted I mark on the
map where my Italian grandparents were born.

'That's not part of the project!' I had protested in alarm.

'It's a lovely additional piece of information, don't you think?'
Mum said it in that bright voice that made it hard to argue.

'You should be proud of your heritage,' Dad persisted.

When I sat down after the presentation, a girl sneered,
'Typical, another wog project from the wog.' I felt my cheeks
turn a flaming pink and I vowed no matter how hard I had to
fight my parents I would never do another project on anything
remotely Italian again.

In the playground, a boy spat biscuit in my face before
running off and yelling, 'Wog!' On a different occasion, a
boy tipped chocolate milk in my schoolbag and said my kind
should go back to where we belonged, which confused me — I
was born in Australia. Another time, a girl cried, 'Dirty wog',
and spat on me. I took out the little hankie Mum always tucked

in my pocket and carefully wiped the spit from the front of my Catholic school uniform, making sure I got my tear-filled eyes under control before looking up. I did not say a word and was not about to give anyone satisfaction by crying. Mum told me 'sticks and stones ...' but I envied her having grown up with an Anglo-Australian name and looks.

Of course not all the children at school made hurtful comments. There were others, like me, on their own private bi-cultural journeys. I also had a firm circle of Anglo-Australian friends, several of whom cheerfully nicknamed me 'Bocca' and asked me to teach them to twirl spaghetti onto a fork. Sometimes I had slices of salami on my sandwiches, which drew attention, other times I had egg and lettuce. Many days were sunny, but some days shadows were cast by those who, from a young age, had learnt to malign anyone without a 'pure' Anglo-Australian heritage. Unfortunately, there was the occasional teacher who acted the same.

My Italian grandparents, Nanna Francesca and Nonno Anni, were no strangers to the sort of thing that was happening to me at school. When I was younger, Nonno Anni was actually 'Grandpop' to me, which he sent up, by crowing, 'Bampop'. At the time 'Nonno' was already taken by my great-grandfather Vitale, who was alive for most of my first decade. I did not call Grandpop 'Nonno' till adulthood. He did not insist on it like Nanna Francesca did (which probably made me want to defy her even more).

Back in the fifties, after Nonno Anni had closed up his shop in the city late one evening, he and my father (then in his early teens) were walking back along Wharf Street when a bloke heard my grandfather talking in his heavy accent and sneered, 'Bloody wog.' With one swift punch Nonno Anni had the bloke on the ground and another bloke backing off. Nonno Anni was a big man, over six feet, tanned, broad, and muscular from years of hard work. (He got his height from his grandfather Demetrio who was around seven foot.) My father told me that, as they walked away, Nonno Anni said to him, 'What does "wog" mean?' When Dad explained, Nonno Anni said, 'I knew from the tone of his voice it couldn't be good.'

Anni means 'years' in Italian but I do not call my grandfather, Nonno Anni for this reason. He shares the same name as Hannibal, considered one of the greatest leaders and military tacticians of all time, who held back and defeated some of Rome's best armies for seventeen years before his own army (including the elephants) faced annihilation around 203BC. Hannibal was regarded as charismatic, cunning, illustrious and articulate. My grandfather could be described in the same way.

It is curious that my great-grandmother Maddalena decided to bestow upon her firstborn the Italian version — Annibale — of this uncommon name. Maddalena dispensed with the Italian tradition of naming a firstborn after their paternal grandparent. Looking back, my own mother did the same thing, despite pressure from Nanna Francesca, who had also resisted naming her sons after her parents-in-law. It seems all the women in my direct line were strong, spirited individuals unafraid to buck tradition or expectation, and yet they all followed the Italian custom of not giving any of us any middle names.

Nonno Anni's hazel eyes crinkle in the corners when he is being cheeky (fairly often) or flash fire in anger. His hands are the most enormous I have ever seen. One hand can easily cover a tumbler of wine. His was a journey that took a peasant boy across four continents to end up a wealthy owner of real estate in Australia, a prominent leader in Brisbane's Italian migrant community, and the recipient of a British Empire Medal, in part for helping other Italian migrants to make the transition to the Australian way of life. He travelled to Australia on a boat called the *Remo* in 1939. Nanna Francesca had made the journey five years earlier on its sister ship, the *Romolo*. Like the fabled Roman twins, Romulus and Remus, my grandparents were destined to live their lives together (albeit with a happier ending).

Some years after arriving separately in Australia, my grandparents met in Stanthorpe in southeast Queensland. Nonno Anni had spent his first three years in Australia alternating work on farms with cutting cane, then in December 1941 he got a job on a farm in Applethorpe which neighboured Nanna Francesca's family property. Nanna Francesca caught his eye when he saw her riding along on her pushbike while running errands to nearby farms. He was then eighteen and she fifteen. They met at a gathering at one of the farms but her father would not let her dance with Nonno Anni because, as my grandfather curiously told me, 'I was a stranger, a stray, you see. Somebody with different eyes.' Nanna Francesca added more matter of fact, 'It wasn't like he was the son of a friend or someone we knew.' Just a few months later Nonno Anni was interned as an enemy alien and taken away to Millmerran. It was not until towards the end of 1942 that he was brought back to the Stanthorpe area to work on a road gang at Pikedale from Mondays through Fridays. On weekends, the internees were permitted to help out on local farms as long as they returned before curfew to be counted. Nonno Anni requested to work on Nanna Francesca's family farm.

Six months later, he was granted a month's leave in June 1943 to marry Nanna Francesca. However, the local Catholic priest refused to marry them, saying he wouldn't let that 'poor girl' marry an internee. When faced with this injustice, Nonno Anni's attitude became 'Right. I'll show *you.*' He took Nanna Francesca to Brisbane and they married in Saint Stephen's Catholic Cathedral. Due to finances, farm commitments and it being wartime, Nanna Francesca's father was the only relative able to attend. (Nonno Anni's father had been interned in a different camp and they didn't see each other for several years.)

During their Brisbane 'honeymoon', Nonno Anni ran into an old friend who got both my grandparents jobs as wait staff with him at the Astoria Café. (Nanna Francesca, just seventeen at the time, insisted she be paid the same wages as the men, and amazingly the owner agreed.) Nonno Anni found he much preferred working in Brisbane, where they could earn a lot more money, so they eventually settled there. The only reason he got out of returning to the enemy alien camp at the end of his leave was because his friend urged a certain doctor (who ate all his meals at the cafe *gratis*) to provide a medical certificate advising that Nonno Anni should remain in Brisbane. Nonno Anni said he had no idea what they officially put on the certificate but it worked. He was allowed to stay, so long as he provided the police with several photographs of himself and regularly reported in at the police station.

The one time I told Nonno Anni about the taunts I was getting at school he was instantly protective. 'I can't believe this sort of thing still goes on. I didn't think people used words like "wog" anymore.' (It was the late seventies and early eighties.) 'Next time, they call you that, you punch them.'

'*Annibale.*' Nanna Francesca shook her head. 'Zoë, come here and help Nonna make the pasta. Don't listen to him. You just ignore them.'

'That's what I do, Nanna.'

'*Nonna.*' She corrected automatically as she finished rolling out the pasta dough. 'Good girl. Now get the broom.'

I retrieved the broom and balanced it across the back of two wooden chairs I dragged into place. Nanna Francesca clamped the pasta machine onto the bench and cranked the handle, winding the pasta dough through several times until it was of sufficient thinness. Then she put it through the fettuccine setting and I gently took the strands at the other end and hung them over the broom to dry. I could just imagine what certain kids at school would say if they could see me doing this.

In my final year of primary school, the class put on an end-of-year play. 'This year we're doing "Christmas Around the World" to show how different countries celebrate Christmas,' the teacher announced, eyes shining. As the teacher gave out the parts I chewed my nails praying that what I suspected was about to happen didn't. 'And in Italy …' the teacher declared, almost bursting with smiles, '… they don't have Santa Claus, they have a *woman*.' Comments and guffaws erupted from the class: 'Gee, that's strange!' 'A woman instead of Santa? Weird!' The teacher pretended to ignore these and continued, 'She's called *Befana*, and is a bit like a witch and brings lumps of coal to the naughty children and sweets to the good. The part of *Befana* has been given to … Zoë.' I didn't know many swear words at that age but I remember the couple I did know popping into my mind, *Bloody shit.*

By my teens, I had so come to begrudge my Italian heritage that I strove to hide it. I even dyed my dark hair blonde to 'look more Australian'. It got on my nerves when Nonno Anni talked incessantly of 'home' — the village of Fossa in the central Italian region of the Abruzzo where he was born.

'You've been in Australia for fifty years,' the belligerent teen in me would counter. 'Why do you still call Italy home? Australia is home.'

Shaking his head, he would wag his finger at me. 'You must go to Fossa. You *must.*'

And being the rebellious teen I was, I vowed I would never go to Fossa, even though Nonno Anni still owned the house in Italy that had been in his family for centuries. Almost all the family, including my parents and sister, had gone over and stayed in the house at some point. Nonno Anni and Nanna Francesca went for six weeks during the northern hemisphere summer *every* year. But I held out, despite the cajoling, the threats, the offered payment of airfare. I held out until I was twenty-three years old.

> *'Everyone has the obligation to ponder well his own specific traits of character. He must also regulate them adequately and not wonder whether someone else's traits might suit him better. The more definitely his own a man's character is, the better it fits him.'*
>
> **Cicero (106–43 BC)** *Roman author, orator and politician*

Recognition

I met Roger when I was twenty. I was very much a 'city girl' and he was originally from a small country town. Roger's Anglo-Celtic heritage and conventional upbringing were a long way from the customs and drama of mine. He struck out for Sydney when he was eighteen and we met in Brisbane five years later. I found him to be irrepressible, sharp and spontaneous, with a confidence both endearing and challenging. Despite our growing up almost 1200 kilometres apart, we shared inherent values, sensitivities and traits of competitiveness, along with aspirations for 'something different' in life, even if perhaps then we knew not what.

Though he knew very little about Italian culture, he was

open-minded and eager to embrace new experiences. Not that I was instantly revealing of many of my family's Italian traditions. For years I had effectively kept under wraps from friends things like 'tomato day', the Italian club, weddings with 500-odd guests, and the many quirky customs of Italian culture. It was quite a while before I even let on that we still had a family house in Italy.

Roger was the only person I ever took to my Italian grandparents' house. At home, I could ask my parents to tone down Italian stuff when friends or boyfriends came over, but with my grandparents nothing was ever 'toned down'. I watched with trepidation as Nonno Anni instantly pressed a stubby of beer into Roger's hand and talked loudly in his heavy Italian accent. Nanna Francesca cried, 'Roger, you're too thin, you should *mangia, mangia!*' Roger looked to me for a translation and I explained she wanted him to eat more. To my surprise and relief, Roger adored them. He rose to the occasion eating Nanna Francesca's cooking like a lord and joining in with the rest of my ever-burgeoning, lively family. I could almost see him being warmly enshrouded in the comfortable cloak that is an extended Italian family. Roger's dark eyes were shining with merriment and I relaxed slightly. Afterwards he told me how he loved the family, the food, the noise and the music. I relaxed more. Then he commented on the plastic covering the hallway carpet, saying he had never seen that before. (The plastic had been there my whole life and I had reached the point I didn't even notice it.) I smiled and nodded but squirmed inside.

Roger and I had been living together for almost three years when we decided to go backpacking around Europe. (Nanna Francesca only tolerated our unmarried cohabitation by telling me that now I lived with Roger I would have to marry him. She promptly bought us a Kenwood Chef Mixmaster as an engagement present, despite our having no marriage plans.) Yet even though I was going to Europe, I continued resisting Fossa.

'I might get there,' I responded irritably to the repeated pleas from the Italian side of the family. 'It's hard to get to without a car.'

It was actually my mother who took me aside and said that I should make the effort to get there, that I should try to discover my heritage or I would regret it later on. She even drew me a map in the back of my blank travel journal before I left so that I could find the house among the labyrinth of village laneways. As much as I did not want to admit it (being in my early twenties I thought I knew it all, of course), my mother was wise in quietly and calmly encouraging me to go. Deep down seeing Fossa was something I needed to do and was long overdue.

Mum, Nanna Francesca and Nonno Anni farewell Roger and me at the international terminal. I will see my grandparents when they come to Fossa for the European summer as they do every year but it will be a long while till I next see Mum. Carrying my pillow, I turn back just before I board the plane to see the three of them standing there. Mum with her flames of red hennaed hair, Nonno Anni so tall, Nanna Francesca so short. Always a crier at farewells, I taste the salt of my tears.

With youthful doggedness, Roger and I travel together through twelve different countries across Europe, all the trials and tribulations ultimately strengthening our friendship, as well as our partnership. It is five months before Roger and I cross the border into Italy on a train travelling from Nice to Pisa. At the French–Italian border the train halts and uniformed men climb aboard carrying machine guns. In my young mind, they resemble 'the Gestapo'. When their attention turns to me, I hand over my Australian passport, too timid to use my Italian one. I have visions of them barking at me in Italian and becoming suspicious if I cannot confidently reply. My Italian surname sparks the interest of one of them anyway. Hopefully, I reply to his question satisfactorily in Italian. I cannot read his smile as he moves on through the carriage.

The rail trip melding the French and Italian coastlines provides an arresting introduction to the country of my heritage. The train bursts in and out of tunnels, revealing stunning vistas every time darkness abruptly gives way to daylight. I blink and take it all in, just as curious about the sight of a woman leaning out her window hanging washing onto a line as the luxurious boats bobbing in a marina of the Italian Riviera. It is as the train pauses at the station of San Remo, the seaside town that shares its name with the song festival and my father, that I begin to feel the first inklings of a connection with Italy.

In Pisa, I have barely stepped off the train when a bird dropping lands with a massive splat on my shoulder (supposedly 'a good sign' according to Italian folklore). Roger doubles over with laughter. Again he laughs when the plain cheese pizza I thought I had ordered appears covered in furry-looking anchovies, which I detest. For my tenth birthday party, Nanna Francesca arrived at my parents' house with several anchovy pizzas. My friends took one bite and stampeded to the bathroom to spit it out with cries of disgust. I did the same but, thinking back, I wish I could have put my grandmother's feelings first or she could have realised my young Australian friends might not like anchovies.

Now that Roger and I are in Italy, I am really looking forward to having a coffee in an Italian café. I gaze longingly into an ambient little bustling *bar*, feeling the blast of warm air in the doorway, hearing the whoosh of the coffee machine, the clatter of ceramic *espresso* cups and the clunk of change in the till. But Roger will not accompany me inside.

'I don't drink the stuff,' he shrugs. 'You go without me if you want.'

I don't. Instead, I am quiet as I bite back my disappointment. So far on our trip Roger has only been interested in drinking different beers in every country, refusing wine and now coffee.

I am beginning to wonder, with trepidation, how he will respond to Italian life in my grandfather's tiny, remote village. I find a phone box and ring the house to say I am on my way to Fossa.

'We thought you'd get here weeks ago!' Nonno Anni bellows accusingly into the phone. 'Where have you been? We'll be going back to Australia soon.'

I feel regretful that I have delayed coming but I am so self-conscious having Roger with me. It is one thing for me to take him along to my grandparents' house in Australia; it is quite another to have him share close living quarters with them in my ancestral village home.

Roger and I arrive in Rome to see our connecting bus pulling away for the ninety-minute trip to L'Aquila, where Nonno Anni will be waiting to pick us up. Desperate, I stand in its path. Fortunately the bus driver stops (a rare concession) and lets us board. As we pause in traffic, I find myself looking down at a small crowd gathered around the prostrate body of a middle-aged man. From my seat high up in the bus, it appears his lifeless blue eyes are staring towards me. It is the first time I have seen, in the flesh, someone who has died. I reflect that indeed the soul or *something* has left the body. The bus lumbers on as I ponder the unexpected news his loved ones will soon receive. Italy has me on my toes.

On the way to L'Aquila, I watch the changing scenery, unaware that my place of origin is about to have its way with me. I am looking forward to seeing my grandparents but remain somewhat reserved about the actual village. In my youthful arrogance, I have doubts about how exciting a tiny village with a dwindling population of 500 people can be. Approaching the border to cross from the region of Lazio into the Abruzzo, my interest stirs. I am about to enter the region where my grandfather comes from, where his parents came from, where my ancestors have lived and died for many centuries.

Three generations ago, two of my great-grandfathers arrived in Australia from different parts of Italy — the Abruzzo and Calabria. My Abruzzese great-grandfather, Vitale, first came to Australia via France in the 1920s. In exchange for his passage, he shovelled coal on the ship *Ville de Verdun* for the voyage from Marseilles to Melbourne. Times were tough for Italian peasants of this era, with farming yielding very little money. More than half of the entire population of Fossa immigrated to Australia or to North and South America between the twenties and the fifties.

Amazingly my great-grandmother did not hear about Vitale going to Australia until she received a letter he wrote from Melbourne. Until then, Great-granny Maddalena had thought he was still in Europe. Vitale managed to find some work in Victoria, but after several years the Great Depression forced him to return to Italy. Had a woman back in Fossa not mentioned that her husband was making good money cutting cane in Queensland, my great-grandfather may never have returned to Australia in 1932. Vitale cut cane in Ingham, and worked on farms around Stanthorpe in the alternating seasons.

By the late thirties, he had sent for his eldest son. At fifteen, my grandfather, Nonno Anni, was off to Australia to join a father whom he had not seen for almost ten years. Europe was on the brink of war when Nonno Anni hugged his distraught mother goodbye, climbed onto the back of a horse-drawn cart, and watched the stone house where he was born, and his father before him, fade into the distance. Uncertain if he would see his mother, his little brother, Elia, or Fossa again, he left a part of his heart behind. By doing so, whether consciously or not, he maintained a connection with Fossa that would permeate the lives of his future family, my life.

Family history and ancestral links have an instinctive pull. Almost sixty years later, I travel for the first time to a place that I may never have visited in my life otherwise. Fossa sits up among some of Italy's highest mountains. Roger pronounces the name of the region almost like 'Arrbuzzo' (as in bee), and I explain it is said in the same way as 'brutal', the double z hard like a t and a z together — *Arbrootzo*. The Apennine Mountains have long stood sentry to the region, isolating it from tourists, development and cultural dilution. Being one of the little-known and least-visited regions in Italy, the Abruzzo is known to have the most untouched mountains and woods of Europe and is regarded as the 'virginal' region: like a young virgin shut up in a tower she has been protected and coveted, her charms untouched.

As we cross into the Abruzzo, the change in ambience is perceptible. The gentle, bosky hills and cultivated fields peter out in the face of imperious mountains. The Abruzzo is the stuff of fairytales — castles surrendering to the elements and dark forests that still resonate with the enchantment of snake charmers, werewolves and witches. Rising arrestingly from the Adriatic Sea, the highest peaks of the Apennines, *Gran Sasso* and *Maiella*, are capped with snow, even in summer. Deep valleys and woods hide huge brown bears and roaming packs of wolves. The sheer, grey mountains tower like the walls of a mammoth fortress hiding all they encompass. No drawbridge is welcomingly lowered.

Entry is through dungeon-like tunnels that pierce the rock. Sometimes we drive in semi-darkness for several kilometres, guided only by an orange glow akin to lantern light. We emerge surrounded by towering rocky outcrops, and speed over perilous, teetering bridges whose pylons plummet into a deep gorge carved out by a river. I glimpse a flash of silvery water far below. We swiftly plunge into another long tunnel and are spat out again, the bus dwarfed by the shadows of the mountain peaks.

I peer up at towns built of stone the colour of sand. Clusters of houses perch on rocky pinnacles, threatening to slide hundreds of metres into the valley below. For every fairytale contains a dark element. The mountains are picturesque and hold still lakes that reflect the deep green forests and snowy peaks, but the area is no stranger to the ominous thunder of earthquakes, the sorcery of the ancient *Marsi* tribes and the bitter, freezing winds that blast the landscape in the dead of winter. I am entranced. It is as though the Italian blood in me has suddenly surged with recognition and I am powerless to resist the magnetic pull that this place has on me. The bus lurches along a mountain road, one side of which plunges to a deep ravine below. Gradually the forested mountainsides of tall pines, chestnut trees and huge Adriatic oaks merge into a valley of orderly vineyards and farms cultivated by the Abruzzese people for centuries. *And this is where my family originated.* I suddenly wonder how Nonno Anni had been able to leave.

A series of houses and shopfronts lining the road indicates the bus is coming into L'Aquila. Despite the warm day, I notice all the locals are smartly dressed in long trousers or dresses. I glance down at my scruffy shorts and unironed T-shirt with a chocolate stain on it. Five months of living out of a backpack and my main clothing concern has become whether I can wear something for the third day in a row. The bus winds its way past the department store *Standa* and I glimpse the colourful markets in L'Aquila's main square, *Piazza Duomo*. With a loud wheeze, it halts near *Fontana Luminosa* where I immediately spot the comforting figure of Nonno Anni. I step off the bus straight into his waiting arms. As he envelops me in a huge bear hug I feel the familiar scratch of his whiskers on my cheek.

'I'm so happy you're finally here,' he says. 'The last of my grandchildren to come here. Now I can finally relax.'

I cannot find any words to reply and simply hug him back ... hard. Nonno Anni wipes away spontaneous tears and swiftly smooths back his hair. He turns and holds out a huge paw to shake Roger's hand. Then he picks up both our heavy backpacks as though they weigh no more than a handbag and bundles us into a taxi he has waiting.

We speed towards Fossa. Nonno Anni and the taxi driver speak in rapid Italian dialect. Occasionally Nonno Anni interrupts the conversation and switches to English to point out different landmarks, or vineyards he once worked. We drive through villages too small to appear on most maps. The taxi struggles up the steep ascent into Fossa, its engine straining as it navigates the narrow snare of village laneways laid with stone long before the invention of cars. As we drive past the *piazza*, a group of villagers all turn to stare. Bells are clanging loudly from the church *campanile*. The taxi lurches to a halt at an awkward angle and the muttering taxi driver jerks on the handbrake.

Nonno is triumphant. 'We are home!'

I smile but I am thinking, *home?*

The church bells continue to toll for a funeral, so we start our visit speaking in a half-shout. A few villagers not attending the funeral come to have a better look at Roger and me. They keep pointing and seem to stare at my bare legs. I presume they are just surprised to see a new face but I feel self-conscious. (At five foot one — and three quarters — I don't have endless legs.) Roger's eyes seem to be sparkling. He has a huge grin on his face, as if he *is* home. I see Nanna Francesca peering from the doorway with her dark, suspicious look. When she sees me, her face brightens and she pulls me down to her height and kisses both my cheeks. For the first time in my life, I readily kiss both of hers instead of one.

'Hello, Nanna.'

'Nonna,' she automatically corrects. 'Come in. Come in.' Her face darkens again. '*Mamma mia,* did people see you dressed like that?'

I look down. Admittedly I am a little scruffy but not indecent.

'*Madonna mia!* Cover your legs. No one dresses like that here.'

I barely have time to change into a pair of jeans before Nanna Francesca is bellowing from the kitchen, '*Vieni qua! Zoë! VIENI QUA!*'

She is turning spicy, fat sausages as they crackle and spit in the frypan. 'Set the table,' she says, beckoning to a wooden drawer of cutlery and a stack of plates in the buffet hutch.

Nonno Anni and Roger sit having a drink. Inadvertently, I double-take at the foreign sight of Roger savouring red wine. I set the table while the men relax. It reminds me of being about twelve and ranting about how unfair it was that Nanna Francesca and I should have to wait on Nonno Anni and other male family or friends.

'Why do I have to help while they get to sit on their bums and eat and talk?' I complained loudly as I trailed Nanna Francesca into the kitchen, noticing out of the corner of my eye Nonno Anni's brother, Elia, nearly choke on his mouthful of pasta.

Throughout their married life, my grandparents had an arrangement that was Nanna Francesca's suggestion. When they moved into their Brunswick Street house in the fifties, she told Nonno Anni, 'Now, I look after the inside of the house and you look after the outside.' Having been born during the rise of the Women's Liberation Movement in Australia I have never been able to understand Nanna Francesca's seeming contentment to serve in her 'traditional' role.

But suddenly, in Fossa, I am feeling magnanimous towards Nonno Anni. 'Do you want to sit at the head of the table?'

He roars with laughter, almost spilling his tumbler of wine as he slaps his leg. 'There is no head of the table here! There is leg, but no head!'

I smile ruefully. *Who is being the old-fashioned one now?*

When we are sitting down to eat, Roger comments on the thickness of the stone walls of the house and how cool it keeps the interior. Pointing to a long, horizontal steel pipe that runs the length of the room before plunging into the foot-thick walls, he remarks, 'It must have been a big job putting in the water pipes.'

'Earthquake-proof rods,' Nonno Anni says around a mouthful, taking a sip of wine and continuing eating without looking up.

Roger's eyes widen slightly but he says no more. Curiously, although I already know these earthquake-resistant rods are there to help absorb tremors and prevent the house from collapsing during a *terremoto*, it doesn't occur to me that this house could be really in danger from a quake.

After we mop up the last of the sausage grease from the plates with bread, I head to the kitchen and reach for a tea towel, but Nanna Francesca shoos me away from the sink. 'Nonno is waiting out front for you. He wants to show you around the village. Hurry now.'

Nonno Anni's face creases in smiles when I join him. He leads me out to *Piazza Belvedere* and we lean on the railings taking in the magnificent view of the Aterno Valley. Nonno

Anni straightens and takes a big breath. He slaps his chest, encouraging me to take some deep breaths of the pure mountain air with him. We walk back down through the village. More people emerge to see 'the foreigners' and I am grateful my legs are now covered. Nonno Anni introduces me to different people who eagerly kiss both my cheeks. For the first time in my life, I have a sense of regret for my stubborn refusal to continue learning the Italian Nonno Anni started to teach me when I young.

While I was growing up, right through my teens, I often stayed at my grandparents' house on weekends or in my school holidays. At breakfast Nanna Francesca would plonk a fried egg in front of me with a piece of white bread to dip into the runny yellow yolk. Nonno Anni had usually already eaten Cornflakes followed by toast and would be sipping a coffee and reading the paper, his hazel eyes enormous behind his reading glasses as the clock ticked loudly. When he finished, he would fold the paper in half, put it to one side and teach me Italian.

'You know what this is?' he would point to my glass of water. '*Acqua*. Go on say it.'

'*Acqua*.'

'Good. *Bene*. And this.' He would point to the basket of sliced bread. 'Bread. *Pane*.'

'*Pane*.'

Nanna Francesca would fetch the milk out of the fridge and place the glass bottle on the tabletop. '*Latte*.'

'*Latte*.'

'And cheese ...'

'It stinks!' I would crinkle my nose. Every time the fridge door opened at my grandparents' house, a waft of cold air carried the strong smell of *Parmigiano*.

'The cheese you don't like,' Nonno Anni would muse, 'is *formaggio*.'

'*Formago*.' I always struggled a bit with that one.

'No. *Formaggio*.' He would carefully enunciate the phonemes.

'*Formaggio*.'

'Right, now show me how you can count to ten again.'

'*Uno, due, tre, quattro, cinque ...*'

Back then, I was four. By grade two, I had become reluctant to participate anymore. I had started at a new school and quickly learnt that it was important to blend in with those who, it was pointed out, were more Anglo-Australian than I was. Until then it had never occurred to me that my name and family background differed from the majority.

Many years later, when my young cousin, almost fifteen years my junior, sat at the kitchen table practising Italian by reading *La Fiamma*, Nonno Anni turned to me and said, 'See how obedient she is? You should have learnt like this instead of fighting me all the time.'

That hurt. Unlike my much younger cousins, I grew up before 'Tuscan mania' hit Brisbane, when tea was drunk more widely than coffee, when footpath dining was non-existent; before Italian food, decor and culture became chic and appreciated. Like a View-Master reel stuck on a click between the previous picture and the next, I knew I needed to press on, and yet it wasn't easy. Before I even knew the word existed I was part of a 'diaspora' — a large group of people (in my case Italian-born) who migrated from their homeland for personal, financial or political reasons. Despite assimilation and resistance, when born into a migrant community there is often a natural compulsion to want to explore the 'mother country' eventually. Perhaps I was a little afraid to discover that part of my identity because it worked against years of trying to 'fit in' and be 'an everyday Australian'. For me, being in Italy was more than a journey through a foreign country. It required looking inward and examining a past that was influencing the present. I was yet to even admit it to myself, but perhaps part of my trepidation was knowing this journey was going to change my future.

Tutto Placido

Nanna Francesca and Nonno Anni return to Australia, leaving Roger and me alone in the Fossa house. Unbeknownst to us at the time, Nanna Francesca has told all her older village friends that Roger and I are brother and sister rather than have the 'scandal' of us staying together alone and unmarried. She has also made up two single beds that she insists we sleep in during our visit, and out of respect for her we do. Roger decides to go for his daily run and receives astounded looks from some of the older villagers. A ferocious black dog chases him down a laneway and I bite back a smirk, still exasperated with him and his continued refusals to accompany me to a *bar* for a coffee. Instead of the strong coffee made by a *barista* that I crave, I am forced to raid my grandparents' giant tin of International Roast (which they bring to Italy from Australia each year) and I don't even drink it in Australia.

Alone in the house for the first time, I wander through the rooms. The kitchen — *cucina* — is an eclectic mixture of past and present. For heat and cooking there are the original fireplace, a wood stove, and the most recent addition — an oven with a stovetop combination of three gas rings and one electric. Interlinked ockie straps hold shut the door of an old squat, brown fridge. A small wooden table and the top of the washing machine double as spots to prepare food. The walls of the *cucina* are two-tone, the top half white, the bottom, a pale lemon. The large, rectangular ceramic sink is divided into two deep, square bowls. On the wall, a bouquet of drying bay leaves hangs next to an out-of-date calendar. Nailed across the inside of the wooden front door is a wool blanket to keep freezing winter air from penetrating the cracks.

The spacious tiled living room, which doubles as the room where Roger and I sleep, is imbued with the lingering scent of charred wood from past fires. A cold draft sweeps down the chimney and over the hearth. I instinctively adjust the makeshift firescreen that doesn't quite cover the empty fireplace, like a frustratingly short blanket on a cold wintry morning. A pair of cross-country skis hangs above the fireplace. On another wall dangling from a hook is a pan to roast chestnuts, its base bearing the distinctive holes. A wide, flat spade for shovelling snow leans near the doorway. The windows are so clouded inside with dust and soot from village chimneys outside they are barely transparent. I clean each one and am met with gorgeous views over the haphazard rooftops of the town, and of the peak of *Monte Circolo*.

The original house had three rooms — a kitchen, a bedroom and a living/storage area. Ablutions were of the 'jug and basin' variety, and the toilet was the stable down the lane until Nonno Anni added a bathroom and tiled the floors when he and Nanna Francesca started coming back here regularly. The tiled floors and white foot-thick walls give the interior cool, still air like that inside a cathedral. Because it was originally a family home and not a holiday abode, the house has everything one would need — furniture, crockery, sheets, books, fridge, TV, sewing basket, pens, paper, tools and hardware, even family photos. (After they migrated to Australia, my great-grandparents' house was lived in by Serafina, a relative who was a spinster. It wasn't until her death that Nonno Anni and Nanna Francesca began coming regularly to stay.)

Nanna Francesca's mania for buying towels is evident from their particular abundance. I hope that even the incongruous tea towels featuring Queensland beaches and the Big Pineapple, which Nanna Francesca brings over from Australia, always remain and are treasured as part of her history, of her time here. I wander between the three rooms, looking, sometimes brushing a chair or a picture with my fingertips. I have a sense of being just one small fragment passing through time. Many have gone before me, and many will come after. The thought is both sobering and humbling.

Whenever we return to the house, Roger and I often discover a little gift waiting on the kitchen table for us. First, it is a basket of fresh eggs, then some tiny bottles of red bitters. On another occasion, it is two small tubs of ice-cream, the kind that comes with a little wooden stick to eat them with. The ice-cream had not yet started to melt. We had missed our mystery benefactor by minutes. Roger and I always lock the door when we go out, so whoever it is has a key. This makes me suspect it is Placido — a distant cousin who has lived his entire life in the village. He watches over the house when it is empty.

Though I have never laid eyes on him I know Placido is a forty-something bachelor who lives alone and works in a factory. His house is the only one in Fossa — perhaps in Italy — with a Hills Hoist clothesline that some cousins, who had immigrated to Melbourne, brought back on one visit. I have been told he is shy and quiet and mostly keeps to himself. When my grandparents have rung from Australia over the years, often a dozen unanswered calls are made before they can get on to Placido. I am touched by his unexpected gifts. Placido does not speak English so I write a thank-you note in Italian and leave it on the kitchen table. Another basket of eggs appears. The note looks untouched. I hope Placido read it.

Nonno Anni rings one day to say that Placido wants to have dinner with Roger and me. It is a quirk that the invitation in this tiny village has come via Australia.

'He'll pick you up at a quarter past seven tomorrow night,' says Nonno Anni.

I tell Nonno about Placido leaving the eggs and other little gifts.

'Oh, he's got his own chickens,' Nonno says matter-of-factly, as though someone you have never met leaving presents for you is the most natural thing in the world.

Roger and I are dressed and ready to go before seven. We sit at the dining table playing cards until we hear a car pull up. Both my parents and grandparents have instilled in me that it is the height of respect to always be ready and to arrive on time. Without waiting for him to knock, we go out to greet Placido. I take one look at his huge lopsided grin and like him instantly. We shake hands in greeting. Placido's hand is warm and dry. He has carefully combed his dark hair over his balding pate. His nose looks too big for the rest of his face and his dark eyes appear both kind and mischievous. He motions for us to hop into his minuscule old Fiat *Punto*. Roger climbs through the front passenger door to squeeze into the backseat. Placido jumps in. The cabin fills with the scent of his aftershave, a pleasantly fresh and spicy cologne with a hint of pine. Sitting in the front with Placido I reach for the seat belt.

'No, no, *no*,' Placido laughs, waving dismissively at the seat belt.

I interpret his rapid explanation as something like: *No one bothers with seat belts around here.* He does a donkey start and halfway down *via del Pallio* the Fiat splutters and lurches into life. At every turn or intersection we come to, Placido has a habit of winding his window down and then up again. I want to turn and exchange glances with Roger, but it would be too obvious. I smile broadly at Placido, whose return grin is wider.

'Australian driving!' he jokes in Italian, swerving onto the opposite side of the road.

We laugh a little uneasily as we fly across the width of the valley in the wrong lane. Along with seat belts, Placido doesn't believe in speed limits.

For a pre-dinner drink Placido takes us to the little town of Pagánica, the very last town in the area to be converted from Paganism. (My great-great-great-great-grandmother Maria Rosa Cincis came from Pagánica before she moved to Fossa after marrying Croce Boccabella in the early 1800s.) Darkness is falling and along with it the temperature. Placido swings open the glass door to a *bar* and stands aside for us to enter. It is filled with people, warmth, the roar of conversations, Italian soft rock music and clinking glasses. Cigarette smoke hangs in the air. We manage to squeeze into a spot at the counter and Placido orders different aperitifs for each of us. Mine is bright red, both bitter and sour, and I deduce it is Campari and soda. I have no idea what the others are drinking.

Back in the Fiat, Placido's inclination to wind his window down and up at every turn or intersection continues. The road begins to climb. We have no idea where we are going apart from 'up'. Placido becomes silent. The lonely mountain road is dark. We do not encounter any other cars. Surely there cannot be a restaurant situated so far out of the way up here. The bitumen abruptly ends and we skid and bounce along a dirt track. The headlights on the dirt road seem to be the only light for miles. I have visions of being taken to some remote spot and murdered. I turn around to Roger who raises his eyebrows.

With a smile on my face, so Placido does not register my unease, I say to Roger in English, 'Where do you think we're going?'

Roger laughs a little shakily. 'Do you think this is definitely Placido?'

Having never met him or even seen a photo, my overactive imagination pictures the real Placido turning up late to our house in Fossa and scratching his head at our absence, unaware we've been whisked away by an impostor. Placido looks at me and laughs, a little crazily. The pitch-dark track becomes worse, with huge potholes that cause the Fiat to shudder and buck. I have to hold onto the handle above the passenger side window.

'Ow!' Roger has hit his head on the roof. I turn to see him sitting in the middle of the back seat with both arms up, palms flat against the car ceiling.

Placido hoots, 'Hey! Four-wheela driving!'

The track becomes so narrow that tall grass brushes the sides of the car, obscuring any view that could let me see where we might be. Then suddenly the track turns sharply left and opens into a clearing. There is a dirt carpark with half a dozen cars already there and, behind it, a charming little restaurant that looks as if it has been lifted straight out of the Swiss Alps.

Roger and I crawl out of the miniature Fiat, feeling both shaken and a little silly. Placido is bouncing with enthusiasm.

He guides us into the dark wood-and-stone chalet, and, considering his easy banter with the female maître d', is obviously a regular. She has shiny, thick black hair that brushes her shoulders as she walks. Her small black eyes are as sharp as her tongue appears to be. In jest, she gives Placido a hard time, then has a go at a burly man sitting at one of the tables we pass. She has eyes only for the men.

We have barely sat down on bench seats at a long wooden table when she taps Roger on the shoulder and wants to know his name. She immediately changes it to its Italian version and grabs his arm.

'*Ruggero, vieni con me.*'

Why she wants Roger to go with her, we have no idea. Placido nods encouragingly, motioning for him to go. She leads Roger through the restaurant and out the back door and they are gone. I return Placido's smile to hide my bewilderment and gaze around the restaurant, which is about one-third full. The walls, floor and furniture are all made of wood the colour of maple syrup. Voices and noise become louder, bouncing off all the hard surfaces. Roger returns carrying a bottle of wine and Placido lets out a cry of delight.

'That was amazing,' Roger says as he sits back down. 'She took me outside where there is a shallow, running stream at the back of the restaurant. Dozens of bottles of wine are lying in it being kept cool. She told me to pick the one I wanted, and then she reached in and got it out of the water.'

The restaurant, called *La Trota*, is known for its fresh trout caught from the nearby mountain streams. The antipasto of roasted bread, tiny pieces of trout and white beans is drizzled with olive oil. Steaming bowls of pasta with trout come next. Then, with a gleam in her eye, the maître d' presents Roger and Placido each with an entire trout. By now I am all 'trouted out'. Worried that I have not eaten enough, Placido arranges for a large piece of fried *scamorza*, the local cheese, wrapped in prosciutto for me. I am already feeling full but don't want to be rude and struggle through it. A big wooden bowl of salad is placed between us all.

At the end of the meal, the perfect skeleton of a trout lies across Placido's otherwise empty plate. On Roger's plate there is a jumbled pile of bones strewn everywhere. He is discreetly trying to pick his teeth with his bitten-down nails. When the black-eyed maître d' clears the table she takes one look at Roger's plate compared to Placido's and bursts into laughter. Placido gives Roger a friendly slap on the back.

Before we leave I really want to see the stream with the wine bottles in it and excuse myself from the table to go to the restrooms, which are in a separate little wooden hut out the back. I close the restaurant door behind me, muting the noisy conviviality of the dining room. I am enveloped in the cold quietness of the mountain. Most of the surrounding peaks are thousands of metres above sea level. It feels high up where I am standing and yet we must only be at about a third of the height of the *Gran Sasso d'Italia* (the Great Stone of Italy), which looms nearby at close to 3000 metres.

The splash of flowing water draws me to peer into the narrow running stream. Under the intense moonlight, I see the bottles of wine lying on a bed of smooth rocks that gleam beneath the surface. Dark forest looms but I am not afraid. I breathe in the crisp air, my exhalations creating a hazy vapour that hangs for a moment. I come across an ornate spout tapped into an underground spring shooting forth a constant stream onto smooth mossy stones. It is numbingly cold under my hands, pure and clear — I drink deeply.

I realise I was always going to come to Fossa. I just wanted it to be of my own volition, not because I was being forced to go. Coming to Italy for the first time feels foreign, and yet familiar. I am not sure I want to admit it to myself — let alone anyone else — but it *has* been a kind of 'homecoming'. There is a paradox in coming 'home' to a place I have never been before. And yet, being a descendant of Italian migrants, I have been brought up with so much family folklore, stories and facts about Italy — the 'mother country' — and so many elements of its culture including food, music, books, paintings, photos, film and religion, that it has always been a major part of my life. Nonno Anni and Nanna Francesca, in particular, made sure of that. For so long have I been suppressing who I am that I feel I no longer know my true self.

Our little party is very merry during the trip home. Placido insists we make a detour to L'Aquila for *gelati*. Between gestures, our limited Italian, a bilingual barman and the English–Italian dictionary I brought along, the three of us have managed to converse and have a wonderful evening. When he drops us back at the house, I kiss Placido's cheek. He blushes deeply. As he drives off, the Fiat strains into a roar, bucking up the hill like a spirited pony.

I have found Placido to be gregarious company, nothing like the quiet, shy, reclusive portrait that had been painted. Roger and I are both keen to replicate the evening, but, strangely, we do not set eyes on Placido again. He returns to his life as a virtual hermit. We venture up to his house. It is all closed up and our knocking goes unanswered. I feel a little sad and tell Nonno Anni so.

'Ah, that is Placi's way.' I can almost see Nonno Anni's expansive shrug at the other end of the phone. He actually finds our evening with Placido hard to believe.

I often look for Placido when I am out and about in the village. He is an enigma. I recall our friendly suggestion that he come and visit Roger and me in Australia and his head-shaking smiles and dismissive hand-waving in response. He proclaimed it was too far, though I also detected a hint of fear in his eyes. Perhaps my ancestors' mammoth journey to the other side of the world has impacted upon my direct family line in that we have all become travellers. And yet, I know Italians in Australia who have never ventured back to Italy, including my own great-grandparents. It was Nonno Anni who inspired in all his offspring a desire to undertake the long journey. Despite my resistance and reservations and fears, it is a journey I am so thankful I decided to take.

'The real voyage of discovery consists not in seeking new landscapes but in having new eyes.'

Marcel Proust (1871–1922) *French novelist*

The Castle

The Castle Ocre perches atop an escarpment, looming over Fossa like a ghost ship sailing upon the eddying mists that sometimes encircle the mountain peak. I am looking forward to taking a closer look since it has featured many times in Nonno Anni's stories. The castle sits directly above the village, the sheer cliff face, almost 250 metres high, forcing Roger and me to walk the winding back roads up to the citadel entrance on the other side of the mountain. It is about a twelve-kilometre round trip. The final kilometre leads us up a snaking lane of chalky white rocks, some like gravel, others the size of cricket balls. We jump across deep crevices where melting snow washed away some of the lane in spring.

Most of the hills in this area are speckled with faded, crumbling castles. For me, there is an undeniable enchantment about castles on mountaintops. They conjure up childhood fairytales and imaginings of being a princess. This notion is dispelled once storybooks are replaced with history books, in which castles are associated with barbaric raids, boiling oil, despotic rulers and some of the most blood-soaked episodes in history. Many Italian towns originated when people made their homes near or within thick, fortified castle walls for their livelihood and protection. This occurred particularly after the fall of the Roman Empire. Barbarians swept through the area around Fossa, devastating towns and forcing the people to take refuge within the outer walls of the castles and monasteries built on higher land.

The early frontiers of the Abruzzo were marked by the precipitous mountains, not by any political lines on maps, and *Castello d'Ocre* was an integral component in the region's defence and safety. This castle above Fossa dates back to at least the twelfth century. In a formal Papal document, or Bull, from Pope Alessandro III, dated 1178, it is stated that this castle was the property of the Bishop of Forcona Pagano. For the next five centuries the castle was resided in and fought over by royalty and religious, until Andrea Bonanni purchased it for 16,000 ducats on 3 May 1626. The Bonanni family lived in the castle until 1806 when they lost their firm grip on the feudal system that kept the villagers, including my own ancestors, in relative poverty.

At the outer gates of the grounds, Roger and I slip through gaps formed by erosion near the supporting stone pillars. The lane narrows to a dirt path overgrown with feathery bushes and the odd overhanging branch, which we brush aside. We cross an arched stone bridge. I notice the sky is beginning to fill with bruised-looking clouds, which makes the grounds feel even more forbidding. The castle stands remote and silent in the gloom. There is not another soul around. As we draw closer, a huge shadow cast by the high outer castle wall swallows us.

Since Garibaldi's men attacked the citadel more than a hundred years ago, *Castello d'Ocre* has crumbled to at least half its size. It once must have been an impressive and intimidating sight, soaring atop the cliff face, some days rising above the clouds, visible from L'Aquila in the distance. Nonno Anni told me of a deep well inside the castle into which the accused were routinely thrown to die and rot. With such grisly goings on within the walls, and the foundations sinking into an ancient burial ground, the bleached ruins are as much bone as rock.

Nonno Anni's grandfather Demetrio, who was twenty-three at the time, witnessed first-hand the attack to liberate the castle from the Papal States in 1870. Nonno Anni's grandfather told him about it and my grandfather then told me. Growing up, I loved hearing the stories of Garibaldi's men hiding in the forest as explosions and fires weakened the castle, giving the soldiers a chance to storm it from the forest. Nonno Anni told me that when Garibaldi's army breached the stronghold, 4000 people inside were massacred. The unofficial version is that the Papal soldiers defending the castle were either sympathetic to Garibaldi's cause or their ranks had been infiltrated, because a number of explosives were detonated from *inside* the castle before the army, hidden in the trees, attacked.

At the imposing castle entrance we are halted by a tall gate of iron bars sporting sharpened ends and held firmly closed with a padlock and chain. We peer up at the castle walls, too high and sheer to scale. Roger rattles the gate but it remains steadfast. The gate bars run both horizontally and vertically; however, in one corner, between two of the bars, there is a gap.

Roger bends down to examine it. 'We might just be able to squeeze through here.'

'Er, you reckon?' I'm dubious. His hips are much more slender than mine.

I look up at the towering stone walls once more. I am desperate to see inside. After some discussion, we decide to breach the gap. Roger goes first. The hole in the gate is at an awkward height so I hold his legs while he walks on his hands on the other side. The only upside to our meagre backpacking budget is that I have lost weight so I may be able to squeeze through. When it is my turn, Roger has to half pull me through (my bruised hips are sore for days afterwards but it is worth it).

Inside the castle walls, the atmosphere is eerie. I get the shivery feeling of being silently observed. Even where entire walls have disappeared their foundation stones remain, allowing us to follow the floor plan of the huge castle. Despite the ravages of harsh winter storms on a roofless structure over many years, I count at least fifty rooms of which the walls still partly stand. Roger drifts off and disappears into another section of the castle. I continue wandering alone. My fingertips graze the lichen-splotched walls.

The castle was built with the perimeter walls carefully calculated to allow all the villagers and their animals to fit comfortably inside during an assault. I lean out of a high stone-rimmed window where others may once have peeped with apprehension. At one outer wall, I can look straight down onto the ochre rooftops of Fossa far below and then up across the valley to the dramatic spectacle of the snow-capped mountains. Meandering through passageways now carpeted with grass, I come upon the deep well. Nonno Anni's gruesome stories of people hurled down there come flooding back. The rocks and mortar laid around the wide circular mouth of the well are in almost perfect condition. I tentatively peer inside. Darkness conceals the bottom. The hairs on the back of my neck prickle. Was a peering face the last sight seen by those whose fate had been sealed? Or were they condemned to darkness when the top of the well was covered to drown out their desperate screams?

Knowing my own great-great-grandfather witnessed the fall of this castle brings this historical event into sharp focus. I imagine the terror when what was meant to be a safe haven became a trap during a successful attack. Maybe it is because so many have died within the walls of the castle, or because these walls are the same colour as gravestones, walking through the ruin is like walking through a cemetery. The air is charged with violent happenings of times past and the whispers of antiquated dialects snatched away with the breeze.

Back outside the castle, we follow a narrow dirt path that runs parallel to the towering exterior wall. At a fork, an intriguing almost overgrown trail leads into a wood. We exchange glances. Roger and I both have a penchant for secret passageways. Unable to resist, we follow the unknown path into a mist. With each step, it tapers even further into a skinny overgrown track darkened by thick brush that scratches our arms as we charily pick our way through. I look up. We still seem to be following the curve of the castle wall. The damp dirt changes to slate-coloured rock beneath our feet. All of a sudden, we come to a clearing and find ourselves looking down — straight down — onto Fossa, almost 250 metres below.

Together Roger and I teeter on the edge of the cliff with the exhilarating, cold mountain wind in our hair. The valley spreads out before us, cupped by some of the highest mountains in Italy. Situated at 900 metres above sea level, the castle dominates both Fossa and the town south-east of it, San Panfilo d'Ocre. It is dwarfed, however, by the surrounding peaks such as Mount Ocre behind us, which soars above 2200 metres, and of course the highest peak in the Apennines, the *Corno Grande*, which towers almost 3000 metres into the sky. Looking over the landscape from this vantage point, the rare piece of virtually untouched terrain of this region in a country long cultivated becomes even more apparent.

In 1921, in his book *Sea and Sardinia*, D. H. Lawrence wrote that the Abruzzo was attractively wild and remote compared to how 'man-gripped and tamed' many other areas of Italy were. 'Life is so primitive,' he observed. 'So pagan, so strangely heathen and half savage. And yet it is human life.' In 1969, H. V. Morton in *A Traveller in Southern Italy* compared the difference between the gentle hills of Tuscany and 'this wild Abruzzo land' to the difference between 'a man of the

Renaissance and a man of the Middle Ages'. When he wrote it, Morton was aware of only two books in English about the Abruzzo: Keppel Craven's horseback tour, *Excursions in the Abruzzi* (1838), and *Through the Apennines and the Lands of Abruzzi* (1928) by Estella Canziani. My searches provide only one more, *In the Abruzzi* (1908), written by Anne MacDonell. I have managed to purchase a copy of this as well as a first editon of Canziani's book which makes fascinating reading. When Canziani visited the Abruzzo in 1913, the locals were so staggered by her different clothes and hairstyle and the paler colour of her skin that they touched her in amazement, even wanting her to take off her hat and pull down her hair because they couldn't believe someone could look so unlike them. Perhaps the open stares and up-and-down looks we endure are a holdover from such sheltered times?

The approaching clouds continue to darken at an alarming rate. Clambering about on the slippery lichen-coated rocks, I am conscious of the nearby 250-metre almost perpendicular drop. Again Nonno Anni's stories are not far from my mind: tales of castle-builders falling to their deaths, the persecuted being thrown over the edge, and even in modern times, the occasional rock climb coming to a devastating end. In about 250 AD, Massimo Levite, a church deacon who was born in Aveia (Fossa's previous name when the village was located a little lower in the valley), suffered persecution by the Roman Emperor Decius, who had Levite tortured and thrown down this ridge in the emperor's bid to suppress Christianity. As a result, Levite became the patron saint of L'Aquila (Saint

Maximus of Aveia). I carefully peer over the edge, my gaze resting on the jagged rocks at the base where a plain cross commemorates the spot where he landed. I am clutching a rock for safety when what looks like a millipede begins to crawl on my hand. Instinctively I let go, then swiftly right my balance, my shoes sliding slightly on the uneven brink. I glance over at Roger scrambling over the rocks in a half crawl. He looks incongruous in a pair of shorts and a big winter jacket, the only dry clothes he has to wear. Most of our freshly washed clothes are hanging up to dry in the house below.

I spy a cave entrance about a quarter of the way down the mountain face. A metal cross stands sentry. Is it for one of the fallen or in memory of the monks who, for centuries, used the caves in these mountains as hermitages? It is hard to imagine how a monk could have safely accessed this remote cave. Heavy rain begins to move across the valley towards us. It has the unwavering determination of an invading army. We decide to retreat, back through the clothes-grabbing brush, along the gullied trail of ankle-twisting white rocks, and down the meandering road to the protective walls of the village.

Before long, the inside of the house is cosy with the smell of pork and fennel sausages sizzling in the pan. Two of the village cats curl up asleep on a rug near the hearth in the kitchen. Outside, the rain marches into the village like a clattering troop of horses. The onslaught hits us head on.

> *'We have two ears and one mouth so that we can
> listen twice as much as we speak.'*
>
> **Epictetus (55–135 AD)** *Greek philosopher*

Lucina and Fulvio ... and Mussolini

During the autumn evenings, the house becomes cold but not yet cold enough to light a fire. I huddle in front of Nanna Francesca's single-bar heater (I feel the cold like she does). I hope the heater is safe; when I turn it on it emits a rusty, burning smell. In the mornings, I make my way around the different rooms, pushing open all the windows. Some of them, stiff with age and lack of use, are at first unyielding to my touch. The morning sunlight pours in onto the tiles, bringing with it warm air fragrant with the nearby pine forest. I lean on a windowsill, basking in the warmth of the sun on my face. In the laneway below, a ginger cat follows a woman back and forth between car boot and house as his mistress unloads her groceries.

A knock at the front door echoes throughout the quiet house. Roger looks up from the book he is reading. As I pass him in the living room he slides a bookmark between the pages. I open the door to see an elderly couple both shorter than I am. This is incredible in itself. It is not often one sees a couple no taller than five feet. I am unaccustomed to looking downwards to speak to anyone except Nanna Francesca or children, most of whom hit my height by ten.

I smile. '*Buongiorno.*'

'*Buongiorno,*' they chorus back and then introduce themselves as Lucina and Fulvio, friends of Nonno Anni and Nanna Francesca.

Lucina and Fulvio both grew up in Fossa and migrated to Australia in the early fifties after they were married. By this time, Nonno Anni had been gone from the village for more than a decade but he was a character no one forgot. Word spread that his fruit and vegetable shop and milk bar in Ann Street in Brisbane's CBD was often the first port of call for many Italian migrants fresh off the boat. Nonno Anni and Nanna Francesca strove to help set up new migrants with accommodation, work and the support of a fellow expatriate community, easing those first daunting weeks for newcomers. Lucina and Fulvio are among many Italian migrants who are eternally grateful to my grandparents. I feel a responsibility to represent Nonno Anni and Nanna Francesca accordingly.

We sit around the dining room table and talk over biscuits and coffee. Lucina's grey hair, pulled back into a bun with bobby pins, reminds me of Granny Maddalena. Lucina's eyes are a deep blue marred by the first hint of cataracts. She tells me she and Fulvio are staying in Fossa with her older sister, Pasqualina, who never left the village.

'It's just so boring here,' Lucina sighs. 'Nothing to do. You must be itching to leave.'

'Well, not really ...'

'I could live here permanently,' beams Roger.

I am flummoxed.

'No, no!' Fulvio has tiny moles which look like freckles sprinkled across his upper cheeks. His hazel eyes dart from Roger to me and back again. 'You wouldn't like the winter. It is terrible cold. Makes your joints ache. The climate in Brisbane is much better.'

As the men continue their discussion, Lucina touches my arm and asks if I will write out some postcards for her. 'For my children,' she explains, extracting several L'Aquila postcards from her handbag and snapping the silver clasp shut. 'I can speak English but I've never learnt how to write it and my children only know English.'

Fulvio and Lucina have two daughters and two sons, all aged in their fifties, who live in Brisbane. It is somewhat strange, and yet also a privilege, to act as an intermediary between her and her children — to be the scribe as Lucina dictates. Despite the length of time she has lived in Australia, Lucina retains a heavy Italian accent. She takes a tiny book out of her purse to show me the addresses I should put on each postcard. When she speaks, her gold hoop earrings move in her lobes.

Lucina invites us to have lunch at her sister's house on the following Tuesday and we happily accept. Roger and I have no idea which house to go to among Fossa's maze of lanes, many of which are unsigned. Fulvio decides it is easiest if he comes to collect us at noon and on the appointed day he turns up on the dot. The three of us walk down *via dei Pallio*, the midday tolling of *Santa Maria Assunta*'s bells almost drowning out Fulvio's conversation. Roger, who towers over Fulvio, must lean down to hear him repeat what he is saying. Getting to Pasqualina's house requires numerous twists and turns along passageways and through tunnels. It would have been nearly impossible to find it without Fulvio leading the way. Pasqualina's front entrance is an arched wooden door that leads into a wide hallway with spotlessly clean whitewashed walls and a terracotta-tiled floor. Roger notices something hanging on the wall half-glued with the whitewash to become a permanent fixture.

'Lucky horseshoe?' he smiles, unaware it is an Abruzzese custom to fix one behind the entrance door to ensure fidelity in the marriage of the house.

Fulvio does not skip a beat. 'Mule.'

On closer inspection, the shape is slightly different, in keeping with the shoe of an animal that is a cross between a donkey and a horse. Granny Maddalena had procured a young donkey when Nonno Anni was a boy. Though the donkey was a working animal, Nonno Anni became quite fond of its gentle nature. They grew up together. During the Second World War Nonno Anni and his father, Vitale, were cut off, far away in

Australia, while Granny Maddalena and her young son, Elia, were stranded in the village. One night, German soldiers came knocking at the door of the Fossa house demanding food. Despite Granny Maddalena's brave protests, the Germans shot the little donkey. Sixty years later, Nonno Anni's eyes still got wet when he relayed this to me. Years after Granny Maddalena had migrated to Australia, she received a cheque from the Italian government as compensation for the donkey. It was for a paltry sum. Granny Maddalena tore up the cheque while having a good vent.

Lucina and Pasqualina are waiting in a spacious kitchen. There are a lot of dark wooden cupboard doors and the same terracotta-tiled floor as the hallway. A delicious smell wafts from a copper pot bubbling away on the stove. Lucina kisses my cheeks and introduces me to her older sister, Pasqualina, who shyly takes my hand. It has been many years since Pasqualina became a widow but she still wears all black and her plain gold wedding band.

Lucina motions for us to sit at the table as Fulvio cracks open an unlabelled flagon of red wine. He fills five squat glasses. Platters of *antipasto*, including slices of locally made *mortadella* and *prosciutto* rolled into hollow fingers, commence what is to become a three-hour feast. This lunch is typical of Abruzzese hospitality. It is, after all, the region of the *panarda* — a customary feast of around thirty courses for a big gathering of family and friends seated around a long table. Traditionally no one is allowed to leave the table until all the dishes are eaten. This lunch is not quite a *panarda* but we do work our way through several courses. An old Abruzzese remedy to cure indigestion is to make a cross on the stomach with a thumb while looking towards the sky and chanting, '*Dimonio cala, col corno mancino, sbucciale ecco.*' 'Demon come down, with the left horn, pierce her.' '*I maccheroni buttali di quà. Il baccalà di là, e isso spediaccialo.*' 'Throw the macaroni this side. The cod fish the other side, reduce it to pieces.'

The Abruzzo is respected throughout Italy and Europe for producing more expert cooks than any other area of the country. It is a widespread belief that those native to the region have a hereditary instinct for cooking. There is a saying: 'Any restaurant with an Abruzzese in the kitchen cannot fail.' In the Abruzzese town of Villa Santa Maria there is even a museum to honour local chefs. In the sixteenth century, Prince Ferrante Caracciolo, whose castle dominated the town, gave a number of impressive parties attracting aristocrats throughout what was then the Kingdom of Naples. The cuisine, prepared by the local Abruzzese cooks, was held in such high esteem that aristocrats living in other parts of the kingdom requested their services. This tradition endured and Abruzzese cooks were sought after by the likes of King Gustaf of Sweden, Italian King Vittorio Emanuele III, Adolf Hitler, and by the great transatlantic liners that plied the seas in the twenties and thirties. To this day, Villa Santa Maria remains renowned for its cookery school which continues to produce some of the world's best chefs.

It seems to me the older women of the villages, women like Pasqualina, who learnt to cook by watching their mothers and grandmothers, and by instinct, should be just as esteemed.

AGNELLO ALL'ARRABBIATA

abruzzese angry lamb

INGREDIENTS
~ Olive oil

~ 1 onion, diced

~ 500g diced lamb

~ 2–3 cloves garlic, finely chopped

~ Several finely chopped chillies (or to your taste)

~ Salt and pepper to taste

~ 750mL dry white wine

~ 1 bunch flat-leaf parsley, roughly chopped

METHOD

In enough oil to coat the bottom of a saucepan, cook the onion until golden.

Add the lamb and brown, then add the garlic and chillies and sauté until garlic is golden. Season to taste.

Pour in 500mL white wine and simmer on a low heat for several hours until meat is tender, adding more wine as necessary to keep from drying out (keep lid on or half-on saucepan). Stir through flat-leaf parsley just before serving.

Serves 4

Pasqualina serves a bowl of short, angular strands called *pasta alla chitarra*. She makes this pasta, characteristic of the Abruzzo, on a *chitarra* — a shoebox-sized wooden box strung with steel wires that must be 'tuned', just like a guitar. A sheet of pasta is laid over the strings and pressed through with a rolling pin, slicing it into strips. Once, every home in the Abruzzo had a *chitarra*. A woman's first task of the day was to make pasta. Girls reaching puberty were encouraged to make the pasta dough and press it through the *chitarra*, as it was believed the action this required developed the bust. As the saying goes, 'A girl who can make pasta and has a splendid chest will easily be able to find a good husband.' Looking at Pasqualina's serene face creased with age I think of her making *pasta alla chitarra* for her husband.

I smile at Pasqualina and praise her pasta. I'm not sure she understands. She stares back, her face expressionless, and then gets up to serve some fat pork sausages that have been frying away in a wide pan on the stove. Lucina brings over bowls of salad, then some bread from the local *forno* — the wood-fired oven of the village bakery where all the women once took the their dough to be baked before houses had their own ovens. Like many cooks in the south, Pasqualina has an ongoing affair with the small red chillies known as *il diavolicchio* — 'little devils' — included in a dish to the point that they are 'strong enough to burn a hole in the stomach'. Her next course is a well-known Abruzzese dish peppered with these little devils and called *agnello all'arrabbiata*, 'angry lamb'. This is cooking with personality but it can be heavy-going for those not accustomed to hot dishes. Pasqualina looks pleased for the first time when she sees Roger and me tuck in with gusto. We seem to have passed some kind of test.

Abruzzese desserts tend to be simple. They include *torrone* (nougat), biscuits flavoured with *amaretto*, and pies that vary according to the season and the mood of the cook. Pasqualina has made two large pies. One is fig and almond, the homemade pastry baked in criss-crossed strips over the top. Roger gets a dreamy look on his face as he bites into it. The second pie has a filling of grapes baked down to a jam-like consistency.

Espresso cups clatter against their little saucers as Lucina places them onto the table. Roger's eyes connect with mine. We are each poured a powerful *espresso*. I expect Roger, the non-coffee drinker, to decline but instead he picks up the tiny cup and quaffs it without milk or sugar. I add sugar, as the rest of us do, and take a mouthful. It is the strongest *espresso* I have ever drunk. Lucina picks up the pot offering to pour another. Roger nods vigorously. I can feel a faint frown etch between my brows and try to concentrate on what Lucina is saying to me. Roger's brown eyes almost seem to be glowing as he soaks up every one of Fulvio's words about grape-growing and winemaking.

Pasqualina serves *ferratelle* with the coffee. These slender biscuits are cooked in a contraption similar to a waffle iron. A thin batter mixture is poured into a crosshatched or diamond-patterned waffle iron and held over the fire. In the time it takes to whisper a Hail Mary, a *ferratella* is ready. I have eaten them many times in Australia made by both Nanna Francesca and my father. Dad has even made *ferratelle* with a portable waffle iron for the classes he teaches Italian to. I happened to be there on one occasion and watched his students' faces light up with curiosity and delight as the aroma of warm biscuits filled the classroom. As the Abruzzo is a region of soothsayers and superstition, spells and incantations have their place in Abruzzese kitchens. There are Abruzzese cooks who stir soups for a specific number of times in one direction, who only pick certain produce if the moon is full and who wear amulets and murmur special prayers while cooking particular dishes. Perhaps Pasqualina employed such methods in her cooking before we arrived.

I am feeling full to bursting and look over to see how Roger is coping. He has eaten a prodigious amount. Still deep in discussion with Fulvio about winemaking, he looks flushed and content. Having spent many years in the company of my family, I guess Roger came to the table with a good grounding in Italian hospitality. Step inside the houses of my relatives and, within minutes, you will have a drink in your hand and food placed in the middle of the table. No one goes to another's home empty-handed, even if you just pop over for a coffee.

Pasqualina busies herself at the sink and I rise to help but Lucina takes my arm saying she wants me to see something. She heads up a narrow spiral staircase, leading me to the bedroom where she and Fulvio are staying. The bed has a colossal bedhead of carved, dark wood. An elaborate embroidered bedspread looks to be made of spun gold from the Rumpelstiltskin fairytale. Lucina reaches into a wardrobe and pulls out several long, flat white cardboard boxes. She lifts the lids to reveal exquisite sheet sets.

'I got these to take back as presents to my daughters and my sons. I know my daughters will like them but, well, one of my son's wives is Australian and I wasn't sure ...' Lucina's eyes search mine.

My fingertips lightly brush the embroidery bordering the edge of a thick white sheet. How can I tell Lucina these were exactly the types of gifts Nanna Francesca brought back that I failed to appreciate as a teenager? And yet now I find myself wanting to seek out such treasures. Who knows if her son's wife will graciously accept the gift, and then in private lament yet another 'wog' present? Or perhaps she embraces her husband's Italian heritage and looks forward to such unique gifts. There are so many ways different people handle the multicultural situation mass migration has produced.

'I think they're lovely,' I say. 'I'd be very happy to receive them.'

Lucina beams and hastily repacks the boxes. 'Come with me.'

I follow her up more steep stairs into a tiny attic. A wooden ladder is propped up against the wall. Without a word, she begins to climb. Lucina is in her mid seventies at least. I pause, my foot on the bottom rung. She swings open a manhole-sized trapdoor in the roof and climbs up. I realise my mouth is hanging open and quickly shut it as she looks back to urge me to follow. I scramble up and out after her.

A blast of cool wind hits my face. We are standing on a section of flat cement, a kind of rooftop patio, without railings, among all the other sloping terracotta-tiled rooftops of the town. The cobblestoned street is four storeys below.

'*Bella, no?*' With a sweep of her arm, Lucina brings my gaze to the startlingly magnificent view of the valley, an arena skirted by snow-capped mountains. Trees lining the canals are turning autumnal shades of bronze and russet-red.

My heart feels light. I nod. '*E bella.*' 'Beautiful' seems so inadequate.

We stand and talk. Lucina tells me how hard it was to leave Fossa when she was in her twenties. She and Fulvio arrived in Brisbane where she worked in a job at the cannery which Nanna Francesca organised for her. 'She is a good woman, your grandmother. Gave up her morning to take me on the tram out to Golden Circle.' Lucina worked there until she and Fulvio saved enough to buy a farm. 'It was terrible in the country town,' Lucina sighed. 'I remember thinking, we left Italy for *this?* It was so dry, a very hard place. The buildings were in worse repair than the ones we'd left behind in Italy. And the people were so racist. Terrible. They did and said awful things to us and we just had to take it. Eventually we sold the farm and moved back to Brisbane.'

'What was it like to be in Fossa during the war?' This is one question Nonno Anni cannot answer for me, having already left for Australia before war broke out.

'Mostly I remember that my mother was very sad. My brother had died, you see.' Lucina looks out at the view. 'Mamma was looking after seven of us. We were very hungry. Sometimes she would faint when the — oh, what it is called? — when her blood sugar got low.'

In 1939, Nonno Anni left Italy, having grown up as part of the fascist youth that believed Mussolini was a great man. All his life until then he had lived within a totalitarian system, which gave the government total power to control every major aspect of life in Italy, whether it was politics, law and order, education, religion, entertainment, the armed forces, even music, art and literature. No opposing political parties were permitted, the press was censored or used for propaganda, and all opposition was crushed, earning Italy the label of 'police state'. The secret police enforced government policy and frightened people into behaving how the government ordered them to. My grandfather was a proud fascist. If he had been in Italy after the war broke out, could he have become one of the brutal secret police? It is a somewhat disturbing thought.

The fascists encouraged membership in a youth group from the age of four when a boy joined 'sons of the she-wolf', *Figli della Lupa*. Each child had a uniform and attended rallies and party-organised entertainment and participated in drills. At eight years old, one joined the *Balilla* and began using scaled-down Royal Italian Army service rifles in drills, moving on to the *Avanguardista* at the age of fourteen. Nonno Anni was a member and memorised all the fascist songs. In fact, he was one of four local fascist youths chosen to sing for Mussolini at the opening of the *Campo Imperatore* hotel in 1934. In 1943, Mussolini was imprisoned and later rescued from this same ski resort on *Gran Sasso*.

I am not sure if I should ask Lucina the next question, but I need to. 'What did you all think of Mussolini at the time?'

'Well, before the war, and during the first part of it, everyone thought Mussolini was wonderful. As the war went on, however, people got more and more fed up and we eventually realised he was not a good man. Once we realised how bad Hitler was we couldn't understand why Mussolini kept supporting him.'

It makes me wonder if Nonno Anni's opinion of Mussolini may have changed if he had stayed in Fossa during the war. After he left, Italy moved on without him, and perhaps by the time he began going back regularly he was too old to change. Nonno Anni remained tied to fascism for the rest of his life, and yet time and again I have seen him exercise generosity and compassion to those in need. He had no qualms about 'stepping in', whether to defend an Aboriginal being racially picked on in a pub or giving a homeless person money and lodging to get back on their feet. Most of his actions were anything but fascist.

I thank Lucina, not just for the view and the lunch, but also for giving me another insight into the village where she was born. She has given me a female perspective of growing up in Fossa that Nonno Anni could never supply. Nonno Anni certainly would not have had the freedoms he grew up with had he been born female.

Roger and Fulvio are still at the table talking when Lucina and I return to the kitchen. Pasqualina is drying up. Again, Lucina rebuffs me as I go to help. Roger and I thank Pasqualina profusely in Italian and receive a toothy smile. She clasps my hand in both of hers. Her palms are as dry and crackly as autumn leaves. Pasqualina stays in the kitchen while Lucina and Fulvio walk us to the door.

'We're here for another two months yet,' Lucina sighs.

Fulvio rolls his eyes and nods. 'Don't know what we'll do with ourselves.'

Lucina and Fulvio seem to view spending their remaining months in Fossa as serving some type of sentence.

'I miss my children and grandchildren,' Lucina continues to sigh. 'But this is our last trip to Fossa. I probably won't see Pasqualina again.'

Having lived a lifetime within a forty-minute car trip of all of my closest relatives, the calm acceptance of separation that I have witnessed among Italian migrants I have known never ceases to amaze me.

A few days later, Roger and I are having breakfast when there is a loud knock at the door. It is Lucina and Fulvio. Their talking overlaps in a rush.

'We've come to say goodbye ... changed our flights back to Australia.'

'... in case you wondered where we went.'

'... Pasqualina is good about it ... we're too old to go on any other trips ...'

'We'll tell your grandparents you're okay when we get back to Brisbane.'

I wish them well, trying to hide my disappointment. We kiss each other's cheeks. Then, they are gone. Lucina and Fulvio are leaving relatives, and the village of their birth, for the last time, yet they seem preoccupied with the life they have made in Australia, particularly their children and grandchildren. For them, immediate family has a stronger pull than a place. I can understand this. I once asked Nonno Anni why, when he loved Fossa and Italy so much, he did not return there to live.

With his customary gesture of open arms, palms facing upwards, he said, 'By the time I made enough money so that I could go back, we were settled here. Besides,' he gave me the cheeky smile he reserved for teasing his descendants, 'you lot all live here and you're not going anywhere, so we were hardly going to leave.'

A few weeks later it is time for Roger and me to move on from Fossa. We are getting a bus to Rome where we will stay for a bit and then take a train on to Venice and beyond. Switzerland, Austria, Germany and Holland beckon before we head back to Australia. I have mixed emotions as I hoist on my heavy backpack and lock the front door of the Fossa house behind me. Roger and I are quiet as we traipse through the cobblestoned village lanes to the bus stop, attracting stares from those we pass.

Fossa and the Abruzzo are beautiful. I definitely feel a connection with this place. It is difficult to explain but it is like something deep inside me surged with recognition when I came here. As much as I wanted to fight it, I felt *home* in several senses of the word, as though back in a sanctuary where one can safely remove their armour. It made me feel closer to my family, my culture, my ancestry. In a stange way I even felt more at home among the green valleys and snow-capped mountains — European scenery I had long had a penchant for though I had only seen it in pictures.

Nanna Francesca is from Palmi in Calabria. I wonder if I would feel the same connection there but I will not have a chance to find out on this trip. Maybe next time ... I somehow know that I will be back. It is not the 'one-off' trip I thought it might be, though I don't voice this aloud. I feel compelled to come back. By coming to Fossa, something has definitely altered in me, but I am not quite sure yet how this will have an impact on my life when I return to Australia. I sneak a look over at Roger. He seems pensive. Fossa has cast a spell that will elicit significant and everlasting change in both of us.

Tomato Day and the Dancing Cassatas

Back in Australia, it starts when Roger asks me to teach him how to twirl pasta onto a fork. Before long he is kneading his own pasta or bread dough. At home or at my parents' or grandparents' houses he raves about things I have grown up with and ceased noticing. The food, the music, the family dramatics — things I had kept strictly under wraps from other boyfriends or friends — he loves and cherishes. When Roger is driving, Italian music blares. He goes to Italian lessons. He reads every book about Italy he can get his hands on. I watch with bewildered amazement. His heritage is strictly Anglo-Celtic Australian. He tells me he had never eaten pasta until he was eighteen. I am astonished when he complains if I do

73

not cook him pasta every few nights. It seems almost overnight Roger has become an Italophile. He says that in Fossa he has found a place in the world where he feels he truly belongs.

Some things he enthuses over — like serving food from the centre of the table rather than dished up on individual plates — leave me perplexed, as these were things I had grown up with and thought were normal. For Roger, our large family get-togethers (sometimes with forty people or more) or our Easter and Christmas traditions are new and interesting. He eagerly eats the Easter bread cake that Nanna Francesca bakes in the shape of a dove with hard-boiled eggs tucked inside. I no longer feel self-conscious if Nanna Francesca rouses in Italian or if the men of the family (most of them, except Nonno Anni, sporting thick, dark, luxurious moustaches) spontaneously break into booming Italian song. Roger clearly revels in it all.

He watches me cook a tomato pasta sauce from scratch using the bottled *passata* from tomato day and soon he wants to come along to help my grandparents prepare and bottle the tomatoes. Each autumn it is tradition for Nonno Anni and Nanna Francesca to make and bottle tomato purée or *passata*. As a child I went with Nonno Anni in his ute to the fruit and vegetable markets out at Rocklea. I would beg to sit in the back of the ute (legal in those days) loving the wind in my face and 'holding on tight' as I was told to, sometimes catching Nonno Anni's gaze as he kept an eye on me in the side mirror. We would both smile at each other.

Since he had a fruit and vegetable shop for more than twenty years, Nonno Anni was familiar with many of the merchants at the markets. Often I stood and waited as he chatted to growers he knew. I wonder how we must have appeared: a big, burly, tanned Italian with his granddaughter skipping along by his side. We would head out early when the price was right and the Roma tomatoes ripe and buy anywhere up to eighty cases. Using a fridge trolley to move the cases Nonno Anni would load up the ute (I had to sit in the front on the drive home). He stacked the cases in the laundry under the house to wash the tomatoes.

Roger beams when he sees the breezeway underneath my grandparents' Queenslander set up for tomato day. Nanna Francesca gives him one of her aprons, which he eagerly dons (we all wear them except for Nonno Anni). Everyone has their specific jobs. Nanna Francesca, my mother and I cut up the tomatoes while sitting on upturned wooden crates in order to be low to the ground to grab tomatoes from the next case. Our chatter is constant as we slice each tomato in three deft strokes and throw them into huge, plastic containers. When these fill, Nanna Francesca moves on to her next task while my mother and I cut up the rest.

My father carries the containers of sliced tomatoes to the gas stove hooked up underneath the house where nine-litre saucepans occupy all four burners. Nanna Francesca watches over and stirs the huge pots of tomatoes which bubble and froth as they boil. She and my father work together pouring the hot pulp into huge ceramic bowls for the next process. Roger puts this cooked pulp through the hand-cranked *passatutto*, a stainless-steel vegetable mill, to remove skins and seeds. It is a messy process with the red liquid making its way over the wooden table onto the cement floor and staining his canvas shoes. (We are all in old work clothes because of tomato spatter.)

After it has gone through the *passatutto*, the tomato mixture is smooth. Roger pours it into more large ceramic bowls and I am responsible for adding a handful of salt. Only one person adds the salt so that oversalting does not accidentally happen. Using a soup ladle and a funnel, my sister bottles the tomato *passata* in hundreds of tall, brown-glass beer bottles that Nonno Anni has collected after Italian dinner dances over the years. These are ideal for bottling the sauce, with new caps creating a perfect seal. Unfortunately, when the beer company changed their bottles to screw-tops the new bottles were unusable. The old beer bottles have become precious and Nonno Anni constantly washes them for reuse.

Nonno Anni completes the last part of the bottling process, capping on shiny new lids with a special contraption and then carefully stacking the bottles in the old copper for boiling. He separates the rows of bottles with strips of hessian. They come out of the boiler piping hot and Nonno Anni grabs each bottle, protecting his hands with an old rag. He lines them up in the storeroom under the house to cool. It is an exhausting, backbreaking enterprise for everyone and takes twelve to fourteen hours with the only break being a quick lunch of bread and cheese eaten on the run. I am sore for days afterwards and marvel that my grandparents and Nanna Francesca's brother Vincenzo, whom she calls Vinchy, conducted the process with just the three of them at times. My mother sometimes helped them if we were at school and my father at work and she was also astounded by the older people's endurance.

Roger is tired but I can tell he does not want the day to end; after fourteen hours, though, by nine o'clock at night, I'm more than ready to head home. He wants to have a go capping the bottles but Nonno Anni won't let him. I laughingly tell Roger he cannot expect to do the 'top job' on the first day. 'Maybe next time,' Nonno Anni says gruffly, but as the Italian saying goes, '*Domani sì fa la barba gratis.*' 'Tomorrow beards will be cut free of charge.'

Another interest provoked by our time in Italy for Roger is wine. He attends a winemaking course and creates his first red wine which becomes an annual practice. He even crushes the grapes by foot himself. Soon after we buy a house together I hear the musical clink of a mallet hitting the top of a three-star picket. I run out onto the balcony and Roger looks up from the area I had earmarked for a lovely garden bed.

'This will be a great spot for my grapevines,' he shouts, turning his back to me to continue hammering.

My lips purse. Did he have to choose the *front* yard? Without intending to I do a near-perfect impression, complete with arm gestures, of Nanna Francesca's histrionics when Nonno Anni has done something to exasperate her. Roger mulishly plants his grapevine cuttings with extreme care. I grab the last one and unceremoniously shove it in some dirt in the *back* yard. Roger is surly. To the astonishment of us both, the vine flourishes along the back fence and into three neighbours' yards, the canes laden with tight bunches of the *Isabella* grapes suited to Brisbane's climate.

Since the lunch in Fossa when Roger was forced to try coffee to be polite and realised he loved it, he has become a regular coffee drinker, always taking it black, the stronger the better. When I tell him Italians add sugar to bring out the flavour of the coffee he adds a teaspoon, takes a sip and agrees. I even see him partaking in shots of *Galliano* accompanied by *espressi* with Nonno Anni at ten in the morning. Together they rhapsodise about Fossa and I am relegated to bystander. Since I grew up listening to Nonno Anni's stories about Italy (many more than a dozen times over), it isn't fresh and exciting for me like it is for Roger. However, the allure that everything Italian has for him is forcing me to start looking at my heritage in a different way. He loves and considers precious the very part of me that has often been demeaned and therefore hidden for much of my life. In a way, having someone love the very things that others have made me feel ashamed of or uncomfortable about is quite powerful.

Now that I have been to Fossa, I can picture where Nonno Anni's stories took place. Even though I've heard them all before, I start listening closely — really listening — and I watch. My grandfather's eyes glaze over, seeing a scene from the past rather than me sitting before him, only returning to the present when his eyes fill with tears at a memory. Tendrils of recognition creep in and curl around me. If I continue to shun my heritage, there is much to lose. Talking to one of my second cousins, who is about five years older than me and who experienced the same sort of prejudice at school as I did, I

78

discover she is coming around to our heritage in the same way. Aspects of our Italian background that once were embarrassing or a hindrance to being fully accepted are becoming precious. The future of an Italian community in Australia no longer rests with the original aging migrants. The descendants of Italian migrants are realising it is up to them to nurture and continue their Italian cultural heritage or it is in danger of disappearing, particularly as migration from Italy to Australia has practically stopped since the mid 1970s.

When Roger and I become engaged, Nanna Francesca gives us the go-ahead to start using the Kenwood Chef Mixmaster she had bought as our engagement present five years earlier. By this time Roger's insatiable enthusiasm and clear delight in all things Italian has intensified with each passing year. His parents travel from interstate to visit and discover their son has become an Italophile. I sense some bewilderment and understandably they need time to adjust and appreciate it is not a phase; Roger has chosen to change his way of life. Some of my family members who have grappled with their own biculturality over the years also need to adjust to this new member of the family so intent on worshipping Italy. I urge Roger to tone it down but Nonno Anni eggs him on, clearly delighted that of all people it is me, who eschewed my Italian heritage, who is marrying an Anglo-Australian striving to be an Italian.

One day, when we are sitting drinking red wine Roger made himself with grapes picked from our backyard vine, a laughing Nonno Anni slaps Roger on the back with affection and says to me, 'He's more Italian than you!'

That's it, I think. I have grown up mainly knowing the Italy presented by my family, portrayed in clichés, or disparaged by intolerance. I realise that I need to form my own connection with Italy that is not influenced by Nonno Anni or Roger.

I quietly begin to explore literature, art, music and cinema created by Italians. I am interested in writers' perceptions. Italy as a subject has attracted many distinguished writers: Coleridge, Voltaire, Hemingway, Proust, Twain and Wordsworth among them. I read Italian works such as Luigi Barzini's *The Italians* (1964) and I adore Giuseppe di Lampedusa's *Il Gattopardo* (1960) and Ignazio Silone's *Pane e Vino* (1936). I immerse myself in the multifarious 2000-year-old tradition of travel writing, some books inspiring, others not so grand. I reread Estella Canziani's *Through the Apennines and the Lands of the Abruzzi* (1928), H. V. Morton's *A Traveller in Southern Italy* (1969), Norman Douglas's *Old Calabria* (1915), *Stories from the Abruzzo* (1993) by contemporary Abruzzese writers, and more recent diasporic writings.

I connect most with Canziani's writings, not just because they are about the Abruzzo, but because she is English-born with an Italian father and an English-born Italian-American mother, and I can relate to having such a multicultural background. It is a revelation to me when someone asks her if she is English or Italian and she confidently replies, 'I am both.' Why did I always think I had to choose? I realise I need to go back to Italy to connect and explore more for myself, not just Fossa but Italy in general, and in particular Palmi, Nanna Francesca's birthplace. I resolve to go (no doubt Roger will readily agree) but in the meantime, I have a wedding to organise and I have to make the decision whether it will be in Italian or Australian style.

The Italian weddings I attended in Brisbane in the seventies and eighties were something to behold. It is rare now that families hold traditional Italian weddings for guests numbering 600, or more, but there was a time when this was expected, despite the exorbitant cost and indulgence, so as not to offend anyone in the Italian community. I quite enjoyed it when our family attended these weddings, which, for a time, seemed to be a regular occurrence. Studio portraits were taken in the seventies of the guests as well as the bridal party. In one photo of Nanna Francesca and me at a wedding reception lounge, I am no more than two or three, she is about forty-nine, and we are both wearing similar white shoes and floor-length dresses, our shoulder-length hair in soft curls. In a family shot, when I was about six, I am in another floor-length dress at a wedding (complete with turtle-neck skivvy underneath), though this time my hair is cropped in an elfin style and is slightly damp with perspiration, and my cheeks are pink. I remember running wild through the reception lounge with a gang of Italian kids of a similar age, and I had been swiftly pulled aside for the photo before running off again.

The weddings all began with a full nuptial Mass at a Catholic church, followed by dozens of staged photos before hundreds of us all travelled in convoy to the reception lounge. The Bride, usually in a huge white satin gown, and the Groom, in a powder blue (or similar) tuxedo, cut a ribbon to enter the reception, prompting the release of several white doves into the windowless, air-conditioned function room. Often, a dove would christen the front of the Bride's *Gone with the Wind*-proportioned skirt, eliciting cries from the seven bridesmaids in hot pink (or similar) taffeta as they rushed forth with dampened linen napkins to clean it. I always felt sorry for the frightened doves swooping back and forth through the cavernous reception lounge looking for an exit before being caught for the next wedding.

An army of waiters wearing black trousers, white shirts and black bow ties would stream out of the kitchen in single file, brandishing silver trays at shoulder height. Platters of *antipasti* were placed in the centre of each table, prompting guests to lean forward to grab slices of rockmelon wrapped in *prosciutto*, marinated black olives, *giardiniera* (mixed preserved vegetables), pieces of cheese and *grissini* — crisp, dry, pencil-thin bread sticks. The table would be cluttered and as guests leant in to put some *antipasti* on their plates it was necessary to manoeuvre around four different glasses, ceramic swan *bomboniere* that hid teeth-cracking sugared almonds under their outstretched wings — pink for the ladies, blue for the men — and carafes of red wine, white wine and orange juice. Usually by then, someone like Nonno Anni with his big hands had already managed to knock over a wine glass, the telltale red stain on the tablecloth now covered by his serviette. (In Abruzzese folklore it is a sign of good luck to knock over or break something at a wedding reception — or so they say.)

Bowls of ravioli would come next, their red, saucy peaks sprinkled with snowfalls of *Parmigiano*. The noise level of the reception lounge would rise as the clatter of cutlery on plates competed with hundreds of conversations in English and Italian, as well as Italian dinner music from the live band in the back. The bridal table would stretch across an entire wall of the room in front of a mural depicting something like the Grand Canal of Venice. The rest of the round tables for reception guests would balloon out around a deathly slippery parquetry dance floor. At times, children bored with sitting at their tables would get up to skid and slide across the empty dance floor, and yes, I was one of them, sometimes earning a soft smack on the backside for going overboard.

The waiters would continue to serve and clear with precision, stepping around running children, obviously used to Italian weddings where the children ran wild. They would move in with the next course, alternate plate drops of Veal Marsala and Florentine Chicken. The latter, marinated in lemon juice and then fried in breadcrumbs, was rumoured to have inspired a certain American to found a fried chicken empire after enjoying a lot of it on holiday in Tuscany (though Italians didn't like to think there was any such link). Vegetables would be served separately and a dinner roll placed on each side plate. Throughout the evening one of the guests would raise their knife and start tapping the side of their wine glass, encouraging others to do the same. The tinkling would grow to a crescendo throughout the entire function room, prompting the bashful Bride and Groom to kiss, to the cheers of the guests.

If any wily guest thought it had been too long since the couple had kissed, the tinkling would begin again in earnest.

'*Pronto!* Can I have everyone's attention please?' By this stage of the evening the reception lounge hostess would tap at a microphone. Her bottle-blonde hair stiff with hairspray, piled high to reveal large, plastic, blue earrings in the shape of birds. 'I hope everyone is having a fantastic evening, yes?' Pause. 'I can't hear you!' She would beam. 'And now for a special treat, dessert is served!' Two of my older cousins and I were recently reminiscing about the 'dancing *cassatas*'. The lights were dimmed and waiters emerged doing a kind of dance while wheeling trays of *cassata* — ice cream containing candied or dried fruit, nuts and liqueur — and saucers of alcohol, lit to create blue, wavering flames.

Afterwards, the hostess would introduce a Master of Ceremonies, who held the microphone too close, giving every one of the other 630 guests an intimate association with his irregularly wheezing nostrils. A pyramid of empty champagne glasses would be stacked high and the Bride and Groom beckoned over to pour a bottle of champagne for the toasts. Together they would hold it and tip the contents into the top glass. As the glass filled, the champagne washed over into the glasses in the row below and so on.

The Bride and Groom would retreat after the first bottle was emptied, leaving the efficient wait staff to swoop in and fill the rest. After the speeches and the cutting of the seven-tiered wedding cake, it would be time for the bridal waltz. Rolls of coloured streamers were passed around the guests and as the

Bride and Groom waltzed, everyone would wrap the couple in streamers (as a child I loved this bit) until they resembled a colourful paper mummy, continuing to shuffle amid the delighted cries as they were 'bonded' with luck and happiness.

With the formalities of the evening over, the band would crank it up a notch and guests would flood the dance floor. The other guests could now move freely among the tables, ignoring the place cards and sitting to chat and drink with whomever they wished. The evening would end with a farewell circle and a guard of honour the bridal couple had to scuttle through. I was never one of those kids who fell asleep across a row of chairs. Bright-eyed, I would be running around up until the Bride and Groom departed in the early hours (and then wake up at six the next morning, much to my parents' chagrin).

When Roger and I get married, I do not want a big Italian wedding (though I think Roger would have happily obliged). I am mindful of how his family might react and I cannot shake feeling self-conscious when none of Roger and my friends or work colleagues are Italian. An extended guest list is dispensed with, along with many Italian customs such as glass tinkling to make the bridal couple kiss or wrapping them in streamers on the dance floor (which I will regret omitting in future years). It is expected that we will have a full nuptial Mass in a Catholic church, which we do, though my dress is ice-pink and my bridesmaids wear black. Nanna Francesca wails over this because in her eyes black is strictly for funerals. She bluntly tells me I'm lucky she's not dead and can attend since I waited so long to get married (I am twenty-seven). One Italian tradition I want to keep is giving each wedding guest a *bomboniera* of five sugared almonds representing health, happiness, wealth, luck and fertility. My future mother-in-law looks confused when the word *bomboniera* rattles off my lips. I sheepishly realise that sometimes it's easy to assume others are familiar with traditions or Italianisms I have grown up with.

Although I'm not following all of the Italian traditions, Nonno Anni and Nanna Francesca have an absolute ball. At the beginning of the night, Nonno Anni tells Roger's country relatives to call him 'Joe' (throughout his life Australians struggled with Annibale and he'd often end up with Annabelle), and they all go on to have an uproarious evening. I suspect that for my grandparents (and my parents as well) it is a relief that my wedding goes off without a hitch. When my parents were getting married they had their own set of issues to deal with — those of the cross-cultural marriage. It was not until my early teens that I began to realise what a major feat my parents had achieved by forging a cross-cultural marriage in the sixties when Australia's acceptance of multiculturalism was still immature. Not long before they were married, the Holt government's then Minister for Immigration, Billy Snedden, proclaimed that Australia must have a single culture, saying, 'If migration implies multi-culture activities within Australian society, then it is not the type of culture Australia wants.' Mixed marriages were looked down upon.

My parents had to overcome some seemingly insurmountable obstacles to be together. Both sets of my grandparents were no shrinking violets, and nor were many in both the Australian and

Italian communities. (Mum told me that someone had actually warned her she would have 'brown babies' if she married an Italian.) At the time, there was a firm belief that all cross-cultural marriages ended in divorce.

My parents never divorced as was predicted. My mother died three months shy of my parents' thirty-ninth wedding anniversary. It was not until after my birth (being the first grandchild for both sides) that my Italian and Australian grandparents started coming together for birthdays and family gatherings. Over the years, I witnessed them having plenty of robust debates as well as good laughs. Such is the richness and intricacy of being in a mixed cultural family.

As newlyweds with work commitments and a steep mortgage, Roger and I cannot afford to go back to Italy for some time. It is frustrating that for so many years I resisted going to Fossa, and now that I want to go I am unable to. Then unexpectedly the opportunity arises when I am granted a research scholarship to study in Italy. If we pool what money we have in with it, we can stay for an extended period this time, particularly as we will live in the Fossa house. Our five-year wedding anniversary will occur while we are in Italy. Naturally Roger is coming with me. I would not want to go without him anyway. He is beside himself with excitement (almost exasperatingly so) and vociferously outlines things he wants to do this trip. In contrast to me, Roger travels to Italy with an outlook unfettered by heritage or a lifetime of feeling caught between two cultures. His over-exuberance sometimes threatens to curtail my own enthusiasm. It is hard to compete with an Italophile 'beating one to the punch' with places to go and things to do.

I am going to Italy without the chip on my shoulder I went with last time. My heart is open. No longer am I against Fossa and all it represents because it signified a part of me I was not yet ready to acknowledge. I strived to take the straight road, more concerned with how I was perceived than how I wanted to be. Looking back I feel sad that the need to fit in with my Australian peers caused me to sacrifice part of my heritage and for so long I have been acknowledging only half of myself. After all, I am an official citizen of both Australia and Italy — half Australian, *mezza Italiana*. I can live, work and vote in both countries.

I realise that this time in Italy I cannot simply play tourist as I attempted to on my first visit. I am not a tourist. Nor am I a native. But the Italy I have grown up with, Nonno Anni's Italy that he left behind in his youth is not the current Italy. I have to discover that for myself. In the mind's eye of a migrant, possible change is not always factored in. A place and its people don't always stay the same as they were many decades before. I carry images of Italy skewed by a build-up of mental pictures and memories not originally my own — an Italy of the twenties and thirties. I have two versions of Italy in my head — the peasant version and the romanticised version of books and films. And so, I will go to Italy with different eyes. I am now thirty-two and almost a decade has passed since I came to Italy last. I imagine carefully and methodically unpicking the stitching that binds me to Italy and my ancestors to discover the underpinning of my make-up. But, as the eighteenth-century poet Robert Burns claimed in his poem 'To a Mouse', *'the best-laid schemes o' mice an' men ...'*

Some journeys simply need to be allowed to flower spontaneously ...

'No man ever steps in the same river twice, for it's
not the same river and he's not the same man.'

Heraclitus (circa 544–480 BC) *Greek philosopher*

Chestnuts and Coffee Beans

I first learnt to roast chestnuts one Sunday afternoon when
Roger and I were over at my grandparents' house to pick coffee
beans from their tree. The coffee tree is fecund, the thin, heavily
laden branches drooping with fruit. Our hands reach in among
the densely growing leaves to pluck the coffee cherries. Nonno
Anni, Roger and I quickly fill plastic bags with ripe red fruit and
any stray bits of leaf and twig that make their way in there too.
Roger's habit is to carefully select each cherry, going for quality;
Nonno Anni goes more for speed and quantity; I am somewhere
in between. Nanna Francesca peers around the tree, watching
us with her usual look — a mixture of worry and menace. The
New Farm soil is rich, dark and fertile, sinking under our feet.

'Oi! Who would have thought you'd be doing this one day?' Nonno Anni pokes me in the ribs a few times, making me laugh and squirm away.

'*Lasciala stare!*' cries Nanna Francesca. '*Lasciala stare!*'

Throughout my entire life I have heard my grandmother shouting, '*Lasciala stare!*' telling my grandfather to let me be when he teased or was cheeky to me.

Shaking her head, Nanna Francesca retreats to the concrete laundry under the house, wheeling her screeching metal laundry trolley in front of her. I glance over at my grandparents' Hills Hoist, which is battered from grandchildren climbing and swinging on it, grey wires sagging from much use. The washing is a mixture of navy work singlets, King Gee work pants, aprons and floral three-quarter length dresses. Towels are treated to half a dozen pegs each. I find it endearing. *If a breeze should lift, those towels won't be going anywhere.*

'Aye! You ever cook chestnuts?' Nonno Anni's voice breaks my reverie.

I look into his eyes — alive, intelligent. 'No.' An adventure awaits.

He nods. 'Come on. Come upstairs. I show you.'

I follow him up the back steps. His gait sways a little but is still sure. Nanna Francesca will come up later, taking each step one at a time. Roger stays behind. Now up a stepladder, he is reaching for the highest coffee cherries.

The spacious kitchen is cool and dark. With age, Nanna Francesca has leant towards keeping windows closed rather than open. She has not been well in recent times and it is the first time in their marriage that she has allowed Nonno Anni to cook in her domain. Piles of clutter are strewn over the benches, a table, even the floor — bowls, tea towels, half-eaten boxes of chocolates, glasses, groceries … Suddenly a mouse runs across the floor. I only manage to half-stifle a squeal. Nonno Anni swings around in time to see it scuttle under a cupboard.

'Bloody ting!' He sounds exasperated. 'I set the trap but it doesn't take the cheese.'

I look around at spilled breadcrumbs and dry pasta.

'Here …' Nonno Anni rattles a brown paper bag of chestnuts. He shows me how he cuts a small slit in each nut to prevent them exploding with the heat. His hands are large and capable, well-worked, but his palms remain fleshy. He gets out a battered old frying pan (he has drilled the holes through the base himself) and noisily pours in the chestnuts. He plonks an anodised bronze-coloured lid on top and in one swift motion deftly lights the gas hob. As the chestnuts cook over the blue flame, Nonno Anni regularly gives the pan a good shake. Amid the dull clatter, a sweet, rich aroma fills the kitchen. I call Roger down from the ladder, knowing he won't want to miss this. I am proud that, even at seventy-eight, my grandfather continues to teach me new and interesting things. Roger's face when he enters the kitchen looks like a child standing in front of the tree on Christmas morning.

Nonno Anni tips the roasted chestnuts into a large white ceramic bowl and places it in the middle of the table. Nanna Francesca pours us each a glass of cold lemonade. Nonno Anni shows Roger and me how to hold the searing hot nut inside a paper towel and roll it between our fingers to loosen the shell. Then we peel off the brown outer layer to reveal the cream-coloured kernels within. The chestnuts are warm, with an earthy, almost meaty flavour.

'You know, when I was about in my teens in Fossa, I used to go with the groups of men on foot up to near *Gran Sasso* where the chestnut trees grew thickly,' Nonno Anni tells us. 'We would pick sacks and sacks of chestnuts. Then we camped there around a fire overnight, roasting and eating chestnuts and drinking wine before returning the next day.'

His eyes mist over and he is no longer seeing the four of us sitting around the table under a fluorescent light. Despite its poverty and struggle, I often see my grandfather's past as a golden era. I strive not to romanticise it as I know times were tough enough to force my family to emigrate, but despite the harshness Nonno Anni remembers growing up in the Abruzzo fondly. I realise that I will always treasure this afternoon with my grandparents and my husband. And I will remember it and the chestnuts and coffee beans when they fade into a golden time of the past as well.

When we get home, Roger asks me what the word for 'chestnuts' is in Italian.

'*Castagne.*' The plural automatically rolls off my tongue and it occurs to me how even a word like 'chestnuts' can sound emotive in Italian.

Translate many English words into Italian and it is surprising how something that is ordinary can suddenly sound lyrical and romantic. 'Floor' becomes *pavimento*; 'soapy water', *saponata*; 'side-whisker', *basetta*; even 'brothel' becomes the much more fetching *bordello*, rolling pleasingly off the tongue. As I sit on a plane on my way back to Fossa, I contemplate the name of the village and wish it meant something profound and beautiful. In the past when I looked up *fossa* in my Italian–English dictionary, I have to say it was a little deflating: 'pit, hole, trench …' And it got worse, with several comprehensive meanings incorporating cesspools and mass graves. Why couldn't it mean something like 'beautiful views' (which it has) or 'winding lanes'? The name Fossa has another meaning, though, to do with topography, and the fact that the village nestles in a hollow halfway up the side of the mountain is most likely responsible for its name.

Rome's close traffic, fumes and horns bombard my senses, already heightened by travel fatigue, given the twenty-four-hour trip from Australia. In our diminutive diesel Fiat that idles like a truck, Roger weaves in and out of lanes on the Roman ring road like a true native driver (another Italian practice he has adopted). He has no fear. I look down to see that my hand has involuntarily clutched the door handle. We take the exit that leads to L'Aquila. A brief pause at the tollbooth and then we accelerate. Buildings, aerials and congestion give way to clear roads and rolling green fields. Rome becomes a smoggy speck in the rear-view mirror. The tension declines markedly as we head back to the Abruzzo.

We enter through the dungeon-like tunnels carved deep through the gigantic mountains that act like fortress walls to the Abruzzo. Out of the dimness, the occasional drop of water hits the windscreen — mountain blood. On the other side, the mountains rise and the valley falls away from the road teetering on pylons. I press my face to the window unsuccessfully trying to suppress a smile. Last time we were here in autumn, this time it is spring. I gaze at waterfalls of melting snow and thousands of red, white and yellow wildflowers, a scene so enchanting that it is the stuff of picture books. It is hard to explain, but an unexpected feeling of contentment is washing over me. I *feel* something in being back here in the Abruzzo that I did not feel when we first landed in Rome.

I know Roger and I are getting close to Fossa when I see L'Aquila, its buildings sprawled at the feet of a circle of mountains. We draw up to an intersection with (I later count) sixty-two signs for different towns pointing every which way. We barely pause yet the cars behind us immediately start beeping, but I remember the road to take. As we speed across the valley floor towards Fossa, Roger and I exchange happy glances. I had forgotten how beautiful it is. This nook in the world is blessed. So much more beautiful in reality than in photos: the charm of Italian hill towns built of stone combine with the Alpine beauty of lush green fields and wildflowers. A backdrop of snow-capped mountains and clear blue skies is reminiscent of the pictures on old-fashioned Swiss chocolate-boxes. Plane trees make a canopy over the road, alongside of which runs a canal. A wooden waterwheel still turns for the mill to which Nonno Anni regularly brought grain and chestnuts seventy years ago. The beauty of the landscape does not divulge its sometimes bloody past, the desperate poverty of peasants locked in feudal systems, the ruthless bandits that roamed these mountains as recently as the first decades of the twentieth century.

Landmarks are familiar to me, whether from the last time we were here or a lifetime of my family showing me pictures. The road is a pale ribbon along the base of the mountains surrounding the valley. I catch sight of Fossa nestled halfway up the side of *Monte Circolo*; the ruins of Castle Ocre perched on the peak of the mountain above the village. The road climbs and then narrows to a lane, bitumen transforming into cobblestones — we are coming into Fossa. When I get my first close-up view of the stone houses punctuated by the church spire, it squeezes my heart. I take a sharp breath.

I am struck by how narrow the crooked village laneways are, even more than I remember. Terracotta pots sit on doorsteps, the red and hot pink flowers of spring a welcome sight, no doubt, after the bleak, snowy winters Fossa endures. Not many people are about. Those who are turn and openly stare as Roger and I go past. We fall silent as the Fiat crunches across white gravel in the main *piazza, Piazza Grande.* It is officially called *Piazzale delle Frainine* but the locals call it *Piazza Grande* as Nonno Anni does, so we always have too. Our street name, *via del Pallio*, which it has been known as since at least the Middle

Ages, has changed since we were here last. It is now called *via dei Beati* in honour of Fossa being the birthplace of several saints. A small sign on the edge of the village marks Fossa as *luogo delle beatitudini*, place of the Beatitudes, also known as a place of blessings, referring to both the spiritual and the quiet peace surrounding the area. To me, it somehow makes Fossa seem even more special. When we stop and Roger turns the engine off I am struck indeed by how quiet and peaceful the village is. The thuds of our car doors sound particularly loud.

It is not the same arriving without Nonno Anni and Nanna Francesca here to greet us. I look up at the house with its deep-set windows and biscuit-coloured stone the same as the rest of the village. One wall abuts the next house. The front of the house was changed when the earthquake of 1915 destroyed the original front section and this area was replaced by a landing (shared with a dwelling above) which we reach by climbing a short flight of steps from the laneway. The exterior has barely changed since. The house sits directly across from the village church *Santa Maria Assunta*. 'Recent' renovations were carried out on the church in the early 1700s (most likely because of damage from a massive earthquake in L'Aquila on 2 February 1703) and Nonno Anni told us the house was built more than ten years earlier, in 1692. (Roger later finds etched into the wall the date that verifies this.) *Santa Maria Assunta* is referred to by locals as the 'new church' even though it is several centuries old. The 'old church', *Santa Maria ad Cryptas*, was built in the 1200s.

Except for the twitter of little birds circling over the terracotta rooftops, the village is almost silent. I look up to see the bell hanging still in the tower, a contrast to the last time Roger and I arrived in Fossa with Nonno Anni. Looking up at the house I recall Nanna Francesca peering from the doorway. My breath catches in my throat, for Nanna Francesca is now no longer with us, having passed away, aged seventy-seven, a year and a half ago. She died less than three months after she and Nonno Anni celebrated their sixtieth wedding anniversary (receiving letters from the Queen, the Prime Minister and other dignitaries). I teeter between the pain of her loss and the warm memories of her, a feeling like the delicate tone elicited by the tap on a crystal glass hovering somewhere between a musical note and an anguished cry.

Wood smoke curls from chimneys, the acrid smell prickling my nostrils. Roger and I climb the uneven stone steps, resting our bags at the top of the stoop. I stand at the wooden door. The key was cut in Australia so I'm relieved it fits. The first thing I notice is that the pale lemon colour which was on the kitchen walls the last time I was here has been covered by an earthy orange. Some of the yellow is still visible where the can of orange paint must have run out.

I put my bag down on the terrazzo floor. There is some cleaning to do, but it is wonderful to have a family house where we can stay. Roger's brown eyes shine like liquid chocolate. Seeing the look on his face reminds me of Nonno Anni jumping out of the taxi in Fossa and triumphantly shouting, 'We are home!' Roger brings in our heavier luggage, unconsciously whistling a tune, a sign he is in high spirits. He tells me he feels an affinity with this house. I wonder if this is instinctive or born from Nonno Anni's nostalgic recollections coupled with Roger's affection and respect for his grandfather-in-law. The loud ringing of the phone carries in the quiet house.

I answer the Italian way. '*Pronto?*'

'*Chi parla?* Zoë, I never thought I'd hear you answering the phone like that!' Nonno Anni thinks this is a great laugh. 'You switched on the electricity, the water, the gas? Actually, I don't think there's any bloody gas left. Have you had a drink of water yet?'

Nonno Anni raves about Fossa water and justifiably so. It comes directly from the snow-covered mountains and is pure and fresh. It is hard to explain, but it is almost sweet and so natural I find it makes my skin perfectly clear and my hair shiny when I drink and bathe in it regularly. The treated water back home seems so much harsher in comparison. The church bells peal as I am saying goodbye and hearing them Nonno Anni becomes wistful. His voice cracks with emotion and I feel tears well in my own eyes. Now in his eighties he no longer feels able to travel the long distance to Italy. I know he misses his annual sojourn in Fossa with Nanna Francesca.

Later, Roger and I walk down the alley behind the house to the grocery shop. If Nonno Anni had not shown us where it was on our first trip we may never have found it. There is no sign. The small, dim shop tucks in beneath the owner's house and hides behind a beaded curtain and a frosted glass door. We call it the 'Boccabella' shop because it is run by a Boccabella family and last time I was amazed to see my surname on their receipts. Since family trees have interlaced in Fossa for many centuries, it is likely we are related to the owners, even if distantly and in centuries past. Today, Graziella, the friendly middle-aged matriarch, is behind the counter. She lets out a cry and runs around to our side of the counter when she recognises me. She gives my cheeks two swift kisses and immediately asks after Nonno Anni and my parents. Roger watches as she and I converse as best I can with my imperfect Italian. I feel gauche and shy.

I introduce Roger as my husband and see a flicker in her eyes. No doubt Graziella was one of the villagers who heard from Nanna Francesca that Roger and I were brother and sister to avoid the scandal of us staying alone and unmarried in the house last time. Some people must have believed it because my younger cousins have told me they've had to explain that Nonno Anni has four granddaughters and one grandson, not two grandsons.

Graziella does not mention the 'brother/sister' factor. Dressed in a stylish suit, her hair coiffed, and stockinged feet shoved into comfy slippers, she is a five-foot whirling dervish of energy, moving round the shop and wrapping our purchases of pasta, bread, eggs, *passata*, juice, *Parmigiano* cheese, long-life milk and coffee with swift precision.

'Since you're family,' she explains with a broad smile as she throws in several little glass bottles of Italian bitters with our purchases.

We thank her profusely. I am touched. It makes me feel, in a small way, a part of the village. There is nowhere else in the world I could travel and feel this sense of belonging.

It is impossible not to be drawn in by the vistas unfolding before me as we career around the countryside surrounding Fossa in the Fiat. I look up at the mountain ridges, the highest and most spectacular of which are still capped by melting snow. Last time, when I was here in autumn, the trees were losing their leaves. But spring in Italy makes the landscape even more beautiful. Everything is lush. I am struck by the varying shades of green. The alpine firs, dark, almost silvery; the brownish green of the gently moving cypresses; and a young chestnut tree with foliage of such a pale lime that the way the sun penetrates its leaves they seem almost luminous. The grass is thick and verdant, growing right up to the edge of the road in thick clumps you could roll around in like a horse. There are fields of it, dotted with scarlet poppies, yellow *ginestra*, violets and the occasional almond tree with limbs clad in pink flowers.

The tiny villages we pass through are mostly the same: stone houses with roofs punctuated by chimneystacks. Wooden shutters are painted various shades of ochre, sand and faded green. Pot plants, always terracotta and mostly containing herbs or flowering gerberas, crowd balconies and front doorsteps. The only concessions to the modern age are TV antennae, satellite dishes and the occasional blue and red street signs. The signs specify 'No parking 0–24', but people still insist on parking and losing their side mirrors or scraping car doors as they force their way through impossibly narrow fifteenth-century laneways.

While I quietly marvel to myself at the beauty, committing it to memory, Roger is effusive and loud. He is getting the 'hand waving while driving way over the speed limit' down pat.

'Look at that building up on the hill.' His arm cuts across my chest and I follow his outstretched finger to a crumbling farmhouse covered in vines. 'Look at that field there.' I swing over to look out his window. 'Look at that man on the tractor.' I swivel round again, starting to feel carsick. 'Look at …'

'Look at the road,' I plead, staring down into a ditch very close beside me.

I don't want to dampen Roger's enthusiasm but I am feeling the need to discover some things for myself.

As we wind back up into Fossa, I can hear the bells tolling from *Santa Maria Assunta*. Not so long ago it would have been a brave or foolish person who refused the summoning of these bells. It is not yet a century since priests commanded considerable influence and respect in these hamlets; in return for blessings the villagers were required to proffer alms, which were collected by these priests and friars. As recently as the twenties and thirties, women still crawled along church floors licking the stone floors, sometimes until their tongues bled, in prayerful hope or in gratitude for divine mercy sparing a loved one.

We barrel along *via dei Beati*, almost home, and nearly run head on into the priest leading a funeral procession. Everyone stands stock-still for a stunned moment. The road is too twisty and narrow for us to reverse all the way back down and Roger and I feel terrible as they all move to let us pass. The bells, which are right opposite our house, sound loudly and keep ringing as the funeral procession winds all the way to the cemetery on the outskirts of town. It seems a fitting way to depart this earth — being blessed and carried through the village where you have lived, those who farewell you quietly following.

The pealing bells begin to poignantly slow.

'Much like a person's life,' Roger remarks.

Nonno Anni later tells us this is exactly the reason for the funereal tolling of the church bells. To show respect for the life that has been lived, the bells begin to toll, gently at first, as though to represent a little one new to this world, and then building, building, to represent life's journey. To signify life's peak, the bells reach a clanging crescendo. Then the tolling gradually becomes slower and slower, until the last chime rings out and slowly ... slowly ... stops.

By the time a pasta sauce is bubbling on the stove, the house, which endures long stints standing empty, gradually comes back to life. Toothbrushes stand in a glass near the bathroom sink, books are placed on bedside tables, shoes kicked off. The long wooden dining table is covered with one of Nanna Francesca's tablecloths, a dark-green paisley pattern. (She bought it from a travelling merchant who regularly comes through the village selling all manner of household goods from a tiny truck blaring music to attract attention.) Roger and I each sprinkle a bowlful of pasta with the *Parmigiano* that Graziella grated freshly for us. It tastes divine.

I click on the TV. The game shows are mostly hosted by bottle-blonde, buxom bimbos partnered by borderline-elderly male hosts spouting corny jokes. I flick to a show just in time to see a woman breastfeeding orphaned tiger cubs. Yes.

We have stayed awake as long as possible to adjust to Italian time. In the shower, the plastic shower curtain is too long. I stand on half on it, the other half wrapping around me. I realise groggily that I have been upright for more than forty-eight hours. It is wonderful to lie down and stretch out. The pine bed is out of whack, and with two of the legs uneven on the tiled floor, bangs loudly every time we turn. Sleepily, I tell Roger I will find some bricks to prop them up in the morning. My eyes are already closed. I fall into a delicious, long-awaited sleep.

At midnight, a piercing, spooky shriek echoes throughout the village.

I open my eyes.

The Serpent Charmers of Cocullo

Before dawn has broken, I gently nudge Roger to see if he wants to come with me and watch the sunrise. Already half awake, he readily agrees. Rugged up against the pre-dawn cold, we quietly slip out of the house and into the deserted street. It is silent except for the birds beginning to stir and our footsteps on the cobblestones. I love the magic of being out and about while the rest of the village sleeps. The tips of our noses turn pink in the chilly mountain air. Early morning spring in these mountains retains prodding wintry fingers.

Leaning on the cold metal railings of *Piazza Belvedere*, we gaze over the outspread valley below. In the distance, the orange lights of other towns wink in the fading darkness.

I look down at the neat fields of crops that appear collaged over the valley floor. The canals are not visible from so high up but neat rows of trees following the waterlines give them away. I try to envisage the valley before civilisation took over, before swamps were drained and the serpentine glide of a wide river was coerced into canals. One of the reasons the villages mostly cling to the mountainsides is the knowledge that the river could capriciously transform into a raging flood. Nonno Anni remembers many of the village elders shaking their heads when obstinate young farmers started building homes on the valley floor. Not far from here, *Lago Fucino* was once the largest lake in Italy, a place where the Romans came to holiday. It is now a flourishing agricultural area after being drained (the third biggest engineering project in the late nineteenth century after the Eiffel Tower and the Suez Canal).

Roger and I stand at the edge of the *piazza* for more than an hour. Little by little the sun breaks over a mountain ridge on the other side of the valley. The photo we take will prompt more nostalgia from Nonno Anni when he sees it, telling us that as he was walking down the hill to begin work in the fields below, he would watch for the sun to come over the mountain. We marvel at the swirling mist teasing the rooftops, the changing colours of the mountains, the streaky sky. Suddenly a car door slams, followed by the rattle of an engine starting as a villager heads off to work. The spell is broken.

We breakfast on the balcony at the back of the house, overlooking a lane and the village rooftops. In the exquisite light of morning, the village is even more charming than it was yesterday, perhaps because now I am seeing it with refreshed eyes. From the height of the balcony, the stone houses and terracotta roofs cluster together, hiding the skinny lanes between them. Where the village buildings end, a band of grass and sparse trees covers the incline of *Monte Circolo* until it suddenly steepens. Pine trees thicken into a forest before petering out at the sheer craggy rock of the mountaintop. The forest is dark and tall. Suddenly the same spooky shriek I heard last night comes from somewhere within its depths. In the light of day, it doesn't sound so ominous but it still makes the hairs on the back of my neck stand on end. What *is* it? What creature roams both night and day? I have never heard anything like it.

After hearing it last night, to get to sleep I convinced myself the shriek at the witching hour was an owl swooping overhead. Roger disputes this. Having heard it this morning he is adamant it is not the screech of an owl. Since he is originally from the country and I am from the city, I take his word. Privately I tell myself it *was* an owl, because today we are heading to Cocullo, deep into the forested mountains of the Abruzzo, to see the snake charmers. I came across this festival when I was reading about the Abruzzo and it is doubly special to me because it is not something Nonno Anni, or anyone in my family, or Roger knew about. In fact, it is the first thing that I have discovered about the Abruzzo, the land of my ancestry, all by myself.

Cocullo is a serene, medieval village with a population of 300 or so — even smaller than Fossa whose population has started to climb again in recent years towards 700. I imagine life is usually peaceful in Cocullo. On an average day the twisted laneways see perhaps a scooter or two, the shuffle of older men as they walk and talk and answer a middle-aged woman's cheerful greeting to them while she hangs her washing from her narrow balcony. The church bells toll each half-hour and only the birds or the bang of a wooden door is louder than the hum of traffic on distant roads. The town is so quiet that even the whisper of a breeze through the nearby woods is audible. Although it seems so tranquil, Cocullo is also prone to the earthquakes of the area, having suffered heavy losses in the 1915 quake.

I have been longing to go to Cocullo since the moment I found out about it. And we must go today ... not any other day, for today, from the church through the laneways to the main *piazza*, Cocullo will be crawling with snakes, literally. The *Festa dei Serpari* celebrates the Feast Day of San Domenico. I have read that the residents of Cocullo venerate — and parade around the town — snakes they have caught from the nearby woods. It is one of the most ancient festivals in Italy; the earliest historical evidence of San Domenico's feast in Cocullo dates back to 1392. Every town in Italy celebrates its own annual festival — the festival of the mushroom, the bean, the flower. In early August, Fossa hosts the *festa* of the steak, the *Sagra della Bistecca*. However, Cocullo's festival of the snake charmers must be one of the more unusual festivals in Italy.

Roger and I head off with a mixture of trepidation and excitement. Neither of us is particularly fond of snakes, but we are not afraid of them either (though we have some concerns about them literally 'being everywhere'). We drive across the valley, taking the back roads to Cocullo. Travelling under a canopy of trees, we pass crumbling open-air churches, the occasional farmhouse, and fields of crocus flowers near Navelli (the Abruzzo provides some of the world's best saffron). Like many Italian hill towns, Cocullo sits high in the landscape, the bleached church like the bow of a huge stone ship, sailing amidst a green sea. The thick, dark forest — from where the locals catch the snakes — grows right up to the edge of the village. During the *festa*, no cars are permitted up the steep road into town. Everyone parks out both sides of the twisty valley road, turning a dual carriageway into a hazardous single lane clogged with pedestrians.

We climb several kilometres of winding hill to get to Cocullo, along with thousands of others. I notice the Italians drive cars fast but they themselves like to stroll. I enjoy the pace considering the walk is uphill and the late spring sun is beating down, though I sense Roger champing at the bit to surge ahead. About halfway up the hill we encounter the first of many stalls. Gaudy figurines and glass-tile photographs of Pope John Paul II sit alongside quaint carved wooden figures and Abruzzese copper work. Costly wooden snakes are the obvious purchase. Three dangle over the village sign, prompting a flurry of people to take photographs.

There are food stalls selling colourful hard-boiled sweets, drifts of pale-yellow spun sugar, and paper bags of peanuts in their shells. Pungent smells hit my nostrils before I see colossal wedges of aged cheeses and cured ash-rolled meats. A powerfully built blue-eyed man draped in too much chunky gold jewellery presides over vats of uncooked fish and octopus — all dyed bright yellow — perhaps from the Abruzzese saffron. I resist the urge to clamp my fingers over my nose. It reminds me of being in the original New Farm deli with Nanna Francesca when, as a little girl, I loathed the smell of the *baccalà*, the dried salted cod.

The most sought-after stalls are *porchetta* vans, each with its own pig on a spit. The pig's head sightlessly stares at customers lining up to purchase *porchetta*. We join the queue. *Porchetta*, a specialty of the Abruzzo, is an entire roast pig, the inside stuffed with all manner of herbs and spices including rosemary, thyme and oregano, and liberal handfuls of salt and pepper, the outside basted to crispy-skinned perfection. Little has changed in its preparation and cooking since medieval times. When I was growing up, Nanna Francesca's sister Nancy and her husband, Roderick, also from the Abruzzo, often cooked *porchetta* in a large brick oven they had built in the backyard behind their Queenslander. I don't think I even knew what *porchetta* was back then as Nanna Francesca simply said something like, 'We go over there for the roast pig,' or Dad would say, 'They're cooking the pig.' Even as a six-year-old my mouth salivated at the prospect, particularly of the crackling. Nancy had five children and there were always people around. At the time I was the youngest.

Along with several Italians, Roger and I carry our *porchetta* 'sandwiches' — *tramezzini* — over to a low stone wall near the entrance to the village. There we perch and eat as people continue to stream by. They appear to be mostly locals and

Italian tourists, with some other European travellers. Ours is the only English we hear spoken, though at least we are not the only ones conspicuously carrying cameras. In *Through the Apennines and the Lands of Abruzzi*, Estella Canziani writes of an Italian photographer who had to run for his life from Cocullo in 1913 because soon after he took a photograph of the procession, a thunderstorm broke over the mountains, with hail flattening the crops, and the locals put this down to the evil eye of the camera. At this time every single person in the Abruzzo, including children, wore amulets to ward off the evil eye, the threat of which obsessed the villagers. Amulets peculiar to Cocullo include three chicken feathers dyed red, green and purple and wired together, and pieces of linen stamped with the image of San Domenico and hung around the neck like a scapular.

The cobblestoned laneways in the village are breathtakingly steep. We all labour up — women and men in their eighties, their walking sticks trembling; middle-aged women old enough to know better than to be wearing their fashionable, but inappropriate, high heels; and parents pulling strollers backwards up the steep incline, toddlers almost slipping out of them. At first glance I think some of the toddlers are holding the wooden snakes I saw for sale earlier — but no, they're holding *live* snakes. The sight of a small child nonchalantly holding a medium-sized live viper stuns me more than if I had seen a grown man handling an enormous python.

We all crowd into the narrow laneways. No one seems to know which way the procession will be coming, but seeing people flanking the walls we assume we must be in the right spot. Roger and I stand in a stable doorway and wait. Half an hour goes by. People continue pouring in, seeking out the best vantage spots. It is now midday and the sun, directly overhead, beats down into the crevice that is our laneway. Another half-hour creeps by. In the distance, near the church, we hear people singing hymns. The *Festa dei Serpari* was originally a pagan festival, but like so many others it has been usurped by the Catholic Church. I hear the beating of a primordial-sounding drum, then a brass band tuning up, then nothing. It is hard to know what is going on. It feels like the moments before the running of the bulls in Pamplona, that tense anticipation filled with jostling and nervous chatter. More alarming still, the locals are starting to push through the crowd, draped in snakes. The procession hasn't even started yet.

Young children have snakes writhing all over them, and these vipers aren't small. It is unsettling to be confronted with so many of these reptiles in such close proximity. Apparently, the Abruzzo is full of serpent men believed to be immune to the venom, who possess power over vipers and can cure those poisoned by snakebite. I have read that the snake charmers or *serpari*, the special clan of men in Cocullo who handle the reptiles, remove the fangs of those used in the festival so they cannot cause harm. Since we are standing in close proximity to hundreds of them, this is some comfort but I also feel for the poor snakes.

The skill of capturing serpents and then removing the fangs is passed down through the generations from father to son. Catching wild snakes usually occurs around the first day of spring, when sleepy vipers are emerging from their winter holes. The *serpari* place the snakes in wooden boxes, sheepskin sacks or terracotta jugs filled with bran. Having removed the snake fangs and grown up with this tradition, both the adults and children of Cocullo have no fear touching the snakes. It explains how during the *festa* they can wander about with vipers draped around their necks and arms as if they were wearing nothing more than a scarf. For onlookers it is a little scary and awe-inspiring. Ripples of excitement go through the crowd.

Suddenly the drum starts up again, beating with authoritative regularity. It is on. So much for waiting patiently in our neat vantage points, the crowd surges forward in a frenzy of cocked cameras and shouting. Roger and I are pulled along with them. A huge green flag, brandished high to mark the front of the procession, disappears around a corner at the end of our lane. The brass band follows. A roar goes up from the crowd as they catch their first glimpse of the statue of San Domenico held aloft on a platform and swathed in live snakes. The rest of us push forward. Caught up in the excitement, Roger and I jockey for positions with the best of them. I even climb onto a stoop with several others. No sooner have we gained a tantalising distant glimpse of dozens of snakes held aloft than the statue turns out of sight with the rest of the procession. Cameras lower. People groan. Abruptly the disappointed crowd turns and meanders back up the lane. Roger and I go with them, our disappointment acute at having missed the official procession.

Pushed along through the village with the crowd, we find ourselves in *Piazza Repubblica*, an open space walled by attractive rendered houses with freshly painted green shutters and wrought-iron balconies crammed with terracotta pots full of red geraniums. The *piazza*, a little larger than a tennis court, is congested with people. I have had enough and resist being pulled along any further with the frenzied crowds. My feet are aching. We stop at the tip of a triangular junction as others continue to teem past, jostling us, but not dragging us with them.

Looking around me, I sense the crowd in the *piazza* to be locals. They begin to clap and chant, their strange warbling somewhat spooky despite it being the middle of the day. I have never witnessed anything like this. Their wails reach a haunting pitch, prickling the hairs on the back of my neck. Then I hear it, the rhythmic centuries-old beating of a drum, and I turn to see the huge embroidered green flag almost hitting the overhead wires.

I clutch Roger's sleeve. 'They're going to come right past us ...'

'*Viva San Domenico! Viva San Domenico!*' the crowd choruses over and over.

I feel my adrenaline surge. Dozens of live snakes are about to pass within centimetres of me. A formidably attired *carabinieri* officer leads the parade. He looks stern, then I see him quickly poke out his tongue and smirk as he passes his girlfriend. The flag comes next, three men trying to control its weight. The young women of Cocullo, prettily dressed in traditional folk costumes of pink and white, follow. On their heads balance huge adornments made up of five large *ciambelle*, a sweet cake-like bread shaped into a ring to represent snakes biting their own tails. The brass band comes next. Passing within centimetres of me, its music blasts my ears. I feel the drumbeats penetrating my chest. I am so close I make eye contact with some of the musicians. An old man follows with a crucifix on a staff. Flowers and feathers are tucked in behind Jesus' body. I see a stylish young woman make the sign of the cross and kiss her fingertips, then teach her three-year-old daughter to do the same. And then ...

Six men shoulder a wooden platform on which stands the large statue of San Domenico. Several live vipers drape around the shoulders and neck, several more coil at its base. Some snakes seem drowsy (apparently they are fed milk before the festival), but others are alarmingly alert. By now the crowd is wild. I feel the rush. Suddenly, two snakes escape, writhing on the cobblestones towards us. The crowd screams. Alerted by the screams the *serpari* pursue the vipers, catch them by their tails, and throw them back up onto San Domenico. From the behaviour of the snakes, the townsfolk read omens: if the serpents favour the head of the statue, that is a good omen and the crowd responds with robust cheers.

Several priests and monks trail the statue. A clergyman in white robes carrying a large coiled snake brushes past me. The tail end breaks free. It is as thick as my arm. I reach out and hold it. It feels all writhing muscle and smooth scales. Roger stares at me, shocked. The villagers bring up the rear of the procession, carrying several vipers each. Some I notice have painted red marks on the top of the snakes' heads. It is exhilarating to be at such close range. I cannot exactly explain the feeling, but Roger and I are both on a high afterwards. Perhaps San Domenico and the snakes have healed us of any ills as the *festa* promises.

Both H. V. Morton in *A Traveller in Southern Italy* and Estella Canziani in *Through the Apennines and Lands of the Abruzzi* describe attending the Festival of San Domenico and the snakes, in 1969 and 1913 respectively, and little seems to have changed since their accounts. In my precious first edition of Canziani's book, now more than eighty years old, her paintings with their overlaying pages of protective tissue paper which intersperse her text are in immaculate order. I study her painting of the San Domenico statue covered in snakes completed on the brink of the First World War, and it appears identical to what I have seen today. The old pages have a hint of smoke in their scent and I wonder if someone once sat reading this book by a fire. I am reminded of when I asked my mother to write down some of her favourite things: one of them was 'the smell of old books', which I thought was superb.

Originally, the festival ended with the killing and cooking of the snakes. Fortunately, the *serpari* now release the vipers back into the forest, although I wonder how the serpents will survive with their fangs removed. Instead, there are anise-flavoured *ciambelle* — fritters resembling little snakes wrapped around each other — and the large *ciambelle* which the young women in the parade wore on their heads. And of course, there is *porchetta* washed down with small cups of the local red wine.

The church bells toll as the festival ends with a blast of daytime fireworks. The bells toll with triumphant joy, like those for the newly married. Faces are wreathed in smiles. We have all shared something still touched by the magic of times past. It has been a once-in-a-lifetime event, definitely worth the pilgrimage to Cocullo.

Late that night as I lie in bed, I reflect on the unusual day. I went to Cocullo knowing it would be full of snakes and embracing the adventure of it all. And yet what caught me off guard and will stay with me for many years is the spectral warbling of the Cocullo locals, their clapping and chanting conjuring the rhythmic, centuries-old deep beat of a drum. I get goosebumps now just thinking about it.

The belltower has stopped tolling for the day … to sleep, to sleep. I do not hear the eerie shriek.

L'Aquila

Nonno Anni went to L'Aquila to get his passport on an unseasonably cold March day in 1939. As he made his way from Fossa along the valley road on the back of his donkey, it began to snow. By the next village, Monticchio, it was snowing so heavily the donkey refused to take another step. After much cursing, Nonno Anni left the donkey in the stable of friends and continued the journey on foot. The fifteen-year-old arrived in L'Aquila just on noon. At the passport office, a brusque civil servant informed him the office was closing for *siesta*. Cold and wet from the snow, Nonno Anni was forced to wait on one of the hard-backed chairs out the front for several hours until the office reopened.

By the time he got his passport and began his trek home, it was getting dark. He made the last part of the journey after nightfall, boots sinking into deep snow. Several packs of wolves regularly roamed the area and their howling could be heard echoing off the craggy outcrops on clear wintry nights. There is the howl of danger a wolf utters when attacked, the howl of love when they find a mate, and the howl of prey, for wolves do not like to eat alone. Nonno Anni told me he was never so glad to climb the steps up to the front door of number ten. Before he could touch the handle, a frantic Granny Maddalena flung open the door, threw her arms around him and cried, 'Annibale! I thought the wolves had got you!' He extricated himself saying she wouldn't be able to worry about him once he was over in Australia. He was to leave the village within a month and the outbreak of war several months later would cut contact with his mother for the next few years.

The municipality of L'Aquila features in Nonno Anni's stories almost as often as Fossa. The name — strange to Australian ears — was familiar to my lips from an early age. L'Aquila means 'the eagle', and though the small city soars at 721 metres above sea level, the surrounding mountains, some of which are nudging 3000 metres, dwarf it. Perhaps it is more aptly named for the eagles that circle in the nearby Abruzzo national park, one of Italy's oldest, which was founded by royal decree in 1923 (the year Nonno Anni was born) to protect the flora and fauna of the Apennine area. The eagles share the abundant woods with Apennine wolves, mountain goats, deer, the Abruzzo chamois (a goatlike antelope) and Marsican brown bears (and whatever makes that spooky shrieking noise which I haven't heard again). The woods are dense and sometimes dark, with trees of chestnut, oak, pine, beech, maple and ash. A wide variety of plants that can be used for medicinal purposes cover the forest floor.

The black eagle featured on L'Aquila's coat of arms is also part of the crest for my surname, which originates in the Abruzzo. (Boccabella means 'beautiful mouth' and derives from a nickname, no doubt sarcastic.) L'Aquila lends its name to the region's capital as well as to one of the four provinces in the Abruzzo — the others are Chieti, Pescara and Teramo. L'Aquila city's origin is more unusual than most. It rose to prominence in the mid thirteenth century with the union of ninety-nine castles. Every castle provided some of its population and was required to build its own church, *piazza* and fountain in L'Aquila (the city still celebrates having ninety-nine of each of these). L'Aquila became so powerful that it even waged wars, and from 1382 to 1556 coined its own money.

The city's symbol, *La Fontana delle 99 Cannelle*, 'the Fountain with the Ninety-nine Spouts', dates back to 1240 and was originally known as *La Fontana della Rivera* — 'the Fountain of the Revered or Respected' — in what was then the main *piazza*. On our first trip in 1996 Roger and I walked through pouring rain to see this historic fountain. The ninety-nine spouts are heads, each one unique, representing the lords of the ninety-nine castles who helped found the city. For almost eight hundred years, the stone heads of the lords have been spitting water, the source of which is still unknown.

In *Through the Apennines and the Lands of the Abruzzi*, when Estella Canziani chronicles her trip to the Abruzzo with her father in 1913, she describes visiting the same fountain where she saw women washing clothes in its troughs, then carrying the clothes home on their heads. Canziani explained the women and children first wound a piece of cloth to pad the top of their heads then loaded up whatever they were carrying — soap, clothing, a copper *conca* full of water, knitting needles or a large iron bedstead! She watched women carry these burdens on their heads up and down steep steps and roadways or while chatting in the marketplace, quite unconscious of their encumbrance, their balance perfect, nothing ever falling. Only the children, just learning, occasionally raised a hand to correct their balance. My great-granny Maddalena, whom I knew well until I was eight or nine, would have been aged about twenty at this time, and would certainly have been one of the women carrying these loads on her head in a nearby village.

The first time, I went to L'Aquila with little knowledge of it other than family stories and the main sights to see. This time I come with more of an appreciation of its history, though I must confess that having an *espresso* in a *bar* (which I failed to do last trip) is just as high on my list as seeing historic monuments. The road into L'Aquila winds up around waist-high stone walls and tall fir trees. Roger and I follow the coil, tailgating and being tailgated, until we emerge through the centuries-old gate *Porta Napoli* into a tree-lined boulevard. With a current population of around 60,000, L'Aquila is a sophisticated urban centre that exports saffron and wool all over Europe and is famous for its copper work, handcrafted lace, wrought iron and woodwork.

The city has experienced many earthquakes since *terremoti* were first recorded in 1315, with most of them occurring in January. The locals say, 'When the cold is at its greatest, the earthquake is at its strongest.' L'Aquila experienced one of its worst earthquakes in 1703, when much of the city was destroyed and 5000 people were killed. That year many people slept in the huge main *piazza* preferring to face death in the open than under rubble. The area is well overdue for another big earthquake but that is not something I contemplate too deeply.

The people of L'Aquila have been called upon to rebuild their city more than a dozen times over the centuries because of earthquakes. Fortunately, beautiful Baroque and Renaissance buildings remain along with a number of thirteenth- and fifteenth-century churches, several *palazzi*, and the fort, built during Spanish domination in the sixteenth century. In the past, *Forte Spagnolo* has housed a military arsenal, and then prisoners, but today, having been repaired after sustaining heavy damage during the Second World War, it contains the National Museum of Abruzzo and is home to a rare million-year-old *Elephas meridionalis*, a prehistoric mammoth found near L'Aquila in 1954. Underneath the fort are hundreds of secret passages, so many they have not yet all been discovered. In the early twentieth century, a colonel was overseeing their exploration when his wife, their two children and the governess, all roped together, decided to investigate one of the cold passages and did not return. The soldiers conducted searches, shouted and fired revolvers but the women and children were never found and no more exploration was attempted.

A permanent stone walkway stretches across the moat to the entrance of the fortress where a drawbridge might once have been. Above the massive doors is a religious cross with a sinister-looking skull beneath it. Ahead of us are two young Italian couples. One of the men breaks into operatic song, his strong voice resonating against the stone wall. His companions giggle. When my parents first came here in 1970, my father took a photo of my mother standing on this drawbridge walkway. Roger takes a picture of me standing in the same spot. Time moves slowly. The background of the photos, taken more than thirty-five years apart, is almost identical. All that has changed is that the daughter stands where the mother once stood.

I peer into the empty moat, struck by how deep it is. 'I wonder if anyone tried to get across. What do you think their fate was?'

Roger smiles and companionably slings an arm around my shoulders. Walking towards the town centre, we pass *Fontana Luminosa*, a beautiful fountain built in fascist times, featuring two naked women tipping a pitcher into the water below. I fell in love with this fountain during our first trip. The water pitcher is a large two-handled vessel made of beaten copper called a *conca*. The *conche* are a major symbol of the region, made by local coppersmiths. When Canziani stayed in L'Aquila in the autumn of 1913 she described how from all around came the clang of coppersmiths working in their doorways beating copper to form huge cauldrons and gleaming *conche*. In the past, the *conche* were used mainly by women to carry water from the wells and fountains, usually balancing the flat-bottomed vessels on their scarfed heads. When I was young, Nanna Francesca would bring me back a miniature version of a copper *conca* from almost every trip to Italy. I generally gave them to my parents (who already had their own extensive collection). Just a year or two ago, I asked my parents to dig a couple back out for me and they now have a place in my home.

Underneath the high arching portico along *Corso Vittorio Emanuele*, I crane to see ahead. *Yes.* The *bar* I wanted to go into for a coffee on our first trip when Roger refused to accompany me is still there. Catching my look, Roger is sheepish. This time he cannot cross the threshold quickly enough. A flurry of customers jostle for standing positions at the sleek black granite counter, crashing empty *espresso* cups back down on saucers, followed by a swift wipe of lips barely moistened by the single gulp. Along the butter-coloured walls, boxes of chocolates and *torrone*, the locally made nougat, clutter glass shelves. Every surface is spotlessly clean. Roger orders two *espressi* and we stand at the crowded counter. Within a minute, the *barista* places them in front of us. I slide over the sugar boat. The *espresso* (not 'expresso') is black, strong and sweet like the Turkish proverb — *coffee should be as black as hell, as strong as death and as sweet as love.* In a couple of swallows, it is gone. Within two minutes we walk out the door and into the lively *Piazza Duomo*.

Almost every day, all over Italy, markets crowd the main *piazze* of the larger towns and cities. We wander among stalls set up under huge umbrellas and carefully erected tarpaulins. There are tea towels, tablecloths, boxes of shoes, racks of clothing, row upon row of cheap watches and CDs, kitchenware and beautifully crafted copperware. In the produce area everything is fresh and in prime condition, ready to be eaten today. Brilliant red egg-shaped tomatoes still cling to their vines, black grapes hang in triangular bunches, delicate zucchini flowers adorn a basket, and mandarins are stacked with their attractive glossy green foliage still attached. Strawberries are an irresistible scarlet, their sweet perfume intoxicating. Purple artichokes lie in pyramids and *cos* lettuces, each of them placed in neat rows, are appealing in their leafy freshness. I cannot resist the *piselli*, peas in the pod. The stallholder fills a bag for me.

When I was a child, I was drawn to the pea patch Nonno Anni planted each year in his New Farm backyard. The pea plants were taller than I was — my own private forest. With the winter sun warm on my shoulders, I would make my way up and down the rows, picking peas. Little fingers with bitten nails became adept at ripping open the pods then cramming the peas into my mouth. I could swiftly open a pod with just one hand, a skill I retain to this day. My grandparents never worried about how many I ate. Nonno Anni tells me that whenever they wondered where I was, they would check the pea patch first. That was back in the seventies. Over the years, the pea patch was replaced by snake beans, chicory, and then a

FIORI DI ZUCCHINI FRITTI
deep-fried zucchini flowers

INGREDIENTS

~ 2 eggs

~ 150g plain flour

~ Salt and pepper

~ 4 tbsp beer or soda water

~ 20 zucchini flowers

~ Olive oil for frying

METHOD

Beat the eggs then add the flour, salt and pepper, beer or soda water, and mix well to obtain a light batter.

Dip the flowers in the batter one by one and deep-fry in hot olive oil a few at a time until golden. (Use a small saucepan for frying to use less oil to a level high enough for deep-frying.) Serve immediately.

stack of bricks. Then, last year, Nonno Anni decided to plant a row of peas, nothing like his past prodigious patches, but simply for the memories.

'Remember how you were always in the pea patch when you were little?' he said to me, his eyes crinkling with mirth and the hint of a sentimental tear. 'I planted these for you.'

My heart swelled. A few weeks later, on the phone I asked him how the peas were going.

'Bloody possums,' he lamented. 'They've almost eaten the lot.'

'That's okay,' I smiled. 'They need to eat something too.'

Roger and I continue walking among L'Aquila's market stalls and I reach into the plastic bag and pull out a couple of the pea pods. Roger, half laughing, shakes his head, declining my offer. I tear open a pod.

'How are they?'

I keep chewing, a little disappointed. 'They're not as sweet as Nonno's.'

I recall that on our last trip, in Venice at a fruit stall (where pigeons hopped all over the produce), I chose a perfect-looking yellow banana. The wily stallholder slipped a rotten one into the brown paper bag and I did not realise until I got back to my room. Considering that on my backpacker budget the banana was my meal for that evening I was beside myself. Fortunately, the produce we buy in the L'Aquila market is first rate — golden apples with a juicy crunch, tomatoes still on the vine, onions, blood oranges that drip with scarlet juice when cut, verdant asparagus, pears blushed with rose and gold, strawberries, black grapes, and garlic with the stalks attached, ideal for braiding. I look forward to cooking.

In his later years, my Australian grandfather, Grandpa Bob, also had a thriving vegetable patch. It is endearing how my grandfathers each planted according to their culture. Where Nonno Anni grew snake beans, rocket, chicory, basil and flat-leaf parsley, Grandpa Bob planted cauliflowers, beetroot, lettuce, silver beet, tomatoes and passionfruit. They both grew grapes, Nonno Anni having given Grandpa Bob some of his vine cuttings. When Grandpa Bob died, Nonno Anni wanted to ensure his grapevines did not die after the house was sold. So he took the cuttings back and planted them in his yard where they continue to thrive. Considering Grandpa Bob served in the Second World War and Nonno Anni was interned as an Italian prisoner of war in Queensland, it was heart-warming for me to watch these two aging men sit together at our family get-togethers and have a good natter and a beer. They were almost identical in age, having both been born in 1923, just four days apart.

Even so, I grew up with one set of grandparents who were staunchly Australian and another who were passionately patriotic to Italy. All of them were very vocal in their views. They may have made peace with each other, but they all carried their national pride to the grave. This added to the confusion and complexity of my cultural identity, but I feel fortunate to have grown up hearing 'both sides of the story'. Nonno Anni was working on the Solano farm in Applethorpe in 1942 when two policemen turned up and told him to report to the station with his belongings. Like many Italians in the area who had kept their heads down working, he was interned by the Australian government as a prisoner of war for posing a 'threat'. During the same war, Grandpa Bob served in both the Australian Army and Air Force, and my Australian grandmother, Lorna, in the Women's National Emergency Legion.

Looking at black-and-white photographs of my two grandfathers at this time, I can see their worlds could not have been further apart. Nonno Anni is a tall, burly nineteen-year-old, standing barefoot among a group of internees in their prison camp in western Queensland. In the background, the makeshift tents they slept in line a sketchy path they had tongue-in-cheek dubbed '*via Veneto*'. Grandpa Bob's photo is a head and shoulders studio portrait taken with him proudly wearing his uniform. His Air Force cap tilts at the slightest hint of an angle, his blue eyes and roguish smile alluding to the popular chap he was.

Grandpa Bob was proud of serving for Australia. Every Anzac Day he attended dawn services, the march, and then the pub with his mates. Mum recalls when she was a little girl that he came home one Anzac Day evening and sat on the bottom step having trouble untying his shoelaces. I lament not marching with him in an Anzac Day parade. When I was growing up, descendants did not march with veterans. By the time they did, Grandpa Bob had aged and preferred a ride in an open-air jeep to my offers to push him in a wheelchair. (He was a 'man's man' and I think he did not want to appear 'weak' by being wheeled along.)

I marched once. It was the very first Anzac Day after he died and, feeling a bit like an imposter (irrational since also my maternal grandmother's father fought in the First World War and his father in the Boer War), I took my place at the back of the Air Force contingent Grandpa Bob had marched with. I wished I was marching with him, but at least I could honour him in the year of his death. When the contingent moved off into the parade, the crowds lining the streets began clapping and cheering for us. I found myself having to steady my breathing. It was such a moving experience.

Curiously, in Australia I feel more Italian and in Italy I feel more Australian. (At this time I am yet to discover that many others feel the same.) And yet there is something different already about this second trip to Italy compared to my first. On that initial trip, although the impact of seeing the Abruzzo for the first time was instant and I felt my heritage in my bones, I was still too self-conscious, with too many bittersweet links and memories to simply embrace and enjoy Italy as Roger felt at liberty to do. But now, standing in the centre of L'Aquila's market with centuries-old buildings flanking either side of the *piazza*, the morning sun warm on my back, I allow myself to be open to what I am experiencing. All of a sudden, the church bells peal out the midday hour, jolting me to appreciate that *yes*, I am here in Italy and it's wonderful, not just because it is a magical place but because it is in my make-up.

Up near the fountain at one end of *Piazza Duomo*, I gravitate towards a trestle table groaning under the weight of old and antique linens. Some must be from deceased estates and some are yellowed with age or have the odd stain, but the cutwork and embroidery is exquisite. Despite his face starting to show signs of masked impatience, Roger comes over and helps me to draw out tablecloth after tablecloth, some large enough to fit tables for twelve, some for a small corner lamp table. After much deliberation I decide on several in white and cream, all with delicate embroidery or lace, and not a stain or a mark on them. We approach a bent, fragile-looking man who is chatting amiably to some older women going through the piles of linens. He's not the stallholder and directs us to two young blokes in designer sunglasses who look like they should be selling stylish clothes, not antique linens. They're doing a brisk trade.

The weight of the bag of cloths is reassuring, gently banging against my leg as we continue on among the market stalls. It almost seems wrong that these tablecloths, which have adorned Italian tabletops for decades, possibly handed down from grandmother to mother to daughter, will be taken far away from their land of origin to Australia. Even more astonishing is that, considering I once shunned anything Italian, let alone tablecloths, I am suddenly seeking out these treasures with single-minded determination.

'I'm starving,' Roger announces and my gaze follows his to the red-painted *porchetta* van which is parked in the same spot at the far end of the *piazza* that it was when we were last here. Nonno Anni told me that every summer he spent in Italy he would buy a *porchetta* sandwich while Nanna Francesca shopped at the L'Aquila market. Eating in the street is almost unheard of for Italians, who prefer the more civilised *alla tavola*. A local woman actually chastised Nonno Anni for eating a *porchetta* sandwich in the street, shrieking at him, 'What's wrong with you?' Both Roger and I are aware of this attitude, having copped disdainful stares our first time here as we ate while walking around, something that seems so normal in Australia.

To keep it succulent, the van owner does not cut the *porchetta* until Roger places our order. With mouths watering, we watch the van owner deftly carve several pieces, including some crackling, slap them between thick-cut slices of dense bread then wrap each sandwich separately in brown paper. He throws in a paper bag some stuffed, crumbed olives like those well known from the nearby *Le Marche* region. We sit on the edge of a fountain in the middle of the bustling market (this seems more accepted than eating and walking at the same time). The *porchetta* is delicious (better than that in Cocullo), the olives, piquant and flavoursome. Our conversation wanes.

In *Standa*, the small, modern supermarket, when Roger and I speak to each other in English everyone stops and turns to stare. We fill a basket with necessities such as milk, cheese, pasta and olive oil, and treats such as fresh basil pesto, chocolate and some moreish little hazelnut biscuits. The washing powder is called *Lanza* (we refer to it as 'Mario'). At the checkout again everyone halts and stares when we attempt speaking Italian. As we walk out, weighed down with shopping, I can still sense eyes on my back. I feel my indignation rising. To my surprise I want it to be known I am not a tourist, that my family are from here.

But of course my only response is two pink spots high on my cheeks.

We emerge from *Standa* to find L'Aquila closing down for *siesta*. The markets have disappeared, leaving behind empty wooden crates stacked on top of each other, and stray lettuce leaves. A *Piaggio Ape* groans under a load of crates. Pronounced *ar-pay*, this three-wheeled vehicle has handlebar steering like a motor bike enclosed in a tiny cabin, and a tray like a ute attached to the rear. *Ape* vehicles can be seen throughout Italy, having replaced mules. *Ape* means 'bee' in Italian, and indeed the familiar buzz of these vehicles (as they bear down on you) is common.

On the way back to the car we make a quick detour to the *gelateria* and walk the rest of the way juggling shopping bags with our *tartufo* and *pannacotta* cones.

The Village Witch

My great-grandmother Maddalena Urbani came from the village
of Poggio Picenze, which sits across the valley from Fossa. Roger
and I did not make it to her village on our last trip, as we didn't
have a car and must have decided not to walk the distance.
Looking back, I can't believe I didn't get there. It's strange to
be only just going almost a decade after Nonno Anni pointed
the town out to me from Fossa's *Piazza Belvedere*. I am aware
of being more motivated to explore the places of my ancestry
on this trip than I was on my first. Perhaps being in my thirties
rather than my early twenties also has something to do with this.

Roger and I are driving across the valley from Fossa to
Poggio Picenze when a shepherd moving a mob of sheep across

137

the road from one paddock to another brings us to a halt. Sheep surround the tiny idling car and it sways slightly as they mob us. Roger gives the shepherd a single wave, like those I have seen farmers exchange in passing where Roger grew up in the country. The shepherd casually lifts a hand in response. His almost toothless smile is broad. A thinly rolled burning cigarette stuck to his bottom lip does not fall.

This valley is part of the *tratturo*, an ancient route used during the transhumance, or biannual migration of sheep to better pastures. From L'Aquila, shepherds guided massive flocks (guarded from wolves by huge, ferocious white dogs with spiky collars) up over the mountains around *Gran Sasso* and through Molise to the plains of Puglia to escape the bitter Abruzzo winter. Dotted along the route are *tholoi*, stone dwellings built into the hillsides since antiquity to provide temporary shelter for the shepherds from weather, wolves and bears. Most of the sheep were bred for their wool, though a few were destined for the pot. The shepherds would never kill and eat any of the animals lest they suffer the wrath of their masters. Their reward for their loyalty was if any animal died of natural causes along the way, the shepherds were allowed to roast it over an open fire. I wonder how many died of 'natural causes'.

When the sheep pass, we drive on through the valley and I say to Roger, 'There's Poggio,' pointing towards one of three villages that sit across from Fossa.

'No, it's this one to the left.'

'I don't think so ...' I recall Nonno Anni pointing Poggio out to me but my reply is vague, Roger's sureness making me doubt. He takes us up a winding road and I start to feel carsick. 'I'm sure it's the other one,' I say irritably.

'No, no, it's this one.'

We pass a sign saying San Martino. I give him a look. We wind back down and drive on further to Poggio Picenze. I am more annoyed with myself. Years of repressing my heritage has made me so diffident that I allow Roger in his enthusiasm to take ownership of things I innately know should I give myself more of a chance.

My great-grandmother came from a fairly well-off family which owned a mill and an entire block in Poggio Picenze, including a butchery, a restaurant and an inn. Independent and full of verve, Maddalena was almost thirty, had broken off one engagement, and was considered an old spinster when she married my great-grandfather Vitale one snowy January Thursday in the church at Poggio (it was considered bad luck to marry on a Tuesday or a Friday).

There are various Abruzzese marriage customs and superstitions pertaining to weddings. A week before the ceremony Maddalena would have arranged her trousseau, while Vitale made his way across the valley to fetch it with a cart drawn by creamy oxen, their horns decorated with ribbons and handkerchiefs. (The owner of the animals could keep these adornments.) The bride wore a vivid red, purple, blue or yellow wedding gown in silk or wool, and the groom wore a jacket to match her dress, his pants generally being a brilliant purple.

After the wedding ceremony there was much merriment amid the throwing of *confetti* (sugar-coated almonds, not paper), mortars being fired, a bottle of wine thrown against the wall of the family house, eating, dancing and a local poet proclaiming the wedding toast. Later, the bride kissed her parents' hands, and as she walked away they would cry and call to her as she followed her husband home. (In Granny Maddalena's case, just her mother, as her father had died four years before in 1919.) Her new mother-in-law would await the cortege to give her best leg of *prosciutto* to the bride's family to appease them. However, as Nonno Vitale's mother had died in 1921, again they would have dispensed with this tradition. Next morning the bride would rush to be the first to the fountain to fill her copper *conca* to show she was looking after her husband.

Despite her town of origin being visible from Fossa, Maddalena was considered an outsider in her husband's village. It makes me wonder how she fared during those first weeks of marriage. I am amazed to learn from Nonno Anni that when he was growing up he was often teased in Fossa because his mother was from Poggio Picenze.

'I couldn't win,' he told me with a shake of his head. 'In Fossa they'd tease me and call me *Poiano*, and when we went over to Poggio to visit relatives they'd tease me and call me *Fossolano*. It was like I didn't fully belong to either.'

I was slightly stunned to hear in his lament an echo of my own feeling of not belonging fully to Australian or Italian culture.

'Yeah, I got teased a lot ...' he continued, his lips suddenly curving into a smile, '... but I was lucky, I was big and I quickly learnt to use my fists.' We both laughed.

He reiterated the fascist sentiment of 'Better to be a lion for a day than a lamb for a lifetime'. I understand the mind-set behind this, but I told him I think the world would be a more harmonious place with more 'lambs'. He pretended not to hear, instead telling me stories of his mother, my great-grandmother Maddalena, growing up with her parents and her siblings. My favourite photo is of her brother, Sabbatino, a cheeky grin on his face as he wields a Tommy gun. He looks as full of spit and fire as Granny was.

'You look a lot like her,' Nonno Anni said, 'when she was younger. I've put photos of you both next to each other and the likeness is incredible. The same nose, cheeks and ...'

He went on but I struggled to see it myself. I knew Maddalena till I was almost nine and I just couldn't picture myself resembling 'Granny' as I knew her, with her wizened face, her long grey hair swept up into a neat bun at the nape of her neck.

Poggio is similar to Fossa, though perhaps a little larger (it has a population of around a thousand compared to Fossa's six or seven hundred). The name 'Poggio Picenze' derives from the castle which was built on the side of *Monte Picenze*, and in turn from the *Piceni* or *Picentia* peoples who settled in the area in about the third century BC. The castle dates back to around the year 1000 and is referenced in documents dated 1173. *Podio de Picentia* had fortified walls and six towers, including one high tower in the middle, but its position made it susceptible to raids. Remains of the castle are still visible in the old part of town.

Passers-by stare and turn around to keep watching Roger and me. Like in many parts of the Abruzzo it seems they are not used to unfamiliar faces. I try to put myself in the shoes of Granny Maddalena who walked these lanes a century ago. She was born here in 1893 in an era when the women still wore traditional Abruzzese folk garb with aprons tied around a cinched-in waist over full skirts and petticoats, and a fitted waistcoat or jerkin over their shirts. Their clothing was mostly coloured in deep blues, greens, reds and white. It is said their Renaissance-style gowns remained almost unchanged for centuries due to their remote geographical location. They wore their long hair in tight nets tucked under scarves or a *tovagliola*, a white lace-bordered local headdress almost like a veil. In her book, Estella Canziani describes going to villages 'not far from L'Aquila' where she saw a 'medieval society' and 'all the women, young and old, wore regional costume'. My Granny would have been twenty at the time. It would be astonishing if Granny had been part of the crowd that gathered to inspect Canziani and her 'strange English clothes'.

Though the location of Granny Maddalena's family home was explained to me back in Australia, now that I am here I cannot find where it is situated. This is frustrating. There was a lot of overlapping family talk at the table one day of 'the third green door on the left' and 'the second corner', none of which are obvious now. I look and look but none of the doors I see are painted green. Granny was fifty-four when she came to Australia to live out her final thirty-four years. She spoke little English and I spoke little Italian, but we communicated. Her kisses were gummy, leaving my cheeks moist. The older she got the more her pasta swam in oil. With her thick accent, she pronounced my name 'Tszue'.

Nonno Anni always credits any of his business acumen to his mother. Maddalena Urbani was an intelligent person, but received little schooling. Girls were not considered worthy of much education in those days. They were merely marriage and housewife fodder, particularly those not living in cities. Both boys and girls were needed as soon as possible to help work the land and put food on the table. It is not that education was not highly esteemed. Many associated it with success because it meant making a living 'without sweat'. Unfortunately, school facilities in areas outside the cities were often few, poorly staffed and ill-equipped.

During her youth, Granny Maddalena slaughtered young lambs and pigs for the Poggio family butchery; in Australia, she would wring chickens' necks. Just thinking about it makes me squeamish. One of my older cousins said she will never forget the day when a pedestal fan would not work properly and Granny Maddalena took to it with an axe. Granny had a cheeky gleam in her eye, was fiercely self-reliant, spoke her mind, and read the newspaper without needing glasses right up until she was eighty-eight (after she died her corneas were transplanted into a five-year-old boy). For her eightieth birthday she requested, and received from Nonno Anni, a wheelbarrow, which pretty much sums up the incredible person she was. (She wanted to use it to muck out her chook pen and fertilise her thriving vegetable patch.)

I was terribly impressed when Nonno Anni told me that in Fossa, Granny Maddalena was the village witch. This title does not carry negative connotations — it was an honour and meant she was a healer. He said people often knocked at the door in search of her enchantments and herbal remedies, whether it was so she could apply a poultice to cure a boil, use medicinal hashish for a toothache, or utter an enchantment. There are healing words that vary for every physical complaint. For example, an enchantment for babies' tummy-ache was said while making the sign of the cross on their navel:

Muglicolò, muglicolà,	Tummy-ache, tummy-ache,
Pan di segale,	(Here is) bread of rye,
Pan di grà,	(Here is) bread of wheat,
Guarito il muglicolà.	(And) cured is the tummy ache.

These words did not work if a normal person uttered them. Throughout the Abruzzo, the healer was considered a special person and they could only learn the words of enchantment on Christmas Eve. If they were taught on any other night they had no power.

The villagers also came to Granny Maddalena so she could remove the *malocchio* or evil eye. Nonno Anni watched her do so on several occasions. Her tools were a water pitcher, a saucer and an oil lamp, which she laid out on the kitchen table. There were various steps to the process but, in essence, she poured water into the saucer and placed a drop of oil from the lamp in the middle to 'read' the oil. If the oil scattered into many droplets in the water, the evil eye did not exist; however, if all the oil droplets joined, the evil eye was present and Granny Maddalena would then set about removing it from the cursed person.

There were also evil witches — both men and women — from whom the Abruzzese were always trying to protect themselves by putting the herb valerian in keyholes or placing a broom behind the door. (Upon entering a house, the witch first has to count the twigs in a broom and this takes so long that dawn breaks and they risk capture.) Over time, superstition, magic and omens have become intricately woven into Italian culture. The Abruzzo itself abounds with a particularly rich tapestry of spells, incantations, the evil eye, witches, serpent charmers, fortune-tellers, sorcery and *lupi mannari* — werewolves. Ovid, Horace, Pliny and other ancient writers have mentioned the Marsi tribe of the Abruzzo, who had a reputation for magic.

In 1913, most of the Abruzzese that Estella Canziani encountered, including the majority of children, wore amulets to ward off the *malocchio*. The most common charms included a horn, a frog, a Pope's head with mitre and crozier, a cornucopia (a bunch of tin or silver charms all hanging from a circle with the number thirteen in it), a hand, cross-keys, a hunchback (*gobbetto*), a broom … the list goes on. The ones I see in the area now are typically a hand with all fingers closed except for the second and little finger pointing upwards, making the sign that wards off the evil eye, and a curved object to represent an ox horn, both in the colour red to imitate coral.

(Since about 3000 BC in Mesopotamia, red coral has been believed to offer protection when worn, to ward off the evil eye.) These days such amulets are often seen on car key rings or dangling from rear-view mirrors.

Since the advent of radio and television, public transport and better roads, some of these traditions have begun to fade. Still, many locals, both young and old, wear amulets for protection against the evil eye. Roger and I both purchase the 'closed hand with fingers extended' key rings and horn-shaped coral. I now understand what Granny Maddelena's squiggly horn-shaped gold amulet was. As a child I assumed it was just a funny-looking piece of jewellery since it was worn on a delicate chain around her neck.

Interestingly, although Granny Maddalena was the village witch, she also had a deep reverence for the Catholic religion and, in particular, San Francesco di Assisi — anglicised to Saint Francis of Assisi. His first name was actually Giovanni, but people called him Francesco, meaning 'from France', because his mother was French (despite he and his father being Italian). Granny Maddalena was a member of the Third Order of San Francesco, a religious order for lay people, now known as the Secular Order. In 1205, Francesco established three Orders — the Friars Minor, the Poor Ladies or Order of Chiara, and the Brothers and Sisters of Penance. The First and Second Orders live a celibate life in their respective communities. The Third Order of men and women, single or in committed relationships, follow ordinary professions and live a dedicated life of service through prayer, study and work.

When Roger and I visit the mammoth, silent basilica in Assisi the opulence of this monument appears in direct contrast to the teachings of San Francesco (his humble, candlelit underground tomb seemed more apt). Some of the frescoes had disappeared after the big earthquake in 1997 but I was pleased to see Giotto's *St Francis Preaching to the Birds* still intact. That San Francesco was ahead of his time in his respect for nature and animals appeals to me. I had no idea when Granny Maddalena was alive that she followed him as a part of the Third Order. My father recalls she would sometimes wear a special brown dress that signified the robes of San Francesco and her affinity to the Order.

My father was, for the most part, brought up by Granny Maddalena. While he was growing up, his own parents were busy running their fruit shop and milk bar up to fifteen hours a day, seven days a week (though Nanna Francesca confided she would rather have been at home bringing up her child). He accompanied Granny to Italian Mass at the underground crypt in Fortitude Valley. The crypt, completed in 1935, was the only part built of what was to be a massive Renaissance-style basilica, but debt, the Depression and funds going 'missing' brought building to a halt. (The crypt was bulldozed in 1985 and built over with apartment blocks, ironically named 'Cathedral Place'). Many Italians easily combine their Catholic religion with traditions of incantation, witchcraft and paganism. It is not unusual to see an amulet warding off the evil eye swinging on the same gold chain around an Italian's neck as a crucifix.

In the main street of Poggio Picenze I spot Granny Maddalena's surname above an inn door. The *Locanda Urbani Ristorante*, the inn and restaurant Granny Maddalena's family ran more than a century ago, continues to be managed by ongoing generations. It has been remodelled since the slides my parents took back in 1970, but is easily recognisable.

My father brought my mother here, turning up unannounced to relatives he had never met and hoping to stay (something I could never imagine doing). It was midwinter and the rooms of the inn were empty so they were given a bed. While the patriarch of the family was congenial, the women were understandably a little riled at having unexpected visitors. My parents spent some freezing nights in a room with no heat. When the women served them up a meal of pigskin — not crackling, just rubbery cooked fatty skin — my father took the hint.

Roger and I walk up to the closed restaurant and peer in a window at red-and-white checked tablecloths on shiny, dark wooden tables. I'm not sure if I'm disappointed or relieved there is no one about (I am thinking of that pigskin). Would they know who I was talking about if I said I was Maddalena's great-granddaughter? She left Poggio in the 1920s, Italy in the 1940s. How many generations occur before those who migrated are ultimately forgotten?

A picture of Poggio Picenze's church has hung in my grandparents' Brisbane dining room for years. *Chiesa di San Felice Martire* is dedicated to Saint Felix the Martyr. Built around the mid fifteenth century, the church suffered severe damage during the earthquake of 1762 and was rebuilt and enlarged, its stone façade finally restored in 1870 with local stone. The valuable white stone that used to be mined from Poggio's caves in past centuries was one of the main materials used in L'Aquila's construction. Like the Fossa church, Poggio's church safeguards the records of life events of generations of my forebears — baptisms, communions, weddings and funerals — in dusty books with yellowed pages, my ancestors' names written to record each new birth made way for by a death. When one looks at such records, trying to decipher a priest's scrawl, it is difficult not to feel like having let down all these generations by dispersing their lineage to the other side of the world.

Standing on the church steps, I look back towards Fossa. For the first time I can see the magnitude of the snow-capped mountains behind *Monte Circolo* dwarfing it. No wonder cold winds gusting down the mountainside make the presence of these peaks persistently felt, even on the brink of summer. The haughty grandeur and stark bleakness of the towering mountains makes me glad Fossa is nestled snugly into the hollow that gave the village its name. I do not know if it is the raw beauty or that my ancestors have walked these mountains through many ages, but as I stand looking out across the valley the significance of this place strikes me. I stand here now, with the cold mountain wind blowing my hair back from my face, and something stirs in my heart. Part of this area of the Abruzzo is within me. I want to tell Nonno Anni and Granny Maddalena and all those before me who are no longer on this earth: I acknowledge you. I may have grown up far from here, but I *acknowledge* you.

'L'ignoranza fa rima con l'intolleranza.'
Ignorance rhymes with intolerance.

Italian proverb

Old (and New) Calabria

Whenever I expressed interest in going to Nanna Francesca's birthplace, the Calabrian seaside town of Palmi, my grandparents' protective wails of 'No! *No!*' went off like duplicate sirens. Three decades ago, they happened to be in Calabria when a nephew was kidnapped by what is largely termed 'the Mafia'. It is no secret that different areas in the south have mafia groups, such as Sicily's *Cosa Nostra* and Naples' *Camorra*. However, for the most part the Calabrese keep their silence about the *'ndrangheta*, acting as though it does not exist, adding another dimension to the Calabrian proverb: *Chi s'occupa coi i suoi propri affari, va continuare per cent'anni*, 'Whoever occupies himself with his own affairs will live a hundred years'.

In the seventies, Nanna Francesca returned to her birthplace for the first time since she left in 1934. She was eager to catch up with relatives and to see the house her family had lived in, her school, the places where she used to play with friends and the shops she had visited with her mother and grandmother. However, her relatives would not let her even walk around on her own. She insisted on going to find her old house only to discover it had been knocked down. She and Nonno Anni visited her uncle, who owned an olive mill, and Nanna Francesca enjoyed seeing her relatives but my grandparents never went back.

Not long after, her uncle was shot in the head. An uncharacteristic frost had destroyed the olive flowers on the trees and there were no olives to press at the mill that season, hence no money to make the regular 'payment'. Apparently, Nanna Francesca's uncle tried to explain the situation, but the *'ndrangheta* does not like to be defied. Sometimes the Italian mafia is referred to in jokes or portrayed with some mirth in Hollywood movies, but living with fear and oppression is no laughing matter. It is slightly gauche even using the word 'mafia' for what is more usually known as the 'business', the 'family' or the 'organisation'.

Despite my grandparents' repeated protestations and my father's attempts to persuade me not to go, I determinedly set out to Calabria and Nanna Francesca's birthplace of Palmi for the first time. On this occasion I am appreciative of Roger's enthusiasm to explore every inch of Italy. Near Pompeii Roger and I see a sign on the *autostrada* saying,

'Roadworks next 596 km'. We both laugh. Then Roger faces some of the most difficult and intense eight hours of driving he has experienced in Italy. It was the first mistake we made in being blasé. The second was thinking any 'mafia presence' was all hype.

Nanna Francesca's father, Domenico Solano, left Calabria for Queensland, arriving in Australia on a boat called *Caprera* in July 1927. He was a cook for a cane gang in Ingham before settling near Stanthorpe, three hours south-west of Brisbane. Domenico painstakingly cleared hectares of scrub by hand to become one of the first Italians to establish his own apple and pear farm. In 1934, after several years apart, my feisty great-grandmother Francesca Carrozza decided it was about time she and her daughter — my grandmother — joined her husband in Australia. She was never to see her mother or her family again.

The Solano family set up house among their orchards on Ellwood Road, Applethorpe, being one of the fourteen pioneering Italian families to settle in the Stanthorpe area between 1925 and 1935. Two more children were born in Australia, a daughter named Soccorsa and a son, Vincenzo. Soccorsa had not even left the hospital where she was born when the nurses, adamant Soccorsa was too hard to say, dubbed her 'Nancy', a name that was to stick for life. Ironically, *soccorsa* means 'help' or 'assistance' and is a common sign in Italian hospitals. 'But Mum and Dad always called me Soccorsa, or Corsa for short at home,' my great-aunt Nancy told me with a smile. 'It *is* officially my name.' Perhaps these Australians had good intentions behind 'renaming'

153

someone's child but now, seven decades later, it reeks of imposed assimilation and arrogance. I could not imagine many Australians putting up with being told what to call their own child, even back then.

I have travelled out to Stanthorpe on numerous occasions over the years and stood across from my great-grandparents' farm. It is a very quiet place. The wooden house is still, with no sign of the current owners. It is painted white in contrast to the dark colour in old family photographs. The large wooden shed that Nanna Francesca's father built still stands. Great outcrops of granite punctuate the landscape. I have walked along the gravelly lane where Nanna Francesca rode her bicycle to carry out errands to neighbouring farms and unknowingly caught Nonno Anni's eye.

Sadly, the apple and pear orchards my relatives planted have all been dug out now, replaced by crops of broccoli and parsley. I am fortunate, though, to have seen them and run between the pretty rows of established fruit trees. When I was thirteen, my immediate family, my grandparents and *zio* Vincenzo had a holiday out at Stanthorpe and we visited the farm. The owners were Italians who knew my grandparents and invited us all to lunch. We crowded around a rectangular wooden table eating pasta cooked in the kitchen my great-grandmother Francesca once used. I explored the packing shed unaware at the time that my great-grandfather had built it in the 1930s. I remember being horrified that the family had only an outdoor toilet, and after peering inside it managed to hold off going for the entire day. When the farmer's daughter, who was about seventeen, gleefully showed me the dam she swam in during summer, I stood looking at the muddy water, dumbstruck.

The Calabrese are known to be 'hard-headed' or wilful but kind-hearted. A common gesture for someone to identify themselves as Calabrese is by knocking their knuckles to their head and saying, '*Testa dura*' — hardhead. In a positive sense, the 'hard-heads' are seen as shrewd, down to earth and practical, but there also is a perception of being stubborn and not easily moved by emotion or sentiment. Sometimes Nanna Francesca exhibited such characteristics, sometimes not. She could give what we termed her 'Calabrese look' — a look that could burn through steel — but she could also cry at the slightest provocation.

When Australian descendants of Italian migrants are asked which region they come from, I have observed many often name the region from where the paternal side of the family originates. I have done this too, perhaps citing the Abruzzo because it is where we still have the familial house. It is only in recent years that, when questioned about my Italian heritage, my prompt reply of 'the Abruzzo' has altered to include 'and Calabria'. The most common reaction I get to the Abruzzo is: 'Where's *that*?'; and to Calabria: 'Ooh, the mafia'.

Unexpectedly, Calabria reminds me of country Australia. Mountains flatten into hills, trees thin and dry grasses cover large stretches of cleared land. Speeding along at 140 kilometres an hour on highways that stand hundreds of metres above the ground on cement pylons is, at times, petrifying. Dusk is falling when Roger and I arrive at our pre-booked hotel on the outer edge of Palmi. Exhausted from the '596 km of roadworks' we postpone exploring till morning.

The hotel is built like a fortress. Security cameras turn their impassive eyes on to every nook and cranny both outside and in. Strangely, the receptionist does not give us one of the room keys on brass key-rings hanging behind the reception desk but one on a plastic key-ring retrieved from under the counter. Our room is well appointed, although everything is covered in a fine layer of dust. I open the top drawer of my bedside table and am startled to discover a sizeable crucifix. From the balcony we look down on to an expanse of concrete and tile that must have cost a fortune. An ornate fountain splashes. There is an enormous pool and adjacent area, again all concreted and tiled. Beyond is a breathtaking view of a rural valley daubed here and there with little villages of stone houses. It is the *Gioia Tauro* plain, the most fertile area of Calabria. We can gaze over it far into the distance until it becomes a hazy scribble of low mountains. I take a deep breath of the slightly sweet, summery air.

The hotel restaurant opens at eight o'clock for dinner. Roger and I wander stretches of tiles and lengthy red carpeted hallways in search of it. It seems we are the only guests. Many luxuriously appointed 'common' rooms are unlit and not in use. An enormous billiard table sits in the centre of a room sixty metres square. On another floor, an opulent bar is set up with dozens of bottles and not a soul in sight. We find the restaurant two floors below the ground floor. At a quarter past eight it is deserted and in darkness. A man appears out of the shadows behind us.

He simply says, '*Cinque minuti,*' and turns on some lights and a TV in the corner.

The restaurant is in an enormous room of another expanse of tiles, fancy lighting and dozens of colossal, gilt-framed oil paintings one would expect to see in a palace. There are enough tables to seat several hundred. Bizarrely we saw no sign for the restaurant, outside or in. The spaghetti with garlic, olive oil and *peperoncini* is one of the most flavoursome dishes I've had in Italy. The strange thing is that each night there is just Roger and me at one table, several morose, standoffish waiters who outnumber us, and a different man eating solo at an adjacent table — just three diners. The men are deeply tanned. I observe that each one of them has the outline of a heart tattooed on his forearm. The atmosphere is tense.

After midnight it appears Roger and I are the only two souls in this massive building in the middle of Calabria. Earlier, I stood out on the balcony scanning the other hotel room windows (all in darkness). I think back to the times I've cursed noisy people in adjacent hotel rooms. Now I sleep only fitfully, feeling vulnerable not to have anyone else around. I am lying awake at two in the morning and hear several chairs being scraped back as though a meeting has adjourned in a room somewhere above me.

Breakfast is served by a tough cookie who looks like she'd be comfortable guarding a nightclub entrance. She has jet-black hair pulled back into a severe ponytail and pock-marked skin. She stands with her impressive forearms crossed next to a breakfast smorgasbord of several cakes, all rich and sweet.

SPAGHETTI CON AGLIO —
OLIO E PEPERONCINI

spaghetti with garlic, olive oil and chillies

INGREDIENTS
~ 500g spaghetti
~ 2–3 cloves garlic, minced
~ 2–3 red chillies, finely sliced, to taste
~ Extra virgin olive oil
~ Flat-leaf parsley, chopped
~ Salt, to taste

METHOD

As the spaghetti is cooking in plenty of salted boiling
water, fry chillies and garlic in oil on medium heat
until garlic is golden. Add parsley and salt and combine
with drained, *al dente* spaghetti.

Sprinkle generously with *Parmigiano* and serve
immediately.

Serves 4

The piece I choose is rubbery. Room-temperature apple juice is a vibrant, cloudy green and tastes of Granny Smiths. 'Tough Cookie' watches us in silence.

At reception a male attendant in his late forties greets us with a black eye, a piece of sticking plaster holding together the delicate curve of skin underneath. When we talk to him we pretend not to notice his eye. He recommends a restaurant for lunch on a lonely road many kilometres away and rasps, 'Tell them Ugo sent you.' I'm starting to feel like I'm in a bad gangster film. He moseys over to 'Tough Cookie', who high fives him.

Roger and I have been warned by people (often non-Italians who have never been here) that if we venture into Calabria our car will either be stripped or stolen overnight. It is gratifying to see the Fiat has survived its first night (and every night after that) parked out the front of the hotel. It dispels some of our unease. Perhaps because this is Nanna Francesca's birthplace and I feel protective I am beginning to feel a little defensive at the bad rap Calabria seems to cop from both tourists and native Italians, especially by those who have not visited the region. I was once having dinner with some northern Italians who enquired about my Italian origins. While it seemed acceptable to come from the Abruzzo, when I mentioned my grandmother was from Calabria there was silence. One woman actually puckered up her face with distaste, which prickled me. None of them had ever ventured farther south than Rome.

It is a warm, sunny morning and I am excited to begin exploring Palmi (Palmi means 'palms', named for the trees around its seaside location). Finally I will see where Nanna Francesca was born and lived her first eight years. She had such fond memories of living in this town with her mother and grandmother. Unfortunately her house was knocked down before I was born, but her cousin has narrowed down its whereabouts for me to either one of two short streets next to the park (she was only six at the time so she cannot remember the precise address). Nanna Francesca once said they had a view of the sea from the rear of the house so I can narrow it down further to one side of the two streets.

As we drive into town, I gaze at the scenes unfolding before me. Litter is strewn across footpaths and in gutters. Buildings are grimy, many derelict. Some newer ones are shoddily built with not enough mortar and the bricks facing all different ways. Many new building projects have been started, stalled and then abandoned to graffiti. The exception is a few opulent residences built in the hills outside of town. Palmi feels oppressed, browbeaten. It is a beautiful spot with an amphitheatre of mountains surrounding a lovely stretch of beach and a clear sea. If the houses had been built into the cliffs instead of above them, it could have rivalled Positano. But it seems the spirit and progress of Palmi is being held under a thumb.

Roger parks the Fiat and we walk up and down the two short streets of houses where, at one address, Nanna Francesca lived. It is a poor area with dilapidated dwellings and the bitumen streets in poor shape, but the views of the lush mountains and the calm sea are magnificent. Nanna Francesca said that her grandparents' house was high up and had an expansive balcony with tall railings at the back of the house. 'You could see all the boats and the whole sea up to the Strait of Messina,' Nanna Francesca smiled. 'A beautiful view!' And seeing it now, I can finally visualise the setting for her childhood stories relayed to me over the years.

In Australia, there is usually a definite horizon-line between roiling grey sea and blue sky, but here in Calabria the sea and sky, both a hazy indigo, almost meld. No wonder locals call it *Costa Viola*, the 'violet coast'. Tall-masted swordfish boats create patterns in their wake on the otherwise flat sea. Swordfish are a speciality of the south, particularly in Calabria and Sicily. The boats are unusual in that a fisherman steers the vessel from a wheel high up on top of the mast so as to spot the swordfish, which can grow up to four metres in length. Another fisherman harpoons the fish from the end of a long, narrow plank jutting out from the bow.

Unfortunately, I have little information about Nanna Francesca's paternal grandparents, Vincenzo Solano and Francesca Rizitano, or her maternal grandfather, Antonio Carozza. Nanna Francesca described her maternal grandmother's house in Palmi as 'an ordinary house'. The front of the house was at street level but inside there were steps that led down to the *forno* (wood-fired oven). Nanna Francesca's grandmother, Soccorsa Misale, was like the local baker in the area, because in those days people did not have their own oven in their house. Women who lived in the vicinity brought their dough to great-great-grandmother Soccorsa's *forno* and she would bake it for them. Nanna Francesca said her grandmother could get up to eight pieces of dough in the oven at a time. The women would leave an initial, mark or a name in the dough so they would know which was theirs when it was ready. Curiously, I look over to see a poster for bread and cakes on the wall of a house.

One end of the street leads into a hostile-looking lane that can only be described as a slum. Roger decides to walk back to move the car to a spot up close to the nearby park that looks a bit safer. Nonno Anni and Nanna Francesca would most probably be horrified that I am standing here on my own trying to get a feel for the area. At the other end of the street sits the sixteenth-century church *dei Monaci* my ancestors presumably attended. It is known as the church of the monks and *il Crocifisso*, and I later discover inside hangs a disturbingly lifelike crucifix carved in the seventeenth century.

There are a few spots where houses have been reduced to rubble. I wish I knew which of these was once Nanna Francesca's. She said her school in Palmi was about a fifteen-minute walk away, and we drove past a school on our way here. Her mother sent her to school at the age of four, even though Nanna Francesca was a year younger than the other children starting (the same happened to me). Being the eldest in a large family my great-grandmother had not had the opportunity of much schooling and she was anxious that her daughter learn to write. Nanna Francesca echoed her mother's words to me decades later in Australia: 'Mum would say, "When we go to Australia I need you to write to Nonna for me".' So in addition to weekday school, Nanna Francesca was sent to a retired teacher for private lessons on Saturdays and Sundays. Throughout her childhood and youth, she would write and read letters in Italian for her mother and, using English learnt at school in Australia, she handled consignment notes, banking and any paperwork her father needed done in English for their Applethorpe farm. She eventually left school at fourteen to help run the farm and tend to her newborn brother.

There is a picture of Nanna Francesca dressed to attend school in Palmi taken around 1930. Her hair is in ribbons and her stockinged feet in buckle-up shoes. She wears a smart skirt and jacket and even a long string of pearls. She holds her tiny school case in one hand and her mother's hand in the other. My great-grandmother Francesca Carrozza wears a dark low-waisted dress finished in dark lace. She too has her stockinged feet in buckle-up shoes, although hers have a heel. She wears a plain cross on a chain so long the cross falls to her upper thighs. She has another chain around her neck with an adornment that rests on her chest. With a magnifying glass I can just make out what appears to be the shape of an upside down triangle with little beads hanging off it. In her left hand she holds a book. It is easy to assume it is a bible but the patterned cover suggests otherwise.

I look up the dusty, deserted street and can almost conjure the hazy figures of mother and daughter walking hand in hand on Nanna Francesca's first day of school. I wonder what has happened to possessions that were so important that they wore them in a rarely taken portrait photograph — a little girl's string of faux pearls, a religious cross, a hair ribbon ... Possessions lost in time, much like the people who once treasured them. For the main part we only know our ancestors' personalities for as far back as someone was alive to remember them. The back of my neck prickles as I get the feeling of being watched. I have sunglasses on and look to the side without moving my head. An older woman, not unlike Nanna Francesca in girth and with a dark, suspicious look, is watching me from a window. When I incline my head slightly to meet her gaze she ducks behind a curtain. I turn and walk up a wide stone staircase to meet Roger at the local park on a scalloped terrace above.

In contrast to the disrepair of Palmi's streets and houses, the park adjacent to Nanna Francesca's street, Villa Mazzini, has lovely cobblestoned and gravel walkways. Roger and I stroll under shady arbours of trees, all European except for one willowy gum. The park is popular with locals on this Sunday morning. They all stare at us. Young boys play soccer with fervour despite the signs banning it. In a corner of the park a wooden hut no bigger than a small garden shed is selling coffees. Roger and I sit among the cigarette-smoking local men at a metal table and chairs on the gravel. We swallow two of the best *espresso* coffees we have tasted in all of Italy and promptly order two more.

Along both sides of Palmi's main street, oleanders have been trimmed to mimic parasols. All are in joyful flower in shades of pale pink and fuchsia. It is just after midday and the foreground of the main *duomo* is quiet and deserted. The cathedral looks closed but I try the big wooden front door anyway. I am stunned when I push it open to see a packed congregation in full song during Mass and hastily close the door. This church suffered much damage in the earthquake of 1908. Incredibly, it is so freshly painted today that it looks almost new, a testament to the endurance of people who live in earthquake zones and rebuild.

Palmi has frequently been destroyed by earthquakes. In 1783 an earthquake razed most of the Tyrrhenian coast of Calabria, killing 50,000, but the quake on 28 December 1908 was even more costly in terms of human life because it struck at 5.20am without warning, catching most people at home in bed rather than in the relative safety of streets or fields. Instruments were just starting to be used to record earthquakes at the time and the main shock, registering an estimated 7.5 magnitude on the Richter scale, caused a devastating tsunami with forty-foot waves that washed over coastal towns and cities like Palmi. Together the earthquake and tsunami killed an estimated 100,000 people. In Palmi, around 1500 people were killed and twice that number injured. The two major cities on either side of the Messina Strait —Messina and Reggio di Calabria — had ninety per cent of their buildings destroyed.

Damaged telegraph and railway lines hampered relief efforts. To make matters worse, there were hundreds of aftershocks over subsequent days, bringing down many of the remaining buildings and injuring or killing rescuers. Meanwhile, steady rain fell on the ruined cities, forcing the dazed and injured survivors clad only in their night clothes, to take shelter in caves, grottoes and shacks built out of materials salvaged from the collapsed buildings. Veteran sailors could barely recognise the shoreline because long stretches of the coast had sunk more than a metre into the Strait of Messina.

Although it is now more than a hundred years since this terrible earthquake, the people cannot afford to forget. Even in our sumptuous hotel, there is a long hallway devoted to framed black-and-white photographs of the damage to Palmi after the 1908 quake. Whether I am in Palmi or Fossa, I do not think much of the lurking threat of earthquakes. It is a silent, unseen danger that is upon you before you have time to react — the deadliest kind. And yet the days are too beautiful, the weather calm, and people are going about everyday life so I don't think of earthquakes. Perhaps that is why the locals endure; they choose not to live in fear.

Each day we are in Palmi, Roger and I traipse the often seedy streets despite the searing heat. In the town centre more than a dozen old men sit around on wooden chairs dragged out onto the footpath. They all stare. We are accosted by gypsies. A man plugs away at a poker machine smack bang in the middle of a tiny newsagency. We check out *Le Palme*, the local shopping 'mall' of six shops. At a *gelateria*, we eat *fico d'india* cones, the gelati flavour made from the fruit of the pickly pear cacti that cover the surrounding hills. Everywhere we go we are watched and assessed.

I buy an old picture of Palmi's *Varia* festival honouring the town patron, 'Our Lady of the Sacred Letter'. *Varia* can mean a procession in honour of the Virgin Mary but this particular festival, dating back to medieval times, also relates to the *varo* or the launching of the fishermen's boats. Palmi shares this tradition with Messina in Sicily, with which it also shares ancient ties of friendship and trade due to the short stretch of sea that enabled frequent contact between their fleets. (It was from the port of Messina that my great-grandfather Domenico left Italy.)

The festival picture taken in 1938 catches my eye, since it looks kind of dangerous because the *Varia* leading the procession is an iron cone-like structure rising almost fifteen metres into the air and it is covered in young girls. They are dressed as angels and cling on among clouds, the sun, the moon and the earth, representing the Assumption of the Madonna. On the highest point sits a child of about ten who is 'taking the soul into heaven' and has the task of asking for the blessing over Palmi. As this is happening the entire structure, which is mounted on a wooden base said to weigh about twenty tonnes, is being pushed through the streets by two hundred locals who cannot pause as that would be a bad omen. (In recent times they have begun decorating the *Varia* with dolls rather than children for safety reasons.)

Roger and I eat lunch down at the lido or *la marinella*, a small beach situated at the base of imposing *Monte Sant'Elia*. There are two parts to Palmi: the main town on top of the cliffs and the beach area down below at the water's edge. The lido is part Miami, part tropical isle, part Third World. Again, litter everywhere and grimy, outdated buildings. A shanty town of tin shacks lines part of the beach. When we park the car, a scruffy young bloke with a dog asks for two euros to watch it. But along the water's edge the natural landscape shines through. Umbrellas made from dried palm fronds line a section of beach. Roger and I sit in the shade for ages watching waves gently fold and splash on the grey pebble shore.

At a pizzeria that isn't serving pizzas, an older woman in a headscarf takes our order. She pats me on the arm as she talks and is congenial, unlike the table of teenagers giving us evil looks. On another day, at a different *trattoria* along this shore, Roger orders *nduja*, Calabria's famous offal, and *peperoncino* — spreadable salami — a local specialty in Palmi and among the hottest in Italy. The owners refuse to bring it to him, much to his chagrin. I guess, unlike me, they have not witnessed just how adventurous Roger's palate is. Along with chilli and pork products, *melanzane* — eggplants or aubergines — are popular in Calabria, and I confess to this black fruit being one of my favourites. I've cooked and eaten it all different ways — simply sliced and fried and sprinkled with salt, in pasta sauces, as lasagne layers, stuffed, baked, grilled, even *melanzane alla parmigiana* (which originates in the south, not in Parma as some believe). Centuries ago *melanzane* was said to cause madness and was banned by authorities in Italy. But the Calabrese continued to secretly grow it and eat it — something I can completely understand.

Driving around the back roads of Palmi it strikes me that in some ways Calabria is almost the opposite of the Abruzzo. Gone are the snow-capped mountains and Swiss-like green valleys. Here it is flatter, hotter and drier. This far south definitely appears poorer and, sadly, it is evident in the roads, the buildings, the lack of upkeep, the struggling farms, even

MELANZANE FRITTE ALLA CALABRESE

fried eggplant calabrian-style

INGREDIENTS

~ 4 eggplants (aubergines) — tops removed and cut lengthways into 1cm thick slices.

~ 1 small chilli

~ 1 clove garlic

~ 1 small bunch of parsley

~ 1 small bunch of basil

~ 150g/1¼ cups *pecorino* (or *Parmigiano*) cheese

~ ¼ cup diced sundried tomatoes

~ Salt and pepper

~ ½ cup plain flour

~ Olive oil for frying

METHOD

Bring a saucepan of water to boil, add a generous pinch of salt and the eggplant slices and boil for 1–2 minutes (maximum). Drain and pat dry with kitchen paper towels.

Finely chop chilli, garlic and parsley and mix in a bowl with torn basil leaves, cheese, sundried tomatoes and a grind of black pepper.

Divide slices of eggplant into pairs and make 'sandwiches' by evenly spreading the chilli mixture between the slices. Secure the two slices of eggplant together with toothpicks.

Lightly coat with flour and fry on both sides in hot olive oil until golden. Repeat until all eggplant 'sandwiches' are cooked, draining each one well on paper towel. Serve hot.

the increased graffiti and number of broken signs. There is a dangerous element too, something that isn't so much there to see but which can be felt. From where does this stem? Is it because the south lacks cypress-lined Tuscan hills or Venetian canals? A quiet, pretty child can be lavished with attention while the cheeky child with the lopsided grin is largely ignored and yet contains untapped promise. Roger tells me the Sardinian teacher of the Italian class he attends in Brisbane voiced her frustration at the lack of tourism in the south of Italy. 'The south is beautiful but it has a reputation for danger,' she said. 'Just like Australia. Before I moved to Australia I was told not to come, as there were dangerous spiders and snakes everywhere, but I have to say after living here for some time I've hardly seen any.'

Before the unification of Italy in 1861, the northern and southern Italians had had centuries of history, and even periods of war, which divided them. In Italy regions mean everything. Culinary traditions, language, climate, vegetation and attitudes vary significantly from region to region, including, however clichéd this might sound, the nature of the people. These regional boundaries even extend all the way to Australia where Italians, especially the older migrants, continue to identify and judge based on loyalty to the region of Italy from where they originated. Most migrants naturally came from southern Italy because it was poorer, but there are also those from the north, and even after decades of living in Australia these localities of origin hold much sway.

The Abruzzo sits uneasily halfway up the calf of the boot in central Italy and with its mountainous, cooler climate is more in line with the northern regions. Nonno Anni used to group it in with the north primarily to tease Nanna Francesca. He joked about a 'northerner' marrying a 'southerner' while Nanna Francesca gave her 'we are not amused' look. Then he'd laugh about needing to sleep with one eye open if he said anymore.

We pause for a shepherd herding his flock across the road. A little black dog snaps at the heels of the bedraggled sheep. The shepherd turns to us and we wave. He gives us an almost toothless grin, his long, dirty white beard flowing across his chest. I am not sure I should venture to suggest Nanna Francesca had a better life in Australia than she would have had if she had stayed in Palmi. She was very happy here as a young girl, protected and doted on by her mother and grandmother. No doubt she may have happily found a Calabrian husband and raised a family, never leaving Palmi. Seeing the current poverty and subjugation in the streets where Nanna Francesca grew up it is natural to feel grateful that my ancestors emigrated to seek out a 'better' life in Australia. And yet I feel hesitant in saying this. If I was born in Palmi I may have been very content with my lot in life, proud to live in this corner of Calabria. I think of the joyful shepherd I just saw, the smiling, chatty waiter with an Argentine wife whom we befriended, the shopkeeper who was so mortified she accidentally overcharged me when I bought several evil eye amulets and ceramics in her shop that she ran around the shelves to find us an item to take for free so we would not think badly of her.

Roger and I drive up a twisting road through bushland and pine woods to get to the top of *Monte Sant'Elia*, which offers a view over Palmi. *Monte Sant'Elia* is known as the balcony on the Tyrrhenian Sea for its splendid panorama of the *Gioia Tauro* plain, the Aeolian Islands, the *Costa Viola*, Aspromonte National Park, the Strait of Messina and Mount Etna. The lookout has a flight of steps leading to the edge of a precipice which plunges hundreds of metres into the sea. Next to it, three large white crosses stand sentry over Palmi. Even up here, taking in a view that justifies being described as breathtaking, we are closely watched by a group of men. Unnerving as this is, their stares cannot dissipate my delight at seeing the smoky crater of Mount Etna in the distance.

It is curious to think that only two generations ago my close relatives were firmly embedded in Palmi. In her lounge room in Brisbane, Nanna Francesca displayed a framed black-and-white photograph of her grandmother who stayed behind in Palmi. She is white-haired and sober-faced in her portrait, her long dress snug around her ample bosom and middle. She holds her purse between two work-worn hands more used to holding a wooden spoon or an oven ladle. How did she cope when her daughter and granddaughter went to Australia? Did she wish she went with them, slowly die heartbroken or stoically carry on? Perhaps she was content not to leave all that was familiar. Did Nanna Francesca's mother see a future in Palmi reflected in a grim past or did she just want to be with her husband and made the sacrifice to go? I am grateful for her nous.

Being in Calabria I definitely feel a connection to this region that I don't feel for, say, Puglia or Sicily where I have no ancestral roots. I have to admit, however, that I do feel more bound to the Abruzzo and in particular Fossa, whether because it has loomed larger during my upbringing or because we still have access to the ancestral home there. I'm not sure if it would have been different had Nanna Francesca's home not been demolished. But I do know it would have been a different experience if I could have shared my visit to Palmi with Nanna Francesca. In some of the decor, the women's mannerisms, the coarseness, the 'making do', the body shapes, I see Nanna Francesca, who in turn passed on such influences and heredity to shape me. How astonishing that genetic make-up can combine people from the sea, alpine mountains, cities, villages, two hemispheres; a melding of cultures, places and customs that I can identify with on so many different levels. Perhaps being different is something to celebrate rather than to lament.

After sweltering days spent in Palmi's poverty-stricken streets it is a little bizarre to return at night to the grandiose hotel with its dozens of security cameras. Roger and I sit beside the huge pool (we are still the only guests). I have never gazed over literally hectares of cement and tile reeking of this excessive wealth. I don't really want to voice what I am thinking, certain it is my overactive imagination, but since Roger is more of a sceptic than me, I have to ask.

'Hey, you know with this hotel, do you ...?'

'... get kind of a strange feeling about it?' he finishes for me. 'Yes, absolutely.'

I am relieved. We swap observations, sometimes chuckling a little nervously. I will never know for sure if we are staying in some kind of 'mafia stronghold', but it is not Calabrian mafia clichés clouding our judgment. We stay in other towns and hotels in Calabria and never get the same feeling. The air is almost dripping with a fog of insinuation. (It is not until 2010 that I come across a newspaper article detailing fifty-two arrests of the *'ndrangheta* Calabrian mafia operating in and around Palmi. Among the multiple charges of mafia association, murder and extortion are allegations of infiltrating work contracts and collecting bribes in relation to the upgrade of the *A3 autostrada* between Salerno and Reggio Calabria — namely the '596 km of roadworks' we drove through to get here. The intimidation extended to supply of concrete from 'certain companies', which, considering the hectares of cement surrounding our hotel, is disturbing to say the least.)

'If this is mafia, they're not going to do anything to us.' I sound more confident than I feel. 'We help make the business look legitimate. We'd only be in danger if a rival business decided to do something to the place.' Still, it does feel a little like sleeping with the enemy.

That evening at dinner (again just us and a sole male diner with a heart outline tattoo — this one wearing the fluoroscent vest of a road construction worker!) there is a friendly, talkative waiter we have not encountered before. He is a native of Palmi who has relatives in Australia. Between the waiter's English and our Italian we have a good chat. I am curious to know whether he knows my family. I still have many relatives here (Nanna Francesca's father was the only one of seven brothers with the audacity to strike out from Calabria) but they are people I have never met who don't know me. When I tell him I am here to see where my *Nonna* came from, he asks what her maiden name was. It no sooner escapes my lips than we see a flicker of recognition and a strange expression cross his face. He then abruptly changes the subject. Roger and I look at each other.

Now, if I only knew what *that* meant.

'The art of winning is learned in defeat.'

Simón Bolivar (1783–1830)
Venezuelan soldier, politician and writer

Language — Beauty and Beast

Fossa seems agreeably cool and serene in its location up in the mountains when we return. Roger and I walk down to the Boccabella shop, as we need more *Parmigiano* for dinner. We're cooking some Umbrian pasta with a tomato ragù I have made with chunks of steak, fresh spinach, onion, herbs and garlic. In the dimly lit shop I stand back and let Roger do the ordering. I've noticed people are surprised, pleased and sometimes even excited when Roger (an *Australian!*) attempts Italian, even if he occasionally gets words wrong. They are not as forgiving towards me. There is the expectation that, being Nonno Anni's granddaughter, I should speak Italian fluently and people are openly disappointed when I don't. Graziella throws in a couple more of the red drinks, Bitter BS, 'since we are family'. Again, touched, I smile and am saying, '*Grazie*', when she says something that wipes the smile from my face.

'Roger *bene, tu male.*'

I understand perfectly that she has said, 'Roger good, you bad.' She is referring to our ability to speak Italian, and though not said with malice it's quite blunt. I laugh good-naturedly and cop it on the chin but feel a little miffed. It doesn't help that Roger's chest has puffed out, a smirk on his face. To me the little red bottles of bitters aren't the only things that are 'BS'.

'Wasn't that great?' beams Roger as we climb the wide stairs back up towards the house. 'She must really understand my Italian.'

'If that's the case maybe you should do *all* the shopping in future.'

'It's pretty funny though, don't you think?'

'Hilarious.'

Regardless of the advent of email, Roger and I still like sending postcards. To reach Fossa's *ufficio postale* (post office) at the bottom end of the village we navigate a web of dim tunnels, steep steps and laneways as crooked as they are narrow. One lane is particularly steep, the worn cobblestones gleaming with slippery smoothness. I hesitate, not wanting to fall flat on my face in front of three men who are working on an electricity box at the junction below. An elderly woman dressed in black pushes past me and grabs a thin metal handrail bolted to the side of a house that I had not noticed. Nimbly, she sidesteps her way down a cement culvert. Roger, now at the bottom having successfully negotiated the incline *senza* handrail, looks around to see where I am. I dither, then go for the handrail, feeling every bit like an old lady myself. Roger is laughing, drawing the amused glances of the workers.

The post office is one of the few buildings in Fossa that stands alone. It is also the most modern — an ugly cream brick number. Pushing through the heavy glass door, we enter a cosy room warmed by sunlight spilling in through the east-facing windows. The postmistress and three women are involved in a vigorous conversation. They come to an abrupt stop and turn to stare at us. The room plunges into silence. Roger and I stand behind the three women, thinking we are getting in line, but they all move away and usher us forward. It seems they are just here for a chat.

I vaguely recall that I may be somehow related to the postmistress, Emilia. Nonno Anni has insisted we say hello to her while we are here. Emilia is in her forties, dressed in a smart uniform — a black tailored jacket and skirt with a bright red shirt. Her black bob is perfectly styled. She peers at me, unsmiling, her dark eyes magnified by large black-framed glasses.

'*Buongiorno. Mi chiamo* Zoë. *Io sono nipote di* Annibale Boccabella …' I falter, unnerved with all eyes on me. Even Roger appears to have shrunk back.

'Ah!' she crows, launching into rapid Italian that goes on and on.

'Uh ...' I look helplessly at Roger, but he has no intention of getting involved with the fast pace of her spoken Italian.

Emilia barrels on. Suddenly I recognise Nonno Anni's name and several other words in among her monologue and am relieved. Her smile is wide. She jumps up and comes around through a side door so that the counter and the glass partition no longer separate us. Emilia puts out her arms and kisses both my cheeks. I'm reminded of how when I was young Nanna Francesca used to take me shopping with her in Fortitude Valley and almost every Italian we'd meet along the way would cry, 'Bella bambina!' and affectionately pinch my cheeks until they hurt. The other women in the post office are nodding and smiling. Nonno Anni is well remembered and liked throughout the village. Roger watches on with a look of bemused amazement at the hugs and kisses I receive. This is where our experiences in the village totally differ: through blood I'm linked to Fossa in a way he can never be. After some stilted conversation during which I introduce Roger, I thank Emilia and smile at the women as we back out the door. They all nod and smile in unison. No doubt they will be gossiping about us the moment we leave.

Roger and I emerge from the post office to see the No. 16 bus to L'Aquila waiting with engine off at the bus stop, the end of the line. We want to jump on but unfortunately the *bar* where the bus tickets are sold is back up at the other end of Fossa. It will be a while until the next bus and we decide to see if the driver will let us on without a ticket. Three women are already sitting on the bus with several empty shopping bags, waiting for it to depart. The driver is in a three-piece suit, a world away from the tailored shorts and short-sleeved shirts bus drivers wear in Brisbane's heat. I stand back to let Roger do the talking. His enquiry about tickets prompts the standoffish driver and two of the women to begin shouting all at once. I stay standing on the road. A most bizarre thing happens as this impassioned discussion about tickets continues. The bus, though switched off, is sporadically going up and down, back and forth on some type of crazy, hissing hydraulic system. Roger, who is standing on the platform at the front of the bus, later describes it like riding a mechanical surfboard. The situation is so ludicrous that I am stifling laughter. We never do find out why the bus was doing this.

Roger negotiates our way onto the bus on the proviso he jumps off at the next village — Monticchio, where Nonno Anni left his donkey that time in the snowy weather — and buys tickets from the *tabaccheria*. No sooner have we sat down than the engine fires up and we lurch away, careering down the hill and out of Fossa. We come into Monticchio and Roger tells me to wait on the bus while he ducks out to get the tickets. Thinking the bus will wait for him, I'm alarmed when the driver takes off. I struggle for the Italian to convey we have left Roger behind. However, before I say a word I notice we are doing a loop around Monticchio and it is a relief to see Roger waiting in the distance and the driver slowing to pick him up.

I am in the kitchen feeding the village cats when a knock at the door sends them bolting for cover. A local policeman stands on our doorstep. Burly, in his forties, he speaks Italian so fast and with so many dialect words that I only get the gist of him telling us he has just returned from a holiday in Australia. Roger, however, keeps nodding and conversing, as if he comprehends everything.

The policeman turns to me, shortening his sentences into things he thinks I might understand. 'Golda Coasta.'

I smile and bob my head. '*Sì, sì*, Gold Coast.'

He points to me. '*Nonno — casa — caffè.*'

'*Sì, sì.*' Yes, he had a coffee at Nonno Anni's house in Brisbane.

He points to me again. '*Papà — professore?*'

'*Sì, sì.*'

'Uh, *Zio* …' He stops, struggling to remember what my uncle does for a living.

'Barrister,' Roger pipes up, almost bellowing. 'Barrister, not *barista*, heh, heh.' He laughs at his own little joke. (No one else does.)

The policeman looks confounded. '*E barista?*'

'*No, no, non barista* …' I wade in, giving Roger a look; his attempt at humour now has the policeman thinking my uncle makes coffees. 'Lawyer …' This doesn't come close to resembling the Italian word for barrister (*avvocato*) which I actually do know but have nervously gone blank on. Perhaps this is just as well, lest Roger try making a joke about avocados.

The policeman gives up trying to converse slowly and simply, and reverts to rapid Italian dialect.

I shake my head. '*Scusa, non capisco ...*'

'No, no, I understand,' interrupts Roger. 'He wants us to go to the post office at nine o'clock on Monday morning.'

'What? What for?'

'I think the post mistress, Emilia, is organising some people to be there to see us.'

I eye him askance. *He understood all that?*

Roger turns back to the policeman. '*Lunedì. Alle nove.*'

The policeman nods and smiles. '*Sì, sì. Buonasera.*'

'*Buonasera.*'

Roger is smiling. I feel grumpy, particularly since Roger will be able to stand back at the post office when the onus will be on me.

Walking down to the post office to get there at exactly nine o'clock, I voice my doubts.

'You're being mean.' Roger is all impatience. 'The villagers are getting together to meet us. I think it's really lovely. There's going to be someone there to speak English for us.'

The arrangements seem to be escalating. Roger strikes out ahead, chest swelled, possibly envisaging the blare of trumpet fanfare as he enters the tiny *ufficio postale*. When we round the corner, the area is parked out with cars. I stop stock still for a moment. It's like when I was given the part of *la Befana* in the school play and the two swear words I knew at that age —

bloody shit — popped into my head (although these days the words have changed).

I nervously push open the glass door and the usual half a dozen hangers-on all stop talking to stare at us. I look around the otherwise empty post office. It seems to be business as usual. No gathering. No fanfare. No policeman either. Emilia looks up, a little frazzled. She is very busy on a Monday and wants to know what we want. In a combination of English and Italian, we take turns explaining the *poliziotto* saying to come here at nine. She looks baffled and irritable. Roger points to his hair saying, '*bianco*'. This confuses me too, but Roger tells me he is hoping to convey the white hair of the policeman. Odd, I thought it was dark grey. Emilia goes back to her computer, leaving us standing in a circle of onlookers staring us up and down. Then, a policeman with white hair walks in.

Roger lets out an excited, 'Ah!' and says something like, 'We're here.'

I have never seen this policeman before. With wintry blue eyes, he gives Roger a long look up and down. With a sinking feeling, I realise Roger thinks this policeman is the same one that came to our door. Although they look a similar age and build, this man is different. The policeman turns to the hangers-on with a look as if to say, *Who is this nutcase?*

'We're here,' Roger persists, with a broad smile. 'You said so, remember?'

The policeman continues to stare condescendingly. I half expect him to get out the handcuffs. Then he smirks and stifles laughter. Roger's face falls.

'Come on,' I grab Roger's arm, not about to give the policeman another opportunity to make fun. 'Let's go.'

Stunned, Roger mechanically pushes open the glass door. I follow him out, casting a glance back. The policeman and the others are openly sniggering. Outside, we realise all the parked cars are actually for something at the community hall next door. Roger is crestfallen.

'I was afraid there was a mix-up,' I say as we walk back up to the house.

'I can't believe it. That bloody policeman, he told us to be there, you heard him.'

'Yeah, but I never heard anything about a gathering. Are you sure you didn't misinterpret, perhaps thinking you heard what you wanted to hear?'

Knowing a little Italian can sometimes be more confusing than knowing none at all.

'Maybe ...' Roger is unsure now. 'I do know that he definitely told us to come to the post office at nine o'clock this morning. I can't believe he pretended not to know us.'

'That policeman that came in, he looked different to me.'

'No, it was him all right. To tell us to come there and then act like he didn't even know us ...' Roger continues his tirade up through the winding lanes.

I struggle to keep up with him throughout the hill climb of at least a kilometre followed by several flights of precipitous stone steps. I am puffing by the time we are nearing the final eight steps to our door.

'Take it *easy*.' Roger gives me a look that makes me feel about a hundred then skips energetically ahead, trips, and nearly falls up the front steps.

I quickly chew my lips to suppress a smile and give him a swift kiss.

We have just flopped down on the orange vinyl couch when the phone rings.

I pick it up. '*Pronto.*'

A woman's voice says something in Italian then hangs up. It seems my accent was so evident she knew it was a wrong number without my saying another word. I put down the beeping phone.

That evening, Roger and I are in the kitchen preparing dinner together when there is a knock at the front door. This time the policeman is not in uniform. Discordant Italian barrels out of him and we both pick up that he wants to know if we went to the post office. Considering the events of the morning this seems rich. His piercing eyes flick to each of us, commanding an explanation. Roger speaks to the policeman in English.

'We went to the post office this morning and …'

The policeman brushes off the English and charges on, his Italian getting louder and more enunciated as though we will miraculously understand.

'Yes, we went to the post office and we saw Emilia,' Roger repeats. 'But there was nobody there to speak English.' He adds this for whose benefit I do not know.

'Okay, *ciao*.' The policeman does not want to stick around when we are not attempting to speak Italian.

I await another tirade but instead Roger is quiet.

I voice it first. 'It wasn't the same man you thought was the policeman in the post office, was it?'

He looks meek. 'No.'

'*Roger!*'

It is not until I speak to Nonno Anni that I realise what has happened. Before we left for Italy, Nonno Anni impressed upon Roger and me that we simply had to go to the post office to say hello to Emilia. Despite our promising to do so, Nonno Anni also told the policeman when he saw him in Australia to tell us to do the same thing when he returned to Fossa and, on top of that, to check up and ensure that we did. I love Nonno Anni dearly, but I could have strangled him on this point. It is a mix-up that might never have happened if he had simply trusted we would do what he requested.

'Perhaps I need to do more speaking in Italian,' I say as much to myself as to Roger.

'Of course. You've known more for longer than I have, you just lack confidence.'

'Thanks.' He doesn't realise what it's like when people have a go at you if you are of Italian background and your Italian is less than perfect. I can't help feeling self-conscious.

'Tomorrow when we go to the bakery I'm going to order,' I tell Roger. 'You stand back and don't say a word, okay?'

'Okay.' He smiles and kisses my forehead.

Fossa is just beginning to stir, enveloped in the opaque fog of early morning when we head down the road to the *forno* to buy bread, still hot, from the Albanians who run the village bakery. I brush the hanging beads aside and go in first. Roger quietly stands back. The wooden shelves are crammed with different styles of freshly baked loaves, their crusts of varying shades of honey. I know exactly what to say in Italian when buying bread; it's easy. I eye the loaf I want and step forward. The woman nods and tilts up her chin, ready to take my order. I open my mouth to speak but absolutely nothing comes out. I freeze. Roger realises I've panicked and steps forward and quickly, smoothly buys some bread. My cheeks are hot as we leave the *forno*. Chuckling, Roger pats my back as we walk back up to the house.

Spirits of the House

Sitting out on the balcony, I love to listen to the morning sounds of the village. A dog with a deep, resounding bark punctuates the mountain stillness and briefly halts the birdsong. There is an occasional crunching of tyres on the gravel of the main *piazza* where most people park, as nearly all of the streets here are too narrow. I can hear a bee buzzing, then someone unsuccessfully trying to start a *Vespa*. A woman is chastising her son — though she could just be talking normally. Italian can be so forceful and rapid at times.

A door opens and closes somewhere below me. I see an old man emerge. Dressed entirely in black, he has a shock of white hair. His walking stick taps on the wide stone steps as he makes his way down to the Boccabella shop. I wonder if it is Graziella or her older husband, Tonino, serving this morning and speculate if they are one of the 'eighteen/twenty-eight' couples. My father told me that it was once common, in some areas of Italy, for a couple to be married when the woman was eighteen and the man twenty-eight so she would be able to take care of him in old age. We know several of these couples in Australia.

As a teenager, the egalitarian part of me was outraged to learn of this tradition. This was about the same time I found out about the arranged marriages — in particular, young girls in Italy being married off to single male migrants in Australia. Some men were crafty, sending photos of their much younger selves to Italy. The proxy brides would step off the boat in Australia to be confronted with a husband considerably older than she had been expecting. The life that awaited many of these girls was often one of subservience, procreation and drudgery on a remote farm. Stories like this did not exactly endear Italy to me. In my adolescent mind, I could only see the present-day liberties to be had in Australia. I was yet to comprehend how the poverty and desperation prevalent in early to mid twentieth-century Italy drove families to put their daughters in such situations. As I got older, compassion grew for these women. I realised how fortunate I was to have grown up in prosperous times with freedom of choice.

When I sit on the balcony in the early evening to write, the village sounds are different. A group of boys play football near *Piazza Grande*. I can hear their ball skidding across the gravel, followed by indignant or celebratory shouts. A prolonged catfight erupts in the distance and sets off every dog in Fossa. *Vespas* return home. The drone of an incoming *Vespa* is the only noise loud enough to compete with the sound of Italian television (seemingly turned up to almost full volume) which wafts down from open windows. Incongruously I can hear the theme song to *Murder She Wrote*, followed by the strident dubbed voices of the characters. American detective shows filmed more than twenty years ago screen in prime time in Italy. I look down into the laneway to see a little cat going to the toilet in a pot plant near someone's front door.

Roger brings out a platter of *bruschette* and pan-fried crumbed artichokes and asparagus, placing it in the centre of the table. Not for the first time I adore that he is a man who cooks. The soft pop as he pulls the cork out of a bottle of red wine marks the start of our evening meal. The half-light of early nightfall is delicate and a light breeze carries with it the scent of a neighbour's pasta sauce simmering on the stove and the faint pine of the nearby woods. Roger pours more wine into our glasses.

Occhio morello e cuore di diamante,	Blackish eyes and heart of diamond,
Se mille volte da questa strada passo,	If a thousand times this road I pass,
Tu sei l'allegria di questo mio cuore.	Thou art the joy of my heart.

From an old Abruzzese serenade.

Roger heads into L'Aquila to find out more about the Abruzzo leg of the *Giro d'Italia* bike race which will come through the valley and finish in L'Aquila tomorrow. Alone in the Fossa house I put on a load of washing. The top of the front-loading machine standing in the middle of the kitchen accommodates pots, a colander, wooden spoons, tea towels and Mario (the box of *Lanza* washing powder). The machine stops when it shouldn't at '11', and I must manually switch it through to '13' in the cycle. I remember Nanna Francesca doing the washing in her downstairs laundry room in the days when she still had a copper and a wringer, even though automatic washing machines had come on to the market. I was too little to help. Nanna Francesca told me to go under the house and get the big blue ball kept there for me. It was a great ball to bounce and to kick. When I kicked it, it would go high in the air, usually landing in my outstretched arms, sometimes landing next door in the yard of the three single aging sisters.

I chop up some ripe Roma tomatoes and day-old bread and make my version of a *Panzanella* salad. Looking in the drawer of an antique dresser for a fresh tablecloth, I am astonished to find some old-fashioned undergarments that had belonged to Serafina, who lived here for many years after Granny Maddalena and Elia migrated to Australia in 1948. Plagued by a lifetime of health problems, Serafina remained a spinster, living here alone. She died more than a decade ago at the relatively young age of sixty. My parents spent an enjoyable Christmas with her in 1970. She insisted on giving up her bed for them and went to stay with her sister, Placido's mother.

I am glad some of Serafina's things are still here. There is something fitting in not removing anything from the Fossa house, for it to remain intact, a part of history. I assume that in the past some things may have been removed from the house; it is a shame since those things are now lost from our family history in Fossa. I find a piece of paper with Nanna Francesca's handwriting on it. It is a list of people she wrote postcards to, dated 1992. I tuck it carefully back in with folded sheets, which are embroidered with Serafina's initials, possibly for a glory box never needed. It is easy to discard 'recent' items, but it is only when such items are kept that they grow in historical significance.

I can almost sense the presence of all those who have lived within these thick walls. Perhaps my imagination is getting carried away in the silent house, but I have a feeling of not being entirely alone in these rooms. It is as though the spirits of those who have lived here before me are quietly watching. They hold no menace. In fact, it feels more like my relatives are all standing behind me, giving me strength, comfort and protection. Perhaps there will be a time when I am watching over one of my own descendants as they sit here alone.

A small religious card — cracked with age — of San Bernardino is half tucked into a light switch. He stares out at me in sepia. Saint Bernardino was born in Fossa in 1420 and lived here in medieval times in a house on the very same street

PANZANELLA
(Zoë's version)
tomato, bread and 'leftovers' salad

INGREDIENTS

~ 1 Spanish/red salad onion

~ 1 tbsp caster sugar

~ 12–14 ripe Roma tomatoes

~ Half a bunch fresh celery

~ Half a loaf of leftover dense bread or sourdough
(better if a little old)

~ 1 small bunch of parsley, roughly chopped

~ 1 small bunch of basil, roughly chopped

~ 1 small bunch of mint, roughly chopped

~ Salt and pepper

~ Balsamic vinegar

~ Olive oil

* Finely diced radish, garlic and Lebanese cucumber
can also be added at the same time with the tomatoes and
celery if desired (or any other leftovers that might go well
in this salad).

METHOD

Finely slice the Spanish onion and toss in a salad bowl with the caster sugar. Dice the Roma tomatoes and celery, and mix in with the onion and sugar.

Cut the bread into rough chunks (about 2cm square) and spread on a baking tray drizzled with a little olive oil. Bake at 180°C for 10–15 minutes or until golden brown.

While still hot, gently toss the toasted bread in the bowl with the other ingredients. Add the parsley, basil and mint, some cracked black pepper and salt (crunchy salt flakes preferable).

Mix 2 tbsp balsamic vinegar with ¼ cup olive oil and drizzle over salad. Mix well, adding more vinegar and oil if desired.

I prefer to serve immediately before the bread becomes too moist, but if you would rather the bread soft, leave the completed salad in the fridge for an hour or two before serving and the flavours will intensify.

There are many different versions of this salad depending on individual tastes and leftovers. Ingredients can be altered to create your own *Panzanella*.

as ours. He is not the only saint from this street in Fossa. In 1873, Saint Cesidio (Angelo) Giacomantonio was born just a few houses up from ours. When still a boy, he discovered his calling during visits to the nearby Franciscan monastery *Sant'Angelo d'Ocre* (built on a jutting cliff face up the road from Fossa). In 1897 he became a priest, and three years later, with the blessing of Pope Leo XII, travelled with various other missionaries to China. Within a month, Cesidio was burnt alive in the Boxer Rebellion. He was twenty-six. Cesidio was canonised by Pope John Paul II in 2000. (My family tree crosses his with the marriage of Girolamo Boccabella and Domenica Giacomantonio around 1750, so perhaps we can claim a saint in the family.)

Fossa's other saint, writer and historian Bernardino, who lived a long life until 1503, is buried beneath the same nearby monastery Cesidio frequented as a boy. When restorations were being carried out on the thirteenth-century stone structure in the 1600s and 1700s, the grave of Bernardino was discovered. In his picture on the religious card, San Bernardino has hooded, staring, unsettling eyes. So unsettling, that I cannot stand him looking at me another moment. I carefully tuck the card further behind the light switch. I can't help feeling a little guilty for doing so (a holdover from my Catholic school days perhaps) and hope I won't be struck down (although Nanna Francesca would probably strike me first). A door slams, making me jump.

Roger comes inside. 'I decided to walk back from L'Aquila,' he announces. 'It was fantastic walking along the side of the road, looking up at the mountains. Sometimes I had to move into the grass by the road when a car came past too close.' After walking about twelve kilometres back to Fossa, Roger seems more energised than exhausted. He holds a bunch of white and yellow wildflowers he has picked along the way.

As I get a vase out of the cupboard and fill it with water, he says, 'You know, coming back to the house after spending nearly two hours walking here, I feel an overwhelming sense of home and attachment to number ten.'

Nonno Anni said almost the same thing when he told me about his ordeal of walking for hours through the snow after getting his passport in L'Aquila back in 1939. Many others have taken the same road but Nonno Anni and Roger walked it sixty-six years apart and, regardless of their similarities and differences, saw it through the same eyes — those of kindred spirits.

From the moment we step off the bus in L'Aquila, the anticipation in the air is palpable. The *Giro d'Italia* cyclists are not due for many hours, yet people are already beginning to line the roads into town. I may not be as into bike racing as Roger is, but I can feel myself being drawn in by the charged, expectant atmosphere. It is clear the *Giro*, Italy's version of the *Tour de France*, is a major event. There is noticeably more than the usual number of people in town today. Roger wants to buy a copy of *La Gazetta dello Sport*, the Italian broadsheet printed on pink paper and dedicated solely to sports. Inside there is a map illustrating the route the cyclists will take into L'Aquila. We flick through the various papers wedged into newsstands along the *Corso* — *La Stampa, Corriere della Sera, L'Unità, Il Manifesto, 25 Ore, Libero* — but no *La Gazetta dello Sport*. Roger asks in vain at four different newsstands and each time he is told, '*Finito.*' It seems every copy has already been sold.

A big white van decorated in the official *Giro d'Italia* pink sits on the corner of *Piazza Duomo*. A loudspeaker on top spews forth a shrill stream of pre-recorded Italian. It plays at an ear-splitting volume, luring buyers to their '*Giro* packs'. Roger parts with his five euros. The pack is a pink T-shirt, pink cap and a fuzzy stuffed toy mascot — '*Ghiro*' — on the end of a chain. Roger dons the pink cap. I rarely watch sport of any kind, not even the sports report on the news, but with the crowds, the blaring megaphone, the *Giro* officials wandering about, and the high police and military presence (all in impeccable, eye-catching uniforms), I am swept up in the moment. I find myself slipping *Ghiro* over my head to dangle from around my neck, much to Roger's amusement.

Viale di Collemaggio, which normally provides a beautiful tree-lined vista framing the pale façade of L'Aquila's cathedral in the distance, is choked with dozens of huge parked buses. There is one for each cycling team. After the race, the mass convoy will bus out of L'Aquila to the start of tomorrow's next gruelling stage. Australia is not a big enough cycling nation to have its own team, but Roger, an avid *Tour de France* and

Giro follower, recognises the bus for the team with whom a handful of Australian cyclists currently ride. The number of people attracted to the last part of a stage in the *Giro d'Italia* is staggering, particularly the size of the media contingent. There are several marquees and media booths set up, truck after truck of equipment, and temporary slim transmission towers rise above the leafy trees in the park. Pink banners strung up across *viale Francesco Crispi* denote the last few hundred metres of the course where all the '*Giro* action' is happening. Music blares from a live band playing on a stage set up near the finish line.

Raucous crowds are already jockeying for positions behind the temporary barricades. Roger and I manage to manoeuvre ourselves into a spot behind the first line of people clinging to the barricades. A third line swiftly forms behind us. We are now wedged in. The race finish is still hours away. We stand on the edge of a cement gutter for hour after hour. My feet in thin-soled boots become sore and numb. We wait … and wait. Roger and I are the only non-Italian tourists. What must be our 'strange' Australian accents attract the usual open stares when we converse with each other. A well-to-do couple in front of us, who look to be in their mid forties, are dressed to the nines. They look us up and down with particular disdain. Others around us are friendlier, flashing the odd wide grin.

Suddenly a motorcade of Italian police cars and bikes surges up the hill with sirens blaring and blue lights flashing. Everyone cranes in anticipation. I am expecting the cyclists to follow, but the police are merely escorting a fleet of garishly decorated vans. I watch as van after van pulls up, parking almost bumper-to-bumper for hundreds of metres. A succession of buxom blondes jumps out, and one after the other, they fling open the back doors of each van. Now begins another facet of big cycling races — the publicity caravan distributing freebies.

The crowd surges forward, almost knocking us over, their arms outstretched, all screaming in Italian. For a split second, it catches Roger and me off guard. I become the recipient of a couple of cheap plastic pens advertising some company I have never heard of and a sachet of the liquid sugar cyclists consume that neither of us wants. The Italians around us, ranging in age from five to eighty-five, are going crazy, grasping for freebies. I even see two *carabinieri* carrying away bagfuls to their parked Alfa Romeo police car, the back seat of which is crammed with their previous haul of freebies. Most ruthless are the well-to-do couple standing in front of us. They grab and stash away a haul of caps, T-shirts, pens and key rings, often several of the same brand, simply because they are free.

My hand is lucky enough to connect with a large packet of coffee thrown into the crowd. The well-to-do woman turns around and actually snatches it from me. I am too taken aback to speak. Roger, livid, is about to say something when the well-to-do husband gets into a fight — actual fisticuffs — with the man next to him over an ugly yellow and black T-shirt. We look on in stunned silence. The buxom girls spilling out of team uniforms continue to hurl forth the freebies. If pens, coffee and caps are so highly prized, there would be blood spilled if they threw anything of real value. The scrimmage goes on for half an hour. Then, at some sign we are not privy to, the vans are simultaneously closed. Engines start and the convoy moves off with horns beeping constantly. The girls lean out the windows waving, their cleavage swaying madly too. The frenzy is over for the moment. People calm down a notch.

More waiting. Threatening, purple clouds gather. I feel a few spots of rain. *Great, that's all we need*, I think, but miraculously the rain holds off. Across the road from us, a fellow climbs up into a tree for a better vantage point. Wedged in the fork of two rough-barked branches, he looks anything but comfortable. Others climb onto fences and building façades, staking out any possible vantage point above the six-deep crowds now lining the barricades for several kilometres. My feet and calves are in agony, but we have been waiting too long now not to stay until the end. A middle-aged man (apparently a past cycling champion) rides up and down the finishing straight with a theatrical look of agonised effort on his face. The locals cheer and scream with laughter every time he does it. For Roger and me it is not so funny after the tenth time ...

With tormenting slowness a tinny loudspeaker counts down how many kilometres away the cyclists are. The rowdy crowd becomes quiet with anticipation. A commentator's tirade climbs to a screech. The cyclists are just *two kilometres away*. We are pushed forward again by the frenzied crowd. Roger has his camera cocked, ready. I will just be happy not to fall down and be trampled to death. Cheap plastic bugles sold to the crowd earlier now trumpet a montonous fanfare. People wave fluoro-green *Liquigas* flags and pointing foam hands. I strain to see. A helicopter filming the event hovers directly above us. Judging by the ripple of cheers, the cyclists must be coming up the switchbacked road into L'Aquila. The cheers climb the hill towards us. Then a flash goes past. Then another. They're gone.

Roger and I look at each other. Even the Italians around us are laughing and throwing up their arms at the absurdity of a fraction of a second glimpse of the cyclists after hours of waiting. The crowd starts to disperse. Some slower cyclists are now coming in, caught with the team cars carrying spare bikes and the weary crowd moving on. We later find out that Italian rider Danilo di Luca won this stage of the *Giro d'Italia*, which is fitting since he is Abruzzese. He rode the 229 kilometres from Frosinone to L'Aquila in six hours and one minute.

It takes ages for the bus to Fossa to turn up. As we sit on a bench, waiting, it starts to rain. Roger and I huddle together under an umbrella watching the bumper-to-bumper traffic inch by. When the bus finally arrives, we leap on but it remains motionless, vibrating strongly for the next fifteen minutes while the driver reads the paper. We are tired and more than ready to go home. A claret-haired woman sits down in front of us. Her aroma of cheap perfume and cigarettes is overpowering. The bus finally roars into action and squeezes into the tailgating traffic. It is slow going and before the bus leaves L'Aquila it makes an unscheduled stop to let on a group of noisy teenage boys. They crowd the back section. We recognise several of them from Fossa and smile, but they ignore us.

On the trip home, the boys start making fun of us. They jeer, '*Non Italiano!*' and then mock in exaggerated English, mimicking us. The boys are all laughing hysterically. I'm sure they don't realise I recognise many of the Italian swear words they use about us. We are aware our presence in the village is a novelty, and that it is most likely the inhabitants talk about us, but until now we hadn't thought we might be figures of jest. Never having been in a minority group or having experienced any type of racism before, Roger is indignant, particularly since he loves Italy so much. He is ready to attack it head on. I touch his arm and discourage any such thing. I know it achieves nothing. I've experienced the reverse racism over a lifetime in Australia and have learnt that remaining silent and pretending to ignore it is usually less problematic.

For me, this experience brings back painful memories of getting the bus home from school. Being called a 'wog' was something I learnt to take no notice of, but being spat on or having rocks thrown at me was not so easy to ignore. There were worse taunts too — deeply insulting things said about my appearance, my family or my heritage. Sometimes in high school I would stay on the bus past my stop, choosing to walk the long way home to avoid a group that hung out on a street corner and relished giving me a hard time as I went by.

Perhaps it is naïve, but I wasn't prepared for the attitude of some Italians who have always lived in Italy towards the descendants of Italian migrants. I later find out some call us 'hyphenated Italians' for being Italian-Australian, Italian-American or Italian-French. Studies on the subject reveal they look down on people in my position for not being 'pure-bred'. Certainly not all Italians share such views, but knowing that these attitudes even exist is dispiriting enough. If the descendants of migrants are considered to be 'half-caste' in both the countries of their birth and their heritage, then where are we ever to fit in?

Beyond the Abruzzo

On Sundays, the Fossa bakery is closed. We have run out of bread. Fortunately, the Boccabella shop is open for a couple of hours. The shelves that normally house the crusty loaves, today however, are empty. When we ask Graziella if there is any bread available, she disappears through a door at the back of the shop into her own kitchen. I am touched when she returns with a third of a loaf she has cut from her own bread. Roger tells her that later in the week we are heading up to Umbria, Tuscany, Liguria and Emilia-Romagna.

'*Ah, bella Toscana.*' Graziella gets a dreamy look on her face as she fiddles with an earring. 'It's so beautiful there.'

But, it's beautiful here, I think.

During our first trip, Roger and I visited many of the chief tourist areas outside the Abruzzo — Pisa, Rome, Venice — but this time I feel a pull to travel more extensively throughout Italy, to discover Italy beyond the Abruzzo. Naturally I have some knowledge of other parts of Italy from my previous travels, my family, and through films and books. It is curious to read about an Italy described either through a rose-coloured lens or, on occasion (especially in eras past), the condescending viewpoint of writers with no ancestral links. Though I try, I cannot put aside my background and see Italy in either of these ways. It is intriguing for me to read of the quirks of Italian 'characters' that non-Italians find charming or baffling, as these are idiosyncrasies I grew up seeing in my relatives or their Italian friends. In the same way, I did not discover basic Italian dishes in 'a charming *trattoria*'. I tasted them as a child at the tables of my relatives. My heritage is always with me, colouring my perception, like an assiduous spouse, for better or for worse.

In a tiny Fiat, Roger and I shoot up the *autostrada* and into the delicate, quixotic haze of Umbria. Orvieto with its dazzling *duomo*, twisty, cobblestoned alleys, painted ceramics, consummate restaurants and dun-coloured buildings will draw us back again and again on future trips to Italy. To me, the narrow laneways conspire to create a gloomy medieval feel. One evening, Roger and I are strolling along an alley when we glimpse a candlelit grotto at the end of a dark stone hallway. There is not a soul about. A statue of Mary, her hands outstretched, beckons. Roger and I step tentatively over the threshold past two colossal half-open wooden doors and silently walk down the long corridor to the grotto. Wax drips from hundreds of burning candles. To my right is an iron gate in front of a cave-like opening. Steps lead down, down ... darkness concealing what lies beyond. My hair lifts as a cool draft hits my face bringing with it a primeval, earthy smell.

The underground passageways tunnelled into the soft tufa rock plateau on which Orvieto sits are so labyrinthine they almost form another city beneath the foundations of the buildings. In antiquity, Orvieto was known as *Oinarea*, 'where wine flows', because the microclimate of these passages was renowned as perfect for storing wine. During the Middle Ages, the inhabitants enlarged the tunnels for a variety of uses. One night we eat in a *trattoria* in part of Orvieto's underground cave system. It has a curved ceiling of whitewashed hewn rock and an impressive cellar lining one cavern wall. When I order vegetables with my meal, the waitress interrupts to make another suggestion, saying something like, '*gretti*', which is not on the menu.

'*E buona.*' She pushes her thumb in her cheek, turning it, which means 'delicious'.

I have no idea what dish I will receive but agree, trusting her judgment.

After the waitress moves away, Roger, with some authority, says, 'It will be grated.'

Grated vegetables? I ponder this. When our *secondi* arrive, we both peer at the dish. It is *agretti*, not 'grated'. I give Roger a look. His second-guessing Italian words makes it tricky at times. The spring greens are much like grass in looks and texture but have a refreshing, mildly bitter taste. We are both enamoured. In the words of French politician and writer Anthelme Brillat-Savarin (1755–1826): 'The discovery of a new dish does more for the happiness of the human race than the discovery of a star.' I find out from the waitress the preparation of *agretti* involves blanching the greens in boiling water, then sautéing them in a frypan with olive oil, garlic, salt and pepper (we cook some in Fossa after finding *agretti* in the L'Aquila market).

Back in the tiny Fiat, Roger and I continue on up the *autostrada* occasionally boxed in by the mammoth trucks and tourist buses that storm north. After navigating remote mountainous areas of central Italy and the potent, congested south, driving in Tuscany feels easy and relaxed with better signage. We crisscross meandering back roads staying at different towns along the way. In Cortona we are stunned to see two huge Nazi swastika flags hanging off the side of a building … until we notice the *Cinecittà* vans, lights and cameras set up for the film *Bartoli*. We both devour heaped bowls of duck tagliatelle. I drift happily among shops lining the *rugapiana*, nicknamed 'flat wrinkle' for being the only flat road in town, and happen upon Roger in an *Enoteca* cradling a bottle of *Brunello* like a newborn.

We backtrack on foot through the lanes of Arezzo on the day of the antiques market (the largest and longest-running in Italy). I buy an elaborate 1880s silver wand-like implement with a pointing finger on the end, which I later find out is a 'yad', a Jewish ritual pointer, used to follow text while reading from

Torah scrolls. On the Chianti trail, Roger and I visit a small farm that has been producing wines since 1720. The tasting room has an earthen floor and smells of wine, damp wood and mud. The owner smiles with crimson-stained teeth. From there we gaze over rows of vines to the nearby *Vignamaggio* estate where Leonardo da Vinci painted the Mona Lisa.

In Siena I lean out the window of our room as the setting sun turns the sky shades of amber and dusky pink. Below me, some local kids kick a football on a grassy field. Their spirited shouts drift up with the insects that rove through the summer air. In the distance a church bell tolls. I can just see the bell swinging in the belfry. Despite hordes of tourists in *il Campo*, along the back streets ordinary town life prevails. In one of these streets at a cosy restaurant Roger polishes off *ribollita* — a hearty soup thickened with bread. He then says that since he is in Tuscany he must have a *bistecca Fiorentina*, one of the enormous steaks famously cut from the snowy-white *chianina* cattle. The waiter nods with understanding, making general soothing noises. He sizes up Roger's trim frame.

'Sir, the minimum size *bistecca* is one kilo, okay?'

Roger baulks. 'That's the smallest?'

More nodding and soothing clicking noises.

'Why not?' Roger breaks into a grin. 'And I'll have a serve of potatoes with it.'

I nearly slip off my chair. 'Are you sure? Why not get some greens or something?'

Wine sloshes around in Roger's glass as he swirls it, smells it, then tastes it. His eyes are alive and happy. 'It will be fine.

We're in Italy.'

Shortly after, the waiter emerges from the kitchen and presents — for approval — a massive raw steak that threatens to breach the lip of a dinner plate.

Roger eyes it for a moment, possibly contemplating the *ribollita* or the side order of potatoes, and then he nods and tells the waiter, '*Sì, grazie.*'

The super-thick juicy steak later reappears with wedges of lemon and a sprig of rosemary after it has been simply brushed with olive oil, seasoned with cracked pepper and then grilled medium-rare over a wood fire. My piece of chicken with crispy, papery skin, and vegetables, looks tiny in comparison. Nevertheless, Roger conquers the entire steak and nearly a whole bowl of potatoes. I am suitably impressed. Then he orders a round of cheese! I sit and watch, nursing an *espresso*. A familiar Italian song starts playing. It reminds me of dinners with my family. I know it is impossible now, especially since my older relatives are gone or can no longer attempt long-distance travel, but I wish that just once my entire extended family could have assembled in Italy together. It would have been a powerfully moving experience.

The *Bersaglieri* band, *Fanfara*, happens to be performing in the *Piazza della Signoria* when we are in Florence. *Fanfara* play their brass instruments as they *run* along, never seeming to tire, leaving a trail of joyful music in their wake. Roger and I saw this band at the Italo-Australian club in Brisbane when they toured a few years back. The all-male ensemble wears khaki military uniforms and distinctive wide-brimmed hats with long *capercaillie* feathers from a black Alpine rooster. The band is linked to the *Bersaglieri* corp of the Italian Army who fought alongside the *Alpini*, the regiment my great-grandfather Vitale belonged to during the First World War. I later see one of the *Bersaglieri* band members off duty, walking along with his trumpet in one hand and a gigantic cone of *gelati* in the other.

In the Uffizi gallery, as I gaze at the artworks, I unexpectedly experience stirrings of pride. I have Italian blood in my veins. I am a part of this culture. It is all here, reflected in the art, in the scenes within the art, a civilisation and society thousands of years old. It is more than okay to be proud of it. In fact, it is a travesty not to be. Assimilation cannot prevail over a birthright. Roger and I visit each floor and look at every painting at least once, gazing at some longer than others. Apparently, Mussolini had planned to retire to Florence and spend the rest of his days looking at the art in the Uffizi, said to be a testament to his love of Italy.

Out among the vendors in the *Porcinello* marketplace I touch the bronze statue of the *cinghiale* (wild boar) whose nose you rub for good luck. The snout feels well worn under my hand (like Saint Peter's foot in the Vatican). Up close, I see the statue is actually a fountain but the water pressure is so low it is operating at a dribble, making it look like a thread of saliva is falling from the mouth of the *cinghiale*. In the Boboli Gardens,

Roger and I sit on a grassy knoll, elbows touching, and look out over Florence as we share a paper bag of fragrant strawberries. The famous dome of the *Duomo* rises from a sea of white and terracotta, rivalled only by the *campanile* and the tower of the town hall. I admire how most European cities haven't succumbed to high-rises. We meander up hilly streets lined with old buildings. A pure voice singing opera drifts down from a wide-open top-storey window.

Along the left bank of the Arno is *via dei Bardi*, one of the oldest streets in Florence where traditional artisans work. A sign in elegantly scripted letters says *Il Torchio* (the press), and then underneath, *Legatoria Artigiana* (bookbinding craftswoman). I push open the wood and glass door hearing a tiny bell tinkle. The smell of paper and oil paint reminds me of the high-ceilinged art room at school. We exchange greetings with the *artigiana*. She tucks a tendril of dark hair behind her ear and continues dipping paper into a shallow tray of watery paint on a huge wooden table. I see a manual printing press, a vice, and several valuable-looking old leather books in various stages of restoration. Sheets of parchment in assorted sizes are pegged along a string, drying. Everything is *carte decorate a mano* — made, decorated, printed and bound by hand using the same traditional methods as in 1700.

Roger buys a small notebook to use for wine-tasting notes. I cannot resist two journals, one with a cover decorated in rich swirls of violet, green and magenta, the other in varying shades of olive green. The pages are watermarked and almost smooth, the colour of clotted cream. The *artigiana* wraps the books in brown paper before adding a ribbon and a red wax seal. As Roger and I continue down the road, I clutch the precious package to my chest and am happy.

Near Poggibonsi, Roger and I come across an olive mill built in 1426. We buy several bottles of oil stored in underground cave-like rooms where the temperature remains steady. The mill has been in the same family since 1585 and they still have the original notary's contract of purchase, the pages yellowed and rough-edged, the elegant script in ink of faded sepia. From outside the mill, the towers of San Gimignano beckon in the distance. It is said San Gimignano has retained its medieval appearance more than any other town in Tuscany. This may be true for Tuscany, but as I look around at all the cafés, tourist shops and modern carparks it seems to me that the small villages of the Abruzzo have retained much more from that time.

In Bellagio, we sit at a café beneath a luxuriant wisteria vine, its trunk thick and knotty with age, its leaves lush among the purple hanging flowers. The deep navy waters of Lake Como sparkle under the mid-morning sun when a wooden water taxi cruises past. Our hotel is the town's oldest such establishment, said to have been welcoming guests since 1788. (It is rumoured that before this there was another inn on the same site that stemmed back to the Middle Ages.) Its famous guests include

Hungarian musician and composer Franz Liszt in the autumn of 1837 and American writer Mark Twain in 1867.

Roger and I have dinner on the hotel terrace overlooking the spot where Mark Twain described swimming in his book *The Innocents Abroad* (1869). The weather is clement with the gentlest breeze. Dusk has fallen, suffusing the landscape in soft light. It is a setting for romance. As evening deepens, the mountains that rise steeply from the lake turn different hues of mauve, indigo and olive. The lights of other towns twinkle from distant shorelines. Moonlight causes ripples on the lake to flash silver. A band starts up with an Italian singer crooning, '*Quando, quando, quando, quando ...*' It would all be so perfect if Roger did not come down with a severe case of tonsillitis that keeps him in bed for days. I bring him lemon granita and *gelati* to soothe his throat and some painkillers and lozenges from the *farmacia*, but it gets to the point that I have to ask the hotel reception to call a doctor.

The *dottore* bounds into the apartment with an energetic step. Aged in his fifties, he looks striking with thick grey hair, electric blue eyes and a deep tan. He speaks no English. Instead of a tongue depressor, he sticks his finger in Roger's mouth to hold down his tongue. Even through his fog of pain, Roger's gaze connects with mine as I stand in the doorway watching in mild disbelief. The doctor roughly pats Roger's tender neck and glands and then gives his stomach a forceful shove. Antibiotics and some type of drink are prescribed and he bounds back out the door. Fortunately, the antibiotics start to work straight away, as we have to leave the next day.

In Parma, I buy a watch which the salesgirl refers to as 'Bigga Benna'. Roger and I both fall in love with the tissue-thin slices of almost sweet Parma ham, served with crisp pieces of *torta fritta*. We go back to a *taverna* called the *Gallo d'Oro* (the golden cockerell) to have it two days in a row. Across from our hotel on the main street is a vast supermarket and I love meandering along the aisles peering at all the Italian products. Above the delicatessen, huge letters proclaim, '*Gastronomia*'. Stout legs of Parma ham swing on hooks along the twenty-metre length of back wall. The glass cabinets are crammed with different shaped cheeses separated by wands of herbs. Roger is compelled to take a photo. Several customers eye him curiously. (In our travels we seem to be taking a lot of photos of food, including meals and drinks.)

We spend several days with some relatives who contacted me in Australia when they discovered we were both researching the same family tree. Our branches cross at Granny Maddalena's grandfather, who was born in 1810. They live with their dog, Baritone, in a three-storey building, with one family occupying each floor. In the internal spiral stairwell, baskets are suspended from ropes to transport items between each floor. There is a big hail storm one evening and everyone is upset. 'The phone lines have been cut for two hours!' We mention that in Australia we have had storms that have left us without electricity for two days. Everyone stares at us dumbstruck.

Near Carrara we slow down, trapped behind near-to-the ground trucks transporting mammoth pieces of marble. At first I think the surrounding mountains are covered in snow, but I soon realise the entire mountains are white marble. I am unimpressed by the clinical feel of the 'designer outlet malls' in the Tuscan hills or the town of Pontassieve where Roger decides we should stay instead of my choice of Fiesole near Florence. Our accommodation is on the top floor of a 1950s-style post-war building. We scale the six flights of stairs in a dimly lit shaft, breathing in the fusty air of stale cigarette smoke and cement dust, the soles of our shoes scraping on each gritty step. At the top, an Italian-Chinese wearing a loud Hawaiian shirt eyes our bags and tells us the hotel reception is up the street, around the corner and up another hill.

The hotel's reception is reminiscent of an Elvis Hawaiian movie set, circa 1962 — bamboo walls, light-shade fringed with straw, pictures of Hawaii and shells. I'm almost waiting for 'Clambake' to start playing. The Italian owner wears colourful board shorts. Are we still in the hills of Tuscany? I feel like I've been transported back to a motel at Surfers Paradise on the Gold Coast in the seventies. I half expect to see a bar called Birdwatchers and a rotating caddy of postcards featuring topless women. Smiling, the owner shows us to our room (back along the street, around the corner, down another hill and up the six flights of stairs). A double bed looks suspiciously like two camp beds pushed together (it is). The bathroom is a plastic cupboard. At least it is clean — except for the water glasses. The owner has such big dark eyes, his head balding in a way that makes him look like Australian actor Garry McDonald as well as my father, that I cannot bear to show my disappointment. Instead, I smile broadly. Knowing this accommodation was his idea, the smile probably frightens Roger more.

The only place open to eat at is a modest pizzeria. A mammoth man with a bushy salt-and-pepper moustache has a burning cigarette perched continuously on his lips hovering above the pizzas he prepares in a slapdash manner. We have a similar experience in the port town of La Spezia when we go to the Cinque Terre in the Liguria region. I can imagine that many tourists who leapfrog from one pretty tourist town to the next may never get to experience some of these industrial or vista-less working towns of Italy. I'm not sure I particularly want to either. However, it does give me a greater understanding of Italy.

For the most part, we find the further we are from any tourist spots, the better the food is. On a return journey Roger and I pick Castrovillari off the map of Calabria knowing nothing about it, and stay in a delightful town of historic buildings concertinaed together like a stone piano accordion. The lanes in the old part of town remind me of Fossa. We eat at a table outside the front of a family-run *trattoria* overlooking the dodecahedron turret of an Aragonese castle where brigands were tortured. Nearby is the oldest convent in Calabria, built in 1220 and heavily bombed in English and American air raids in 1943. It is a hot night, still 32ºC at 9pm. A little further on from where Roger and I sit, three elderly people open folding chairs and sit out in the narrow lane talking loudly. Across from them, another older couple perch on their front step shelling peas together. I would take a photo but Calabria is the one region in

Italy where I've experienced extreme reluctance by most people even to be in the background of photos.

Guidebooks claim Positano is three hours from Rome. A quick zip down the *autostrada* and you will be lying on a sun lounge, cocktail in hand, gazing over the Amalfi coast. Fossa is an hour and a half from Rome so I envisage a four and a half hour trip, allowing an extra half-hour if we encounter heavy traffic. When I say this to Roger, he shakes his head. 'Look, I've mapped out all the secondary roads …' I can barely conceal my dismay. The serpentine squiggles on the map are a bull-angering red. My aim is to get to Positano as quickly as possible — since we are paying both arms and both legs for beachfront accommodation.

'Via the back roads we'll get there in the same amount of time or less.' Roger's eyes are imploring. 'Imagine the towns and ruins we'll pass. I want to see the "real *Italia*".'

I mull this over for a moment, chewing my bottom lip. His enthusiasm wins out. I feel almost ashamed for even suggesting the 'clinical' *autostrada*. How unadventurous of me.

Seven and a half hours later, we limp into Positano. The secondary roads with their bad signage get us lost or take us into the heart of bustling, smoggy cities we did not intend to visit — ever. We argue in Sora as we circle and circle and are then stuck in bumper-to-bumper traffic for two hours. Ah, the '*real Italia*'. After extricating ourselves from another snarl at Frosinone, we head for the *autostrada*. Truck after huge truck surges by and in their strong wind drafts the little Fiat shudders and struggles to keep all four tyres on the bitumen.

'I'm approaching the Amalfi coast from the end near Salerno,' Roger says.

'But won't the Sorrento end be quicker?'

It will be four years before I am vindicated, when we revisit Positano via Sorrento and find that winding road shorter, wider and easier. Approaching from Salerno takes longer, but in hindsight I'm pleased to have seen four times more of the Amalfi coastline even if we must negotiate 160 hairpin curves along forty-one kilometres of road. Unfortunately, motion sickness is something I have never grown out of (as a child I got sick on most car journeys). At fourteen, on my first plane trip (a one-hour Brisbane-to-Sydney flight with Nonno Anni and Nanna Francesca), I threw up. Twice. As I had my head in the bag Nanna Francesca was insisting I look out the window at the Opera House at the same time. I once accompanied Grandpa Bob on a six-hour fishing trip on Moreton Bay. I caught one whiting before I got seasick and was told to go down to the hull where I spent the next few hours breathing the smell of fish guts, petrol fumes and synthetic carpet. I thought that was to be the end of me. Even when Roger hired a small wooden boat for a romantic row around Lake Windemere in England's Lake District, I had to be taken back to shore after fifteen minutes I was so seasick. Roger spent the remainder of the hour rowing around alone while I watched from a tiny pier.

Navigating the Amalfi coastal road, Roger faces razor-sharp curves, beeping buses, maniacal drivers who blithely drive in any lane, and massive trucks lurking behind tight corners. The driving requiring the most concentration comes after seven hours in the driver's seat, yet Roger handles it with equanimity. Compared to the road, the *Mare Tirreno*, Tyrrhenian Sea, is an azure mantle of calm to our left. Craning out the window, I can see above its folds, the sharply rising land is almost completely terraced with groves of lemon trees. I glimpse a small waterfall shrouded in deep-green glossy foliage and a cat bounding up an uneven rock staircase. Hip-high walls hug the road to stop cars from plunging into the Gulf of Salerno. This is an Italy remote from my grandparents' peasant stories of the Abruzzo and Calabria, an Italy previously not so well known to me in Australia.

A curtain of dark cloud draws across the sky. Nearing Positano, it begins to pour. Our groans turn to sighs of wonder as the misty rain reveals clusters of fairy-lit pastel-coloured buildings clinging to cliff faces, encircling a cerulean cove. The façade of our hotel is a glowing haven, our room sumptuous with lofty white-washed ceilings and tiled floors smooth beneath my bare feet. A private *terrazzo* with terracotta pots of red and fuchsia-coloured pansies overlooks both the beach and the buildings clinging to the cliffs. When I lie in bed, I can gaze through the French doors past the translucent curtains floating on the breeze and on to the sea. The *Mare Tirreno* stretches far to a misty horizon where Sicily lies out of sight. It is the perfect place to celebrate our wedding anniversary. As Swiss painter

Paul Klee once said, 'A single day is enough to make us a little larger or, another time, a little smaller.'

While I sit surveying the dark-coloured beach at Positano and the sea spangling in the morning sunlight, I think how when Nonno Anni left Italy by ship on the *Remo* it was the first time he had ever seen the sea. And yet he easily succumbed to the Australian coastal way of life, of 'the beach'. My father recalls in the fifties it was a Boxing Day ritual for his family to load up the ute with a dozen relatives, some cooked chickens and a watermelon and head off to Suttons Beach at Redcliffe for the day. Eventually Nonno Anni bought one of those fifties-style holiday houses at Nobby's Beach on the Gold Coast.

When I was growing up, Nonno Anni often wore his 'Venice' shirt to the beach on our family holidays at the Gold Coast. I have treasured memories of swimming in the surf with my father, my grandfather and Nanna Francesca's younger brother, my great-uncle Vincenzo. I'd look across the waves to see the two balding, bobbing heads of my dad and Nonno Anni, and then Vince, whose thick black hair always looked slicked back whether it was from seawater or Californian Poppy hair oil. Nanna Francesca stood at the shore, refusing to go more than knee deep, shrieking at me to be careful. Embarrassed, I dived under waves, probably adding to her worry, while Nonno Anni yelled back to her, '*Lasciala stare!*' This made me even more self-conscious, as several freckled Australian faces would look over in surprise to hear a foreign language shouted across the waves. In those days before fake tanning products, I slathered myself in coconut oil. Having olive skin that tanned easily, I was glad for once of my Mediterranean background.

I think back to the night before when Roger and I had dinner at a restaurant on Positano's esplanade. The sloe-eyed waiter made such a fuss when he discovered we were 'Australiani': 'Such a long way to travel', 'Don't often see Australians here', and so forth. It *is* a long way to travel and I can't help pondering that if I had been born and grew up in Italy, I may never have ventured all the way to Australia, particularly if I had no links there. Roger and I wandered around hand in hand after midnight. Along the beach beside a black, velvety sea, up alleyways, down steps and up again, we did not pass a soul. It was thrilling to feel like we had Positano to ourselves while others slept. Back in our room, Roger closed the shutters but left the windows open so we could still hear the sea. Gentle waves lapped with hypnotising monotony. Before I went to bed I stood out on the terrace and saw an old man sitting on a chair on the beach with his little dog beside him waiting for a fishing boat to return. I fell asleep listening to his contented lone whistle, a melancholy tune drifting up …

Our tiny Fiat has traversed more than 5000 kilometres, crisscrossing Italy from north to south. We have visited almost every region, but before Roger and I return to Fossa there is one more place I need to see. Ever since my parents took me along to a once-off travelling exhibition of Pompeii relics in Brisbane City Hall when I was seven, Pompeii has fascinated me. The plaster casts of people and animals that had died had an effect on my young mind because I realised terrible things could happen to innocent people, a valuable lesson.

Standing in the Pompeii ruins among what had been houses and shops, it is sobering to look up and see Vesuvius looming, to feel in its path. Curiously, it is late morning, about the same time the eruption detonated in 79 AD. Fine trails of smoke emanate from the crater of the volcano. I turn my back to cross the threshold of a Pompeiian house more than 1900 years after its inhabitants perished or fled. The mosaic floor is smooth. The fresco of an angel still flutters her wings on a wall. In a common room, an open section of roof allows light to fall upon a shallow pool designed to catch the rain. The walled garden with a large agave flourishing in the centre is a peaceful retreat from the dusty streets.

One day the volcano will erupt again and re-cover the ruins and along with it this bustling city with all its tourist spots and souvenirs. Perhaps someday archaeologists will uncover the relics of souvenirs depicting a volcano which have themselves been covered by an eruption. I'm not sure I could live in the shadow of such a threat. The giant boom from a distant quarry is enough to start me imagining the same sound bellowing from Vesuvius. Each night when I lie in bed in a third-floor room in the heart of Pompeii I know that if the active volcano decided to erupt now, there would be chaos and it is likely Roger and I would be trapped.

The quiet lanes and pure mountain air of Fossa beckon us both. Roger agrees we will take the *autostrada* to get 'home' swiftly. On the *autostrada* near Naples, many of the cars around us are noticeably covered in dents and scrapes. We are all driving far beyond the speed limit (if there is one) when suddenly a car squeals to a stop and begins reversing rapidly along the freeway. Another three do the same, all reversing in convoy back to the last exit off the *autostrada*. Roger and I are both laughing at the 'mad, Italian drivers' when we are brought to an abrupt halt, faced with a wall of bumper-to-bumper traffic that appears to stretch for kilometres. No one is smiling now. For the next forty-five minutes we creep along. The other cars drive out of their lanes, filling the emergency lane and even pushing through the middle of the white lines. After several kilometres the *A1 Autostrada* — the busiest road in all of Italy — is totally closed and to our dismay we are being forced off onto an exit.

The makeshift detour signs peter out after several dizzying roundabouts and we are left to our own devices. We don't even know where we have been directed to so cannot locate it on the map. Prostitutes stalk footpaths with lurking pimps nearby. Rubbish lines gutters. Modern run-down blocks of flats look forbidding. Roger and I keep driving (with the doors locked) and, after almost an hour, find ourselves in Caserta. There is a striking palace but the main street, with most shops boarded up, is decrepit — sinister even. Here there is none of the charm of the Italy depicted to the rest of the world in travel brochures.

We pass a desolate industrial estate and alarm starts to set in. There are no signs. Our map shows none of the individual streets of Caserta. Feeling vulnerable is the worst. I tell Roger to do a U-turn. To my chagrin he presses on. The landscape becomes bleaker and less inhabited. In the tiny Fiat cabin there is an argument similar to the one in Sora. Roger turns the car around. Back in Caserta we see an *autostrada* sign and the relief in the car cabin is palpable. We stop at the very next *Autogrill* for a strong coffee.

Seven and a half hours after we set out, we limp into Fossa.

> *'What really happens is trivial in comparison to what could occur.'*
>
> **Robert Musil (1880–1942)** *Austrian author*

Bones of the Dead

Roger remains sound asleep as I quietly get up and walk over to the window. I look out over Fossa's terracotta rooftops, shiny with rain, and am struck by how contented I am to be gazing at this almost timeless scene once more. A strange thing has been happening to me since I have been staying in the family house in Italy. Ordinarily, when I travel there is a natural compulsion, from time to time, to appraise a destination in relation to home, meaning my life in Brisbane. However, in Italy I find myself thinking of the village as 'home' compared to the rest of Italy. I feel almost like an Abruzzese in that when I venture into other Italian regions I become aware of myself comparing them, not just to the Abruzzo, but also to our province of L'Aquila. From somewhere deep within, a loyalty, pride and protectiveness for 'my' region is emerging, as though Nonno Anni's feelings have manifested in me. Through our extended travels that have now covered most of the other regions, I have discovered that Italy can be stunning and quirky, but also abrasive. Sometimes I may pass judgment on Italy, but if I hear a person or tourist of non-Italian background criticising Italy I become suddenly defensive. It is a strange position to be in.

Misty clouds swirl around the village. The top half of *Monte Circolo* is not visible at all. Today is Friday the thirteenth. I wander around the silent darkened rooms. The foot-thick stone walls and the drizzle combine to muffle any sounds of the village. I do not even hear a *Vespa* or the usual shouts in Italian. I switch on the naked bulb hanging above the dining table and sit down to write. About an hour and a half later, Roger emerges. He makes French toast for breakfast and then heads to L'Aquila, having no intention of being made housebound by the rain. His love for Italy and all things Italian only grows in fervour and he is determined to make the most of every minute here. He may not have Italian blood, but for Roger the words of English poet Robert Browning truly apply: '*Open my heart and you will see, Graved inside of it, "Italy".*' I am content to stay in the dry, cosy house, high in the mountains, during foggy, rainy weather. For me it is perfect weather for writing.

At one o'clock Roger bustles back in, full of verve. From the bags of produce he has collected, he unpacks a round of sheep's milk *pecorino*, made at a local farm. It is just like Granny Maddalena used to make when she lived in this house seventy years ago. Zio Elia told me that one of the sheep they owned and milked was very smart and would come to them like a dog.

'When I was buying the *agretti*, two *carabinieri* were getting tips from the grocer for a particular salad,' Roger tells me. He loves this Italian way of life.

The rain has stopped and the temperature is lifting so we decide to have lunch on the balcony. I make linguine with butter and sage. Unlike the rainy quietness of the morning, the clearing weather brings the village to life. Just as we sit down, a chainsaw starts up in the nearby woods, shattering the serenity. Then a power tool begins to whine in one of the houses further along. Near the main *piazza*, a man wields a relentless, droning whipper snipper, despite the long grass being wet from the rain. The theme song to the American detective show *Colombo* blares from an open window above us. And, just when I think it can't get any noisier, a young guy comes out onto his skerrick of a balcony below us to yell into his mobile phone. We sigh and twirl our pasta.

A moment later, it becomes comical. A convoy of about twenty cars suddenly bursts through the village, all of them blasting horns in a celebratory manner. They take the road up towards the monastery. Minutes later, they drive back down the mountain, snaking their way through Fossa once more, all honking their horns in a jumbled cacophony. We start laughing. Roger speculates that their team has probably just won a football match. I wonder whether I glimpsed a bride in one of the cars. We are wiping our plates clean with the last crusts of bread when a white van lumbers into Fossa. Recorded piano accordion music bellows from its rooftop speakers. The van pulls up outside the church. Roger and I lean over the balcony railings to watch. It is a dry-cleaning service attracting its customers with music, much like an ice-cream van does in Australia. People come out in droves. I can literally hear doors banging and running footsteps on the cobblestones. A dying rural town with an aging population this is not. Several years ago on our first visit it seemed to be, but now it is bustling and full of younger families, though it still has its fair share of the aging. I notice several *nonni*, dressed all in black, some with headscarves, making their way to the van.

Heading down the road for a walk later in the afternoon, Roger and I come across a trio of women sitting on wooden chairs around a doorstep in a cosy sewing circle. We smile and greet them. The two old women raise their heads to reveal kind eyes like squashed raisins.

'*Buonasera,*' they chorus back.

The younger woman, who looks to be in her thirties, keeps her head down, intent on her lacework. A little further on in the lower reaches of the village we come to Fossa's original church. Built in the early thirteenth century, *Santa Maria di Cryptas Chiesa* is guarded by two small lions, now chipped with age. With a low-pitched roof and tiny bell arch, the almost windowless façade is more forbidding than welcoming. This unassuming shoebox of a building has none of the outward ornateness of other Catholic churches we have seen, yet inside 800-year-old frescoes cover the walls, typical of Gothic–Byzantine art in the Abruzzo. They follow a logical sequence: the

Creation; an agrarian calendar; a cycle of Christ, with the stories of the Passion, the Crucifixion and the Sepulchre; and then twelve episodes from the life of the Virgin Mary. I love that the fifteenth-century fresco of the Madonna and child depicts the baby wearing evil-eye amulets around his neck; an Abruzzese touch perhaps. The frescoes of the saints and crusaders Giorgio and Martino, and their protector, San Maurizio (represented as usual with his right hand of six fingers), lend support to many theories that the Templar Knights came here.

Assuming that the village would have had no more than a few hundred people when they built *Santa Maria di Cryptas Chiesa*, the detail and workmanship in the frescoes is astonishing. I particularly like the concept of the agrarian calendar with each month depicted by local activities significant to that time of year — something both important and relevant to a rural community. These paintings were not merely decoration; they illustrated stories for the illiterate. The colours have now faded to earthy ochres, sand and auburn. Sections of plaster have detached, caused by the earthquakes the area has experienced over time, leaving ghost-like pale gaps in several frescoes. The thick stone walls contain only a couple of slits for windows, which let in very little natural light and weather, perhaps explaining why these frescoes have survived eight centuries so far. Legend has it that Dante Alighieri visited this church and was so overwhelmed by the Last Judgment frescoes, particularly the scenes depicting hell, that he was inspired to write *Inferno*. It can be substantiated that he visited L'Aquila and the churches there, making this legend plausible.

On the outskirts of Fossa, the houses thin out to unkempt paddocks containing tussocks of grass and trees gnarly with age. We come across an abandoned vineyard with rampant grapevines escaped from their trellises to crawl across the thick grass. Roger stands beside a drunken fencepost, its wood now weathered to silver, as he surveys the neglected vines.

'It would be my dream to get one of these vineyards into working order again.'

I smile. Who knows what the future holds.

We continue along the bleached road. Since the women in the sewing circle, we have not seen a soul. Two neat rows of pines stand tall, planted for Fossa's men and boys who have died in war. Nonno Anni told me our family has lost one male for each major war. My great-grandfather Vitale was conscripted to serve in the First World War for five years. He said he hated every moment of it. He was one of the *Alpini* — soldiers trained to fight in steep, snowy mountains. Formed in 1872, it is the longest active mountain infantry in the world.

They rose to prominence during the First World War for the three-year campaign they fought in the Alps against the Austro-Hungarian *Kaiserjäger* and the German *Alpenkorps*. This battle became known as the 'war in snow and ice', as most of the 600-kilometre frontline ran through the highest peaks and glaciers of the Alps. Twelve metres of snow was a usual occurrence during the winter of 1915–16, and thousands of soldiers died in avalanches, their remains still being discovered. I read a *New York Times* article from 1917 which conveys the sense of utter desolation and huge losses in these mountain battles. It also praises the combined efforts and success of the *Alpini* and *Bersaglieri* (the corp with the *Fanfara* band we saw in Florence).

During one battle, my great-grandfather Vitale found himself face to face with an Austrian soldier. Both had their bayonets raised but Vitale was in the slightly better position. The Austrian soldier threw down his gun and begged for mercy, taking photos of his loved ones out of his tunic pocket, saying he had several children. Vitale thought for a moment, looked around, then told him to run and get out of there. It is a story that makes me feel very proud of my great-grandfather for his decency and compassion. Bayonet warfare is so grisly. It must have been unbearable to a conscript who did not want to be fighting in the first place.

At one stage of the war Vitale was guarding a railway tunnel in northern Italy and he carved his initials into the cement entrance. Nonno Anni told me that almost sixty years later he searched for, and found, his father's initials, still clearly visible, at the cave-like entrance. Around ninety years after Vitale fought in the First World War, I came across an album of songs the *Alpini* sang as they hiked in their grey-green uniforms and distinctive grey felt hats with a black raven feather sticking out (officers' hats had a white eagle feather). As I listened to mellifluous voices singing *Quel mazzolin di fiori* it was a little emotional to think of my great-grandfather as a young man walking along a mountain road, his voice raised in song with his battalion. The song called 'This Small Bunch of Flowers' was about a woman who has picked them for her love but he doesn't come home. Perhaps not the best lyrics for the soldiers to be singing going off to war. I knew Nonno Vitale a lifetime later as a white-haired, white-whiskered man who shuffled with a walking stick, drank beer from a tall glass, put a raw egg in his morning coffee, gave me sloppy kisses and was hard to understand if he didn't have his teeth in.

The road ends at the entrance to the cemetery. Rendered stone walls three metres high completely enclose the graveyard. The iron gate, which is the only entry point, hangs open. I notice a newish-looking padlock and chain hanging near the sliding bolt. When I step inside, I understand why the sexton locks up the cemetery at night. The high walls encircle elaborate vaults, many decorated in marble and gold with stained glass windows and noble statues. Fossa's cemetery is serene and beautiful with its series of chapels and vaults, burning candles and religious figurines. The well-kept paths and mown segments of grass are lined with deep green cypresses. My mother told me the evergreen is a symbol of immortality. She said that in ancient times the custom was to place fresh boughs on a coffin during funeral rites as a salute to the departed and a consolation to the bereaved — such a lovely tradition that it makes me want to resurrect it.

Roger and I are the only ones in the cemetery. I am not overly superstitious but I cannot avoid being conscious that it is Friday the thirteenth. It was not our plan to visit the cemetery on this date. Our rambling *passeggiata* unwittingly brought us down to this spot. At least it is not All Saints' Eve when it is believed the dead return to their homes and candles are put on their graves for them to see their way. Then the returning spirits form a procession up to the village to visit the church. Macaroni and minestrone flavoured with saffron are placed on the windowsills of houses for the spirits when they pass (and later given to the poor). Children carve out holes in pumpkins for eyes, lighting them with tapers inside to represent the heads of their departed grandparents. The wandering souls can stay in their homes until Epiphany and then must return to the cemetery.

We silently walk around the graves in the twilight, peering with interest at the names. The number of graves that bear my surname make me pause for thought. I am so accustomed to having a relatively unusual and unknown name in Australia it is unexpectedly heartwarming to be in a place where my name is more common. I stand at the graves of some of my relatives. Each has a photo of the deceased on the headstone, an Italian custom. Sombre faces stare back at me with strong jaw lines and august noses and large dark eyes, some crinkled in the corners with mischief.

The vaults are well-tended with arrangements of flowers and flickering red candles. Some of the more elaborate vaults are the size of small houses. I peer into one family crypt and count spots for eighteen individuals. There is something almost appealing about a family being together in death as well as in life (if they got along of course). For some non-Italians these elaborate vaults must seem strange. However, as my family has one in an Italian section of a cemetery in Brisbane, I am used to them. Our family vault accommodates eight. It has a small chapel housing an altar, several statues, candlestick holders and vases. Nonno Anni jokes it is 'first in, best dressed'. It is currently half full. On certain anniversaries we place flowers and light candles in the chapel. For the rest of the time it remains locked.

All Saints' Day is big. Every year Italian migrants and their descendants make their pilgrimage to the Italian section of this particular Catholic cemetery in Brisbane, along with picnic blankets and deck chairs. A marquee shading row upon row of plastic seats for Mass stands on a large grassy area in front of the vaults. Marquee seats quickly fill, so many families sit in the shade of their ornate vaults on folding chairs or a rug spread out on the grass. I think back to the one Roger and I attended with my family the year before. A ute with a makeshift altar on the back reversed up to the front of the marquee. I struggled to refrain from chuckling at the incongruity of a portly priest being assisted up onto the back of the ute. I leant over and whispered to my cousin about the altar on the ute and she replied, 'It's been *blessed.*' *The altar or the ute?* I wondered. Perhaps both.

It was almost impossible to hear the priest saying Mass in the makeshift open air 'church'. Everyone outside relied on the responses of the congregation under the marquee. Certainly, Roger had never attended anything like this, but to his credit he slotted into the experience with respectful acceptance. I felt slightly ridiculous standing, kneeling and sitting as required throughout Mass, all on the family picnic rug. Still, it was a refreshing alternative to the usual Mass in church, something I had to attend once or twice a week until I was sixteen but rarely attended anymore. The homily seemed to go on for ages. Those

OSSI DEI MORTI
bones of the dead

INGREDIENTS
1 cup finely ground almonds
½ cup plain flour
⅓ cup sugar
55g butter, room temperature
2 tbsp honey
Pinch of ground cloves
Pinch of ground cinnamon
¼ cup toasted hazelnuts or almonds, coarsely chopped
Pinch of salt
2 tbsp Grappa or Marsala

METHOD

Preheat oven to 200°C.

Mix all ingredients to make a paste (add a little more Grappa or Marsala if mixture is too dry).

Pinch off small pieces the size of a broad bean, form into bone shapes and place on a greased and floured baking tray.

Bake in oven for 20 minutes.

Best served with (and dipped in) coffee or an Italian liqueur such as *Frangelico* or *Amaretto*.

sitting at the back in the shade of the crypts couldn't hear a word. Bored, the older Italians talked in hushed tones among themselves.

After Mass, the crowd scattered into different cliques, some standing to talk, others, including the older generations of my family, roaming up and down to catch up and talk with people in front of different vaults. As I waited in front of our crypt chatting with Roger and my cousins, I said, 'I'd die for a coffee. All these people standing around talking … all that's missing is the coffee and the biscuits,' to which one of them laughed, 'I bet a stall would make a killing here.' With a wicked look, Roger added, 'We could sell *ossi dei morti*.' (These biscuits, known as 'the bones of the dead', are so hard you must dunk them in coffee or risk breaking a tooth.) We all dissolved into stifled laughter concealed from the generations above us, not meaning to be disrespectful.

It may seem peculiar but in Italy families visit cemeteries and will even have picnics near the graves of their loved ones, sometimes placing *ossi dei morti* on the grave. It is not meant to be morbid, since the Feast of All Souls is a celebration of life and not death. These biscuits, shaped as little bones or broad beans, have associations dating back to Egyptian times when it was believed that *fave*, or broad beans, contained the souls of loved ones.

On what would have been Granny Maddalena's 110th birthday, the family gathered at her vault in Brisbane to toast her with champagne, something that may seem odd to some but was a poignant show of respect for a woman who had been cheeky, caring, stubborn, full of vivacity, and the village witch. It was the same year that I turned thirty, my uncle fifty, Nonno Anni eighty, and that he and Nanna Francesca celebrated their sixtieth wedding anniversary.

There is much Abruzzese ritual surrounding dying and burial. When someone is ill, for example, if the lamp flame in the church burns steadily all will be well, but if it flickers death may be expected. After a death in the house a basin of water is thrown from the window, a sign of tears. In the past, in some steep villages the coffin was carried on the head of a woman used to transporting heavy objects this way. In Granny Maddalena's time all the peasants would take their old clothes to the home of the dead and dye them black in a big cauldron; if you didn't do it you were considered an enemy. Everyone went to the funeral wrapped in mantles. The women would cry and recite *stornelli*, rhymes or verses, and the menfolk let their beards grow. If a man died unmarried, flowers were put in his mouth. And if a man was murdered, all his relations dressed in mourning, his widow and his parents for one year, and the others for six months.

As I walk around the Fossa cemetery, I reflect on how my great-grandparents must have originally thought they would rest here, not on the other side of the world. It is a moving reminder of how migration breaks a chain of ancestral links and history spanning centuries. Roger and I are right in the far back corner of the cemetery and it is almost silent, bar the hint of a zephyr whispering in the cypresses. Suddenly I hear the chain on the front gate rattle …

We exchange alarmed glances. It must be after 5pm. I glance with trepidation at the three-metre-high walls. I may not be overly superstitious but adrenaline surges at the prospect of spending a night in the cemetery, particularly on this inauspicious date. Neither one of us utters a word yet the briskness of our pace towards the entrance gives away how little we want to spend a cold night among the vaults and headstones. Roger, I notice, is walking particularly swiftly, his strides carrying him further ahead, leaving me behind.

We round a row of dense cypresses to find the sexton has reopened the gate. Roger and I sigh and exchange silly smiles of relief. We hear a hose running but cannot see the sexton around. It seems the cemetery was closed for the night but, fortunately for us, he must have come back inside to do something. Or perhaps the noise of the chain was the gate reopening after realising they had locked us in. Roger and I hurry on up the road into Fossa.

We come across a woman on the brink of old age eating handfuls of bottle-green unripe nuts from some almond trees heavily laden with an immature crop. She is dressed for comfort in a floral calf-length dress and apron, her stocky legs thrust into sturdy boots. She talks animatedly, telling us to 'mangia, mangia' — eat, eat — the 'mandorle'. She walks back up to her house, holding her apron double so as not to spill her haul of half-grown almonds. I like almonds — raw, roasted, in chocolate. I have never eaten them when they are barely half-grown. I look uncertainly at the lurid-green fuzzy skin before biting into it. It is both bitter and sour. The still-forming nut tastes of bitter almonds, reminding me of dry Italian biscuits and marzipan. Roger is carefully chewing but does not look enamoured. He so readily wants to love every single thing about Italy that when I press him on it, he says the green almonds taste okay (but I notice he doesn't pick any to take back up to the house).

The ancient streets have a lovely feel in the gathering shadows when we walk back into the heart of the village. Warm light spills from small deep-set windows like lanterns in the darkening lanes. Pleased to be home for the night and not locked in the cemetery, we create our own cosy atmosphere in the brightly lit kitchen. Roger cuts up some chicken breasts we bought in L'Aquila (interestingly the 'wish-bone' is always left attached to the fillets). He sautés the chicken pieces in olive oil with garlic, onion and a splash of red wine. I trim the muddy roots off a bunch of *agretti* before blanching it in boiling water and transferring it to a pan of foamy butter and olive oil. The village cats duck in and out, clawing the mats and tussling with each other.

The first time I stayed in Fossa, Friday the thirteenth also occurred, and on that day I happened to write a poem about Fossa. The poem — my first and only draft — hangs from the earthquake-resistant rod in the lounge room, the paper and sticky tape yellowed with age. Nonno Anni was delighted when he saw it. Now, again, it is Friday the thirteenth as I sit down to write another poem. Under the cobwebby naked bulb that I sat beneath at dawn, I hunch over the dining room table, my pen sometimes getting stuck on the breadcrumbs underneath my piece of paper. The wall clock ticks loudly.

AVEIA

The house is still dark.
The village silent,
Except for our footsteps
On the cobblestones
As we walk to Piazza Belvedere.

Out across the valley
The orange lights of other towns
Wink in the grey mist of dawn.
We wait.
For the sun.

It is cold.
A breeze stirs the Italian flag
Standing sentry to the war memorial.
The sky lightens.
The sun, creeping over the Apennines.

Shops close for siesta.
The TV next door blares.
Linguine with butter and sage.
Montepulciano d'Abruzzo wine
Piano, piano … slowly, slowly

The church bells toll,
A dog barks.
Someone is trying to start a reluctant Vespa.

Old women cluster to gossip,
The loud dialect echoes down the lane.

A plate of leftover pasta for the village cats.
The balcony beckons.
Eyes lift from the village to the mountain.
Passeggiata.
Twilight.

A football skids across the gravel.
Espresso in Bar il Ponte.
A glass of wine on the balcony,
Some olives, some formaggio, crusty bread
From the village forno.

Darkness falls but the orange glow
Of village streetlamps shines the cobblestones.
Dinner is late.
Windows closed against
The night chill.

The village is silent
Without the titter of spring birds.
Then the crack of a rifle shot.
One, two …
Then silence.

Written in the main room of the Fossa house, Friday, 13 May 2005.
It remains hanging from the earthquake-proof rod in the living room.

La Cucina

The backyard of Nonno Anni and Nanna Francesca's home had the usual Australian concessions — the Hills Hoist and a strip of lawn (not all Italians concrete their yards, despite popular belief). But when my family set up long tables on the grass to eat *al fresco*, it was under the shade of fig trees, a bay tree, an Arabica coffee tree and three tall, silvery olives, the cuttings of which had been brought out from Calabria, via Stanthorpe.

It was a charming scene. The autumn sun filtering through the leaves of the trees creating speckled patterns on the tabletops, the long row of tables joined together, their varying heights and widths not quite masked by the long, white tablecloths. The chairs were mismatched too, a combination of vinyl-covered metal-legged chairs and wooden paint-flecked holdovers from the fifties. Whoever was sitting either side of you could be higher or lower to a great degree. If you were unlucky, your chair was too high for the tabletop, causing your thighs to rub the rough chipboard underneath. If you were *really* unlucky, you sat through the entire meal, hours of it, with a table leg wedged between your knees.

The family's conversations were loud. Someone would put on some Italian music and turn the volume right up. Sometimes Nanna Francesca was inclined to clap and step out a *tarantella* Calabrese while bossily trying to make me learn the folk dance from her. Yes, it was a charming scene ... but one that made me feel so self-conscious. At least behind closed doors it could be hidden, but when we ate *al fresco* it was on show for the whole neighbourhood to see. I was all too aware of the curtains of non-Italian neighbours twitching.

Nanna Francesca's meals are now the stuff of legend. She would cook for up to forty of us on her modest four-burner gas stove. I have an enduring memory of her in the kitchen of her Queenslander, busily cooking, perspiration beaded on her brow. In the high-ceilinged room a fan beating rhythmically overhead barely stirred the oppressive heat. My mother, *Zia* Caterina and her three daughters and I often helped. *Zio* Vincenzo, Nanna Francesca's brother, and my father were usually the only men who lent a hand in the kitchen.

Huge serving bowls of pasta were carried down the back steps to the tables. People took turns hauling mounds of *fettuccine* into individual bowls and sprinkling it with

POLPETTE E PISELLI AL SUGO —
meatballs and peas in sauce

INGREDIENTS

~ 400g beef mince (or pork)

~ ½ cup grated Parmesan cheese

~ ½ cup breadcrumbs

~ 2 cloves garlic, minced

~ Parsley, chopped

~ 1 egg

~ Salt and pepper, to taste

~ Olive oil, for frying

~ Peas (fresh if possible)

~ 750mL bottle passata/tomato puree or leftover pasta sauce

Extra salt and pepper

1 tsp sugar

Dash of balsamic vinegar

METHOD

Combine the meat, cheese, breadcrumbs, garlic and parsley, then add the egg, salt and pepper. Combine ingredients by hand, adding another egg if dry or more breadcrumbs if too moist. Form the mixture into egg shapes about the size of a chicken egg (not round). Shallow fry in olive oil.

Simmer fresh or frozen peas in passata (enough to cover peas to serve four) with salt and pepper, a teaspoon of sugar, a dash of balsamic vinegar and some chopped parsley. Simmer for 45 minutes. Serve *polpette* with peas and crusty bread.

Parmesan, then commencing the clattering of twirling forks. Shallow baskets overflowed with crusty bread which Nanna Francesca taught me to cut on the diagonal. Bright-red sauce soaked into the white bread as we wiped our plates clean. Next came platters of crumbed veal and cut-glass bowls of iceberg lettuce dressed with oil and vinegar. (For years Nanna Francesca kindly made me a special bowl of plain lettuce until I developed a taste for the dressing.)

Carafes of wine were plentiful, as were bottles of mineral water and Kirks lemonade, sometimes mixed with red wine to make pink lemonade for the kids, or used as a chaser when the wine, sun and hours of eating became too much. Nonno Anni kept two extra full-size fridges going underneath the house and these were full of drinks. There always seemed to be another course to come — Nanna Francesca's homemade meatballs, *polpette*, more egg-shaped than round, along with colossal bowls brimming with peas in more of the homemade sauce.

I have inherited Nanna Francesca's sweet tooth. She and I were fans of the chocolate *cannoli*, although the vanilla ones seemed more popular with others. For big family gatherings Nanna Francesca made mainly Italian sweets such as *zippoli* (butter-coloured little doughnut balls), the embossed *ferratelli* biscuits and *sfogliatelli*, light and crisp pastry ribbons sprinkled with caster sugar. As a child, I'd watch the adults down cups of *espresso* and thimble-sized glasses of *Galliano* or *Sambuca*, sometimes garnished with a coffee bean and lit, creating a wavering blue flame (although Nonno Anni could never see the point of such fads).

To me, the heart of the Fossa house is the kitchen. From the front door, you step straight into it. I imagine all the shoes that have scraped its threshold. Work-worn boots after a day spent in the fields, the light skip of children's shoes after school or Australian-made shoes pausing on the doorstep when Nonno Anni returned for the first time after thirty-six years. I picture a roaring fire in the cavernous fireplace as my great-great-grandmother Maria Luisa Coletti stirs a copper cauldron of stew that hangs from a hook above the flames. My great-great-grandfather Demetrio, somnolent from toiling in the fields and a flagon of wine, snoozes in a chair by the hearth. When he was about ten, Nonno Anni took advantage of such dozing and stole a handful of his grandfather's roasting chestnuts. The nuts were so hot they burnt a hole in Nonno Anni's trouser pocket but he tells me it was worth it. 'I've always loved food,' he chuckled, giving me one of his looks. Perhaps it is a gene that prods us to cook, consume course after course and have the ability to eat even when really ill or upset.

A wooden table sits in the kitchen of the Fossa house, the top worn to a smooth patina from years of use, its legs having borne the weight of many meals, many elbows. Whether or not it is the original table, I think of it in this kitchen as a place from which the evil eye has been removed, and over which discussions may have occurred to determine if Australia was the best country to relocate to. How foreign and faraway Australia must have seemed from this cosy kitchen in Fossa.

Most of their descendants would travel to Fossa but my great-grandparents, Maddalena and Vitale, were never to return to Italy, living out their days in Brisbane. They spent more than two decades of their marriage apart due to economic circumstance and then the war. I wonder if Granny Maddalena sat at the kitchen table after her sons had gone to bed, taking stock of their situation or reflecting on the last letter her husband had sent from Australia. Perhaps her thoughts were interrupted by the sound of her boys fighting. My great-uncle *Zio* Elia told me he was a terror of a little brother to Nonno Anni, who was around eight years his senior. *Zio* Elia said he would sneak a pin from his mother's sewing box and when Nonno Anni had fallen into a deep sleep would poke his brother with it. Nonno Anni would wake with fists swinging and Granny Maddalena would have to intervene.

Granny Maddalena roamed the mountainsides around Fossa picking spring greens for their supper table. Each autumn, she killed a pig and made salami to last them throughout the snowy winter. When the task was finished, she would tie the fat-seasoned sausages with string and hang them in the *cantina* to cure. Imagine the howl that must have escaped her lips when she came in one day to find many of her salami gone. Then she spied *Zio* Elia, curled up asleep in a corner, a piece of salami string sticking out of the corner of his mouth.

Another winter staple Granny Maddalena cooked was polenta. I have a vivid image of her standing at the fire with a wooden spoon in hand, swiftly beating the polenta in a bright copper pot. I find it comforting cooking in the Fossa kitchen. So many of my fellow family members have cooked within these walls. Nanna Francesca cooked the first meal I ate here.

I clearly recall her standing at the stove, turning the fat, spicy sausages with a fork as they crackled and spat in a pan. While accepting that her lot in life was to stand at the stove, it was also something she cherished and in which she took pride. During our first trip, Roger snapped a photo of me, at age twenty-three, stirring a pot of simmering *passata* at the Fossa stove. Nanna Francesca was incredulous when she saw it.

'You're cooking the gravy?' she cried. '*You.*'

Her disbelief prompted one of my irritable replies but I saw her mouth curve into a smile, secretly pleased. I admit that during my first trip to Italy, something in me had started to change, a gradual breaking down of resistance. I had been helping cook in my parents' and Nanna Francesca's kitchens since I was four. I always liked to cook. I just did not like my grandmother forcing it on me as my lot in life. If she could see how I have now embraced cooking, Nanna Francesca would no doubt say something to get my back up, like, 'See? I knew you'd come around to my ways. A woman's place is in the kitchen.' Roger enjoys cooking in Fossa, too. He turns on the radio, humming along with Italian soft rock, giving tidbits of the meat he is cutting to the clowder of village cats that crowd the open kitchen doorway. It is just like cooking in our kitchen in Brisbane where neither of us can cut up meat without our cats circling.

I always unfasten the wooden shutters when I am cooking in Fossa. The window opens onto *via dei Beati* looking towards the side wall of *Santa Maria Assunta.* I am disappointed not to see Checkpoint at her usual post anymore. Checkpoint earned her nickname for knowing all the comings and goings of the village. During my first trip to Fossa it seemed I could not leave the house without Checkpoint suddenly appearing. She would be either sitting on a little ledge outside her door or come running out if she saw me pass. (I'm sure Nanna Francesca told her to keep an eye on me.)

Checkpoint always seemed to be smiling, her body plump but firm, an apron stretched over her tight stomach. Her dark eyes darted about, missing nothing. When she spoke, her voice had a gravelly tone. I politely rebuffed her constant attempts to feed me. Unable to understand much of what she said, I felt awkward and shy with her. One day, she got so exasperated that as I was walking past she literally grabbed my arm and dragged me towards her front door. Her cries of '*Mangia! Mangia!*' caused her spittle to fleck my face. I found myself looking into a mouth that contained gold and gaps. Roger doubled over with laughter. I envied his distance from it all (unaware at the time that he was beginning to envy my connection with the village).

Nonno Anni recently said she has left the village to live in a nursing home. *Via dei Beati* seems empty without her. I feel sad that Checkpoint and Nanna Francesca, two women who amiably chatted with hands on hips beneath the morning sun, will never again cross paths on this street. I wonder if Checkpoint will make her final journey down *via dei Beati* as the church bells toll.

I place a handful of chopped onions into a hot pan, the resulting sizzle accompanied by their sharp scent with the steam. A pinch of salt helps them soften. Then I add some chunks of

VITELLO ALLA FRANCESCA
Francesca's crumbed veal

INGREDIENTS
~ 6 slices of veal (about 160g each and 1cm thick)
~ ¾ cup plain flour
~ 2 eggs, lightly beaten
~ 1½ cups breadcrumbs
~ Olive oil for frying

METHOD

Pound each slice of veal with a meat tenderising mallet.

Place flour, eggs and breadcrumbs in separate shallow bowls. Working with one piece of veal at a time, dip in flour, then egg, then breadcrumbs to coat, shaking off excess between layers. Repeat with remaining veal slices.

Fry crumbed slices in olive oil over medium-high heat, turning once, until golden and cooked through.

Transfer to a plate and keep warm in oven. Cook remaining veal. Serve immediately.

I have named this recipe in honour of my grandmother Francesca, though I'm aware it is an age-old dish cooked by many. (My mother cooked mounds of Weiner schnitzel — for years I requested it for my birthday dinner.) This recipe uses six slices; however, if it was served in my family or especially at Nanna Francesca's, the ingredients would need to be multiplied by at least six. Leftovers are delicious cold the next day, especially with a dollop of *aioli*.

steak and several cloves of garlic. As they cook with the onions, the aroma brings me back to Nanna Francesca's New Farm kitchen. I throw in a handful of roughly chopped parsley, followed by the glug, glug of tomato *passata* escaping the glass bottle. Salt, pepper and a teaspoon of sugar, and I am done. I do not manage it every time but today I have replicated the exact smell of Nanna Francesca's 'gravy'. I lean over the simmering pot and inhale deeply. It seems the simpler I keep the sauce and with the right amount of olive oil, it mirrors her way. I leave the sauce to simmer on the stove all afternoon, checking it now and again as the tidemark moves down the sides of the saucepan. By dinnertime the meat is so tender it breaks apart on the fork, the *passata* permeated with all the flavours.

Cooking is something that seems ingrained in my immediate family. My grandparents cooked, and my mother and my father. Roger loves cooking. Everyone has their unique strengths. My father loves grandiose cooking. When I was about five he scorched the carpet when a flaming *Bombe Alaska* he was carrying amid much fanfare to the tabletop went awry. I love that my dad has scribbled me out a recipe for a banana cake and that he introduced me to filo pastry with his *Galaktoboureko* and *Spanakopita*. Only he would attempt making chocolate spaghetti … and only he would eat an entire molasses dessert that everyone else deemed inedible — and as a result be sick for days afterwards. My father abhors waste. He does not let any leftovers or foodstuffs be thrown out, preferring to come up with an entirely new meal based around them.

In my childhood, my mother did most of the cooking. In line with her Australian heritage, she cooked 'meat and three veg' and dishes like pea and ham soup and shepherd's pie, though we had meals like fondue and quiche too (it was the seventies). She regularly cooked pasta, mainly *fettucine*, perhaps because she had married an Italian. I was always asking for lasagne but she deemed it too labour intensive so she got me to make it for family meals from the time I was about twelve, which I was happy to do. Mum's cooking changed when she became a qualified herbalist and she peppered our meals with dandelion, nettles or seaweed disguised in sauces and stir-fries to do us 'no end of good'.

My mother's homemade birthday cakes were artworks — castles, clocks, trains, dolls and, as we got older, chocolate and fig, angel or lumberjack cakes. One of her greatest works of art was her trifle, the colourful layers concocted with patient, meticulous precision, oozing with homemade custard and port wine jelly. Grandpa Bob proclaimed it his favourite. It wasn't until after she died that I first attempted trifle. My mother had passed on her recipe to me verbally and I took a huge trifle to my second cousin's place at Easter and an empty bowl home.

In his bachelor days, Roger's cooking range and kitchen were pretty elementary, but when he served up a bowl of pasta garnished with a sprig of broccoli I thought, *hmm* ... These days he has totally immersed himself in *la cucina*. He cooks mainly European dishes. For his homemade bread, he experiments with different flours, such as spelt, and makes a tasty loaf with salami and three hard cheeses cooked into it. He cranks the homemade pasta sheets through the machine and I wait at the other end to take the strands and hang them over a floured broom handle to dry, just as I did for Nanna Francesca and my father when I was growing up.

Roger's soufflés rise every time, his Portuguese tarts have just the right amount of spice, and his Hungarian pancakes are rich and divine. He even cooks from Nanna Francesca's hastily scribbled Italian sweet recipes, swapping tips with the other Boccabella women at our large family gatherings. His cooking has blossomed in recent years; however, I wonder if this passion began when as a young boy he took out second place with his rock cakes at the annual show in his country town. When I was the same age, I loved cooking cakes and biscuits with my mum — especially licking the beaters at the end. On cold, rainy afternoons, Mum and I would make gingerbread men together. After we slid the tray into the oven, she would read me *The Gingerbread Man* as the delicious baking aroma wafted throughout our Queenslander.

It was in my teenage years that my interest temporarily waned. Along with tablecloths, cookbooks were another birthday present from Nanna Francesca that I did not appreciate. Before I had begun to unwrap the coloured paper, the hard cover and weight would give them away. Now I cherish those cookbooks and tablecloths, for I can no longer receive them from her. In my mushrooming collection of cookbooks, those with Nanna Francesca's scrawl inside the cover, half in English, half Italian, are my most treasured. My first cookbook from her, printed in the sixties, has all the recipe measurements in ounces. My second was an original Margaret Fulton. Despite this collection, for the most part I cook the Italian way of a handful of this here, some of that there, a taste, more seasoning, a little sugar ... Nanna Francesca often summoned me to the kitchen to watch and learn from her. There was no mention of measurements. I dutifully listened as Nanna Francesca moved around her kitchen with organised determination. Perhaps she imbued me with a love of cooking after all. It's said that Italians often compare restaurant food to the cooking of their mothers and *nonni* — and that restaurant food usually comes second. I have to say it's true.

For fifty years, Nanna Francesca did not allow Nonno Anni to put one toe over the threshold of their New Farm kitchen — it was strictly her domain. After her death he cooks for himself and is surprisingly proficient for a man entering his ninth decade. He cooks up pasta sauces (he still calls them gravy), which he alternately teams with rice or pasta, and he has taught Roger and me to cook pork and fennel sausages in the pan with red wine. Pan-fried steak he serves with bitter greens he grows in his backyard. He and I were sitting in the dining room one day having a coffee, when I commented on a strange hissing noise coming from the kitchen.

'Ooh, by God!' He jumped up and loped into the kitchen as I trailed behind to discover he had a huge pot of these greens boiling away on the stove.

Memories of a loved one's cooking can stay with you long after that person has gone. My Australian grandmother, Lorna, was astute, stylish and kept her figure (for fifty years she mostly had a cigarette in her hand). She also made perfect fried rice which she served up in smoky brown glass bowls. Grandma Lorna put more garlic in spaghetti bolognaise than Nanna Francesca. I recall the comforting, old-fashioned cooking smell pervading Grandpa Bob's house when he lived alone in his later years. Upon my enquiring, he said he had 'some corned beef going in the cooker for the afternoon', smacking his lips and giving me a wink and a look with his blue, blue eyes and his broad smile.

After watching the film *Big Night*, about Italian-American restaurateur brothers, my parents, my sister, Roger and I left the theatre inspired to cook the impressive *timbale* or *timpano*, the *pièce de résistance* culminating one long epicurean scene. We had no recipe (and no internet to look it up back then); instead we replicated it from what we saw in the film. (I later discovered this dish is considered one of the most labour intensive of Italian dishes.) Difficult to describe, impressive to look at, it is a cross between lasagne and a pie (but several times the size and height).

Together we set about making fresh pasta and meat sauce, boiling eggs and grating cheese. We were all involved in assembling the dish, working side by side at the round kitchen table, talking and joking. My parents had bought a huge silver bowl especially, which we lined with homemade pasta dough. Then began the layering of different cheeses (*Romano*, *Parmigiano*), meatballs, sausage, hard-boiled eggs, *ziti* pasta and cured meats (*prosciutto, capicola, salami*), all bound together by a rich beef and tomato *ragù*. Typically made in regional Italy for a wedding, it is not a dish normally seen in a restaurant. After it was baked and turned upside down onto a large serving platter, we sliced it at the dining room table. Some meals are special in many different ways.

Inadvertently, the cherished recipes and memories that stand out the most are those dishes cooked from scratch. Before we were even aware it existed, Roger and I had adopted many of the philosophies of the Slow Food movement — fresh, organic, chemical-free produce, meals prepared from scratch, supporting local farmers and fostering diverse cultivation. Slow Food is not in favour of unripened apples sitting in supermarket cold rooms for months on end, tomatoes picked green for easy transportation, tasteless, miserable battery chickens and packets of food with ingredients listing more chemical numbers than produce.

Slow Food is contrary to takeaway junk food or zapping a frozen packet in a microwave — meals that look 'dead' on the plate. Some people are amazed that Roger and I don't own a microwave oven. My parents have never owned one. Preparing a meal from scratch does not need to take long. It is how our grandparents and their preceding generations ate. In regards to altering food with chemicals and science, perhaps food activist and bestselling author Michael Pollan summed it up best when he described nutrition science today being about where surgery was in the year 1650.

Over the years, Roger and I take more than one side trip to the town of Orvieto, which is one of Italy's leading 'Slow Cities' promoting local traditions and a leisurely pace of life.

In Orvieto fast food outlets and neon signs are banned. There are car-free days and noise pollution laws. The inhabitants have decided to control the rhythms of their lives rather than have them dictated, particularly by technology. This town has long enjoyed an association with food, considering Simone Prodenzani's *il Saporetto* published in 1415, which includes sonnets devoted to food. Orvieto is where Roger and I have had some of our best meals — thick strands of the local *umbrichelli* pasta in white truffle sauce, *pappardelle* with *cinghiale* (wild boar) sauce, spinach and ricotta *ravioli* with walnuts and black truffles, and a slow-cooked beef dish in a red wine gravy so reduced and rich it was almost like dark chocolate.

The *cucina* is the heart (*cuore*) of the house providing warmth, nourishment, a place to share troubles or joy, or simply the news of daily life. Here in Fossa, I sit at the wooden table and spread out my hands, palms down, feeling the wear of years of use beneath my fingertips. I imagine a young wife sitting here and surveying this kitchen as her new domain; the place where her life would unfold as she cooked and cleaned and sustained the lives of her husband, her children, her grandchildren and anyone else who stepped over the threshold. And she had the same blood as me.

'The worst decision is indecision.'

Benjamin Franklin (1706–1790) *US physicist and politician*

Pilfered Figs

A long piece of nylon rope arcs in front of the fireplace from one end of the living room in the Fossa house to the other. In winter, it would be the perfect spot to dry clothes but today is a beautiful storybook day. The birds are singing, the sun is shining and wispy clouds float across a blue sky. I decide to hang the sheets on the old pulley clothesline, situated just outside and below the window. The first time I stayed in Rome I actually took a photo of a busty woman suspended half out a window, hanging her sheets on one of these pulleys. Such an iconic image is frequently used in films set in Italy. I am looking forward to hanging out my own.

Within the first minute, any romantic notions are quashed.

The sheets I haul over to the windowsill are white and heavy. They are embroidered with a deceased relative's initials and sewn many decades ago when sheets were thick and strong and made to last. Being wet naturally makes them even heavier. Roger is not home so I cannot call on his help. I struggle to lift one sheet onto the line in an untidy clump. Then I have to spread it out neatly for it to dry properly. Being short, I am struggling just to reach out of the window. I balance with my feet on two stacks of bricks on the floor beneath the sill. A knot in the rope keeps jamming the pulley. I have to reposition the sheet precisely to move it along far enough to fit the second sheet on without the knot getting stuck. My arms are aching. I am perspiring. I am suddenly thinking fondly of my Hills Hoist clothesline in Australia.

When I finally have the sheets hanging neatly pegged, I wipe the sweat from my brow and lean out to admire my handiwork. The morning sunlight turns them a blinding white as a warm breeze wafts up along the alley and gently stirs them. I think, *How lovely.* In the next draught, they hit against the stone wall of the house and the clean sheets are marred by filthy marks. I am cursing under my breath when the local priest comes strolling along and looks up.

'*Buongiorno!*' he calls out.

I smile, a little flustered. '*Buongiorno.*'

Within a minute of exchanging pleasantries, he establishes I am Nonno Anni's eldest grandchild from Australia for a visit.

'You don't speak fluent Italian?' he chides, switching to English. 'It's your mother tongue.'

'I was born in Australia.'

'Yes, but Italian is your mother tongue,' he persists.

He tells me he was born in Africa and was posted to Fossa after completing his studies in L'Aquila. As we converse, I am aware that at this moment in time I am like one of those Italian women leaning out their window hanging sheets and chatting to the local priest.

'What date are you leaving?' he asks.

When I tell him, he says, 'Oh, that's a shame. I was going to invite you along to a gospel night, but you'll be gone then. You might have heard us practising?'

That's for the gospel night? For weeks, Roger and I had been cursing a local rock band for frequently disturbing our sleep.

Being Sunday, the priest is in his black robes. On other occasions, I have seen him in ordinary civvies, hanging out with the youths playing football in the main *piazza*. I am conscious that Roger and I do not attend Mass. As if picking up on this, he volunteers the Mass times. I do not tell him the house the village provides for him to live in once belonged to Nonno Anni's aunt. She was childless and Nonno Anni was to inherit her house. The priest at the time convinced her to leave it to the Catholic Church instead, promising to say a special Mass for her once a month to 'guarantee her passage to heaven'. That priest was still in Fossa when I first stayed here. He died at age ninety-nine before I came back.

When Nonno Anni returned for the first time in 1975, this priest put out his hand and said, 'Welcome back.' My grandfather stared at the priest's hand and said, 'If it wasn't for you we would never have had to leave.' Nonno Anni was not a religious man and only stepped inside a church when invited to weddings or christenings or to honour someone at their funeral. He still laments losing that house, although, if he hadn't he may never have come to Australia, and I would not exist. The priest bids me farewell and saunters on in his self-assured way, hands loosely clasped. His scalp glistens with sweat through his short bristly hair. It is a warm morning to be strolling about in long black robes.

I wonder what the priest would think if he knew my great-grandmother, Granny Maddalena, though devoted to Catholicism, was also once Fossa's resident witch. That as an altar boy Nonno Anni skolled a bottle of the altar wine to get out of serving on cold, snowy winter mornings (much to his mother's mortification). I first attended an Italian Mass not in Fossa but in Brisbane when I was a little and the family all went along to the underground Italian Church. My father had to take me outside because the 'wailing' hymns frightened me.

I am still leaning out the window, balancing on the two stacks of bricks, when I spot Roger coming up the lane carrying a number of brown paper-wrapped parcels. He has been down at the Boccabella shop again.

'I was lucky to walk in as Tonino was making sausages,' he calls up, beaming. 'He let me come out the back to watch him.'

I smile as I step down from the piles of bricks. It is inspiring to see Roger develop an unquenchable interest in Italian culture later in life. I hope to have the capability of continuing to seek new knowledge and experiences far into old age.

Roger and I come out of the house one morning to find an old woman sitting in a chair on our shared landing. She holds up her hand to stop us from taking another step, puts down her lacework and struggles to her feet. Despite being around eighty, her skin is dewy and quite smooth. Her pale grey hair, verging on white, is pulled into a neat low bun. With alert grey-green eyes she locks her gaze on me, sizing me up. I smile back, a little self-conscious. She is our neighbour who lives upstairs. Her name is Speranza, which means 'hope'.

Speranza's accent is so thick that even when she uses the little English she knows, communication proves difficult. The name Roger, transformed into the Italian form 'Ruggero', she understands, but she cannot seem to get the gist of Zoë, which has Greek origins.

'Zoë. *Zoë*,' Roger perseveres, phonetically sounding it out, long after I have given up. 'Zed — like *zucchero*.' (*Zucchero* means 'sugar' in Italian.)

'Ah, *zucchero!*'

This she understands. Unfortunately, Speranza thinks my actual name is 'Sugar' and the name sticks whenever I am in the village. Back in Australia, Nonno Anni thinks this is a great laugh and nicknames me *Zucchero*. I call him 'Honey-ball' in return as it rhymes with the Anglicised version of his name — Hannibal. From this time on, his effusive greeting is always followed by a teasing debate over which is sweeter, sugar or honey. It is a grown-up version of his merry greetings when I was a child, which were, '*Nasi, nasi*', noses, noses, and an 'Eskimo kiss', a child's tiny nose no match for his large, hairy-tipped proboscis.

After a general conversation about my family, with Speranza enquiring after Nonno Anni and my parents, we tell her we are going for a walk. She is more concerned about me patting the village cats that are swarming around my legs.

'Don't bother,' she says. 'Food, yes, patting …' Speranza screws up her face.

I disagree. The little mites seem to seek out food and love in equal measure. I don't want to deprive them of either. As we set off, I look back to see Speranza has returned to her chair and her lacework. A cluster of cats sprawls in the morning sun around her feet.

We are not ten metres up the road when Roger spies a board depicting ice-creams outside the only other shop in Fossa, a smaller version of the Boccabella grocery. Roger and I push through heavy green strips — a cross between plastic beads and garden hose — to get into the dank little shop. My nose twitches at the pungent smells of ripe cheese and the huge leg of *prosciutto* sitting out in the open air on a chopping block. Bottles of laundry detergent, tinned chickpeas and household items line shelves on one wall. A refrigerated row of shelves is filled with soft drinks, salami and buckets of tomatoes still attached to vines. Underneath, sitting on the cool terrazzo floor, are garish plastic crates of five-litre flagons of red wine. I recognise them as the ones Nonno Anni would steadily consume during his trips here. He only ever drank at meals and could consume two litres a day without getting drunk.

An old chap shuffles out to serve us, looking a little miffed that we've drawn him away from the men huddled in the back room playing cards. A pall of stale cigarette smoke hangs in the drab, viewless room of 'Bar Belvedere' (Belvedere meaning 'beautiful view'). The ice-cream Roger has his eye on looks like a layer of ice-cream between two biscuits in the picture. I don't feel like one but Roger asks for two anyway, which the shopkeeper insists on getting for us. I compare this with buying an ice-cream from a corner shop in Australia. As a youngster, it was usually in bare feet, slightly sandy from the beach and stinging from hot bitumen, opening the freezer while the shop owner hollered, 'You kids pick what you want before you let all the cold air get out in this heat!' In Italy the locals would be horrified if anyone ventured into a shop in bare feet, even in coastal holiday towns. In Australia, the shop owner would have hysterics if you expected them to leave the counter and select an ice-cream from the freezer for you.

I look dubiously at the large pale-blue freezer that looks like it is from about 1950. There are dark blobs of things frozen in that freezer that I try not to think about, considering the hunters' shotguns we sometimes hear at night while we are watching TV. The old chap gets the two ice-creams out. He puts on his glasses and, even with these on, he has to put his nose a centimetre from the board as he tries to read the price — ninety-five cents each. Six months after we buy these ice-creams, Nonno Anni tells us this little shop has closed down. The old chap running it is in his eighties, and after several decades of serving the Fossa community, he decided to call it a day. I wonder if the shop will stand empty or if someone else will reopen it someday. I hope the latter is true.

Outside, we bite into the ice-creams — a malty biscuit sandwiching stripes of chocolate, vanilla and *zabaione* ice-cream. An Italian cartoon is stamped onto the outside of the damp biscuit. I am wishing there was a 'use by' date stamped on the outside of the wrapper.

'This is great,' Roger raves, as he does about everything Italian.

We continue walking, Roger eating most of my ice-cream as well as his. We take the road out of Fossa that wends south. If one looks up at Fossa from the valley, it appears to have a triangular crown with the Castle Ocre as the centrepiece, a convent to the left and a monastery to the right. We head towards the convent, *Santo Spirito*. Dozing cats scatter as we pass. Having fed his chooks, a man smiles at us as he emerges through a wonky chicken-wire gate held together by timber nailed in the shape of a Z. Bright blue sheets hang on makeshift lines strung up on the side of the road opposite the owner's house. We pause at an old wine barrel left sitting in long grass, and look back at Fossa's pale stone buildings and terracotta-tiled roofs.

The late morning sunshine is warming but not too hot. Wildflowers line the road. Some are very delicate and white with silvery-grey furry-looking leaves and stalks. Taller flowers tower over these with bouffant crowns of dozens of tiny bright yellow buds. There are hundreds of red *papaveri*. Their spiky-looking stalks cause me to refrain from picking one just as I bend to do so. The most beautiful are purple flowers, which are part of the iris family. In May, the Abruzzese mountainsides come alive with wildflowers, entire hills a motion of colour as the blue, yellow, white and red hues of violets, primroses, cyclamens, *ginestra* (broom), cornflowers and forget-me-nots sway in the gentle breeze.

No cars pass us during the leisurely half-hour walk up towards *Santo Spirito*. The only sounds are our footsteps and voices, the occasional loud buzzing of a bee, or a bird cawing as it flies high overhead. Roger and I frequently pause to soak up the view of the valley and the Apennines as we climb higher. Fossa is far below us, not quite hidden behind a coppice of almond trees. The village seems high up when we are in it, but from this vantage point it looks low compared to the towering, craggy peaks above us. We are partway up the north-eastern slope of *Monte d'Ocre* which rises more than 2,200 metres into the clouds.

Verging on summer, everything is leafy and full of fragrance. Bright green lizards scuttle away at our presence. We pick up small mountain rocks that are chalky and white and take turns throwing them, penetrating several empty caves that dot the mountainside. Other caves have wooden doors at the entrance like the *tholoi*, shepherd huts, where some of the locals keep potatoes all year round. I imagine monks hundreds of years ago shivering through long wintry retreats in such caves. These uninhabited mountains did indeed beckon many ascetic hermit-monks, seeking silence for prayer and meditation among the silent rocky outcrops. However, it was the nuns who were first to build a convent among these isolated peaks, in 1222. When I see the fortress-like stone façade and massive wooden doors of the convent, *Santo Spirito*, I am not surprised the film version of Umberto Eco's novel *The Name of the Rose*, which is set in a monastery in 1327, was filmed in the Abruzzo for its resemblance to medieval Italy.

Santo Spirito, constructed of rough-hewn rocks, has soaring walls and tiny mullioned windows of which one apparently has a leaded spy-hole. I place my palm against one rock in the oldest section of wall and contemplate the person who placed it there almost 800 years ago. This spot would have seemed so remote then, only able to be reached by a narrow track suited to donkeys. The convent is shut up tight. Our footsteps on the white gravel seem jarringly loud in the almost silent surrounds. Only the bees vie with us for making noise. I stop beside Roger to stand and gaze at the craggy mountains and the valley. This ancient knoll is devoid of modern sounds. I can hear only nature — the insects, the birds, and the wind in the trees.

'If you were to live a life devoted to prayer and meditation, this is the place to do it,' I say.

Roger murmurs in agreement. As we stand in silence, a kind of peace seeps into us. It is a pity the nuns are long gone from this convent, but in the next few years the cloister will reopen as an inn after extensive renovations. The nuns' two dormitories will be converted into twelve guest rooms and it will become a unique place to stay, with activities for guests extending beyond the usual to include falconry, 'mountain climbing with crampons and ice axe', and rides around the mountainside in a horse-drawn carriage, depending on the season. It is fantastic that new life is being breathed into the 800-year-old building rather than it being abandoned to eventually decay into a crumbling ruin.

Nonno Anni told me that during his first trip back to Fossa, he and a friend walked up the mountain to this convent one morning, just as we have today. In a grassy clearing close by, Nonno Anni found a fig tree laden with fruit. He instinctively went towards it, struck by mouth-watering excitement at the abundance. Before he could take more than two steps forward, his friend grabbed him by the sleeve and pulled him back.

'You can't eat those!' His face registered alarm. 'This used to be a cemetery. The roots of that fig tree ...' his voice lowered, '... plunge into graves.'

Nonno Anni knew the area was the old cemetery. His own grandparents Demetrio and Maria Luisa had been buried there. In fact, the cemetery had been used and reused so often over the centuries that, in times past, after fifty years the bones would be dug up and placed in an *osso sala*, or 'bone room', so the graves could be used again. Not wanting to upset his friend, or cause a scandal, Nonno Anni refrained, but those luscious plump figs stayed in his mind. Back at the house, he mentioned the figs to Nanna Francesca. She too was mortified.

'I could never eat something growing in a cemetery!' she proclaimed.

So Nonno Anni decided to execute his mission, solo.

Mid-morning, when most people were at work or shopping, was the time he chose to steal away. He carried a bag, his step jaunty, out for an innocent morning walk ... Concealed in the bag was a basket. When he came to the heavily laden tree, he decided to first taste the figs. They were spectacular. The tree had not been touched for many years and its load was particularly sweet. Nonno Anni was still kissing his fingers at how delicious the figs were as he told me the story thirty years later. 'The best figs I ever tasted.'

After gorging himself, he filled the basket to the brim and carefully manoeuvred it back inside the bag. With feigned nonchalance, he walked back into the village. His step was indeed even jauntier. Nonno Anni did not take the usual lane up to the house; he took the lower, darker route, threading through twisting, tunnelled walkways at the base of the village to get to his *stalla*. Inside the stable, the air is cool and dry, a perfect spot to store fruit. He did not tell anyone at the time. Occasionally, he would steal away to have a fig or five. I am sure the fact that they were clandestine made them all the sweeter.

Fossa has one *bar* — *Il Ponte da Ascanio*, perhaps getting its name from its proximity to the town bridge, under which flows a stream of cobblestones rather than water. Although *siesta* is over, the *bar* is deserted when Roger and I step inside. I am struck by its masculine feel — black and grey terrazzo tiles, black granite counters, a foosball table, and the *Giro d'Italia* blaring away on a TV bolted to the ceiling. The *barista* emerges from a door at the back. He seems curious about our presence. Roger orders two *espressi*. The *barista* makes them, clatters our coins into a metal cashbox, and disappears back through the rear door. A teenager in a black leather jacket and gold jewellery breaks away from a group watching a slap-up game of football out in the main *piazza* and comes inside, intent on eyeballing us until we leave.

I never tire of walking around Fossa. How could I not love walking in a place that could easily illustrate the township in a fairytale? Better still, a place where the stories of my own flesh and blood have unfolded. It is said that the lives of migrants and their descendants follow a pattern. For the migrants themselves, life is all about survival, coming to a new land, generally with no work or home, and building a new life, most often through manual labour, to nurture a family. For the second generation, life is about integration into the new country, leaving the old country behind, gaining an education and following a profession. The third-generation descendants often pursue university and careers in the arts, having the distance to be able to look back at where their family has come from. I am not convinced this applies to every individual but I can see this has happened with many.

Since we set out southwards to the convent on our last walk, this time we head north towards the monastery. Roger and I climb precipitous steps and alleys that kink and wind up to the *torre*, the highest point of the village. This tower is the oldest structure in Fossa, dating back to the twelfth century, and is still relatively intact, including apertures designed to shoot with a crossbow from. It began its life as part of a castle, *Il Castello di Fossa*, which is a much smaller, more fort-like castle than the main castle, Ocre, perched above. The Fossa Castle consisted of this circular tower and three square-based towers connected by tall, protective stone walls still standing centuries later. It was most likely built to defend the slope beneath Ocre and to house livestock they couldn't get up to the main castle safe from attackers, but was used primarily as a lookout post. Situated at the highest point of the village, the tower commands an impressive view of the valley, practical in the days of marauders. The Abruzzo is dotted with hundreds of castles, mainly because of its strategic location between the Adriatic and Tyrrhenian seas. Roads built by the ancient Romans crisscross the region. After their empire fell, these roads provided perfect access for foreign invaders, including the Lombards, Saracens, Normans, Hungarians, German Hohenstaufens, French Angevins and Spanish Aragonese.

With an attack impending, the villagers would round up their livestock and scuttle up the hill, leaving their humble dwellings behind. Sometimes they had to camp within the castle walls for months, surviving by slaughtering the sheep and cattle they had brought with them. Most castles were built about halfway up the slope of a mountain because temperatures and conditions at the pinnacle were too severe for villagers to survive in improvised housing. It was also too far from the village to afford a safe retreat. This explains why Fossa, which began its life as a castle, is built halfway up *Monte Circolo*.

Not far past the *torre* is Placido's house. There is no sign of his tiny white Fiat. We knock on the door anyway. No one answers. Continuing up the road, Roger and I head in the opposite direction to the road we took to the convent. This road leads to the monastery. It is deserted and much darker due to the tall forest looming all around. It is so quiet we can hear the wind in the pine trees. The local people planted these pines in the early 1930s when Mussolini introduced a tree-replanting program in areas throughout Italy where deforestation had occurred. Nonno Anni helped plant this forest when he was young. His job was bringing up bundles of small pines on the back of his donkey. Now, almost seventy years on, these same pines tower over us, creating a thick, dark forest. It is a great privilege for me to walk through a forest that my own grandfather helped to plant.

The Abruzzo forests are the abode of wild animals, particularly bears and wolves. I am trying not to think of the eerie shriek I heard on our first night and what might lurk within the darkness. Strange that we have not heard the shriek since our first twenty-four hours here. I wonder if the cry heralded our arrival or was trying to warn us away. I'd hoped to hear it again if only to work out what it is. I tried explaining it to Nonno Anni on the phone (doing an inept imitation). He had no idea what I was talking about so, feeling a little foolish, I let it drop.

Roger and I step around overspills of white rocks splayed across the road, the result of minor landslips. They remind us that nature rules here, no matter how much humankind tries to inhabit. This is earthquake territory. The face of the landscape, while beautiful, can express rage. The mountains are so steep that when drifts of snow melt in spring, they take vegetation and rock with them. Twilight, and a cool wind, makes the road feel even more desolate and inhospitable. Roger and I both get a fright when a huge dog suddenly appears out of nowhere and runs towards us. I scan the hills for a hunter, but along comes a man out for a jog, carrying a dog lead. We do not pass anyone else.

Emerging from a bend, we come across a shrine to the Madonna seemingly in the middle of nowhere on this lonely stretch of road. A little light in the form of a plastic candle illuminates her statue behind the glass. Had I been travelling on this remote pitch-black road at night, I am sure I would have been more than a little spooked to see this glowing grotto in the distance. And that is before I read of encounters with *lupi mannari*, werewolves, in the area, which occurred less than a hundred years ago as told by local farmers.

One night, two friends were apparently guarding some threshed corn when one said to the other, 'Dear friend, the hour is at hand but do not fear, go and remain on top of the straw rick and when all is safe I will call you down.' His companion, very frightened, climbed up and watched his friend sprinkle water in the dust on the ground and roll thrice in it, howling furiously as the transformation occurred, and attracting other wolves to hunt with. Sniffing the air he looked up with bloodshot eyes at the terrified man before running off with the pack of wolves. After some time, he returned with half a sheep, then rolled three times in the dust and resumed his human form. He called his companion down saying, 'It is all over,' and the two friends cooked the half sheep but the lupo mannaro *ate very little for he was satisfied with the raw meat he had already consumed.*

Calm acceptance often features in Abruzzese folklore, even with talk of werewolves. To me a particular point sums this up: it is said the *lupi mannari* would take precautions not to injure their own cattle by shutting them in a stable with a watchdog inside and the key hidden in a safe place — so matter-of-fact. I have often seen this calm acceptance in Nonno Anni when he relays stories that seem incredible to me. No wonder the Abruzzo proverb is the pragmatic, '*Chi nasce asino non può morire cavallo*', which translates as 'Who's born as donkey can't die as horse'.

Around the next corner, there is a clearing and the monastery comes into view, rising from a steep rocky outcrop. The blonde stone wall of the monastery appears to be a continuation of the sheer drop of the cliff on which it stands. *How many men died to build it?* I wonder. What a long fall to a painful death hundreds of metres below. The monastery keeps disappearing and reappearing from behind trees as we walk on towards it. *Il Convento di Sant' Angelo d'Ocre* was founded by Countess Sibilla d'Ocre in the thirteenth century, originally for a community of Benedictine nuns until 1480 when it became a Franciscan monastery. Built in 1284, it houses the body of San Bernardino — the saint from Fossa with the scary eyes in the holy picture back at the house. (The card remains tucked behind the light switch. I hope I have not angered him.) Roger and I are only two kilometres from the village, yet in this notch of the mountains it feels like there are no other humans around at all. Far below I can see the vaults of Fossa's cemetery. The final curve in the road becomes very dark as dense foliage grows from one side of the road to the other, forming a low canopy. Tall wrought-iron gates stand open at the entrance to the monastery. A sign proclaims *Oasi Francescana: Silenzio, Modestia, Rispetto* — a sanctuary for the Franciscan order asking for 'Silence, Modesty, Respect'.

Our shoes crunch up the gravel driveway. I peer down on to terraces of land where the monks have extensive *orti* — vegetable gardens — and a crowded chook pen. A donkey grazes on grass growing around his small stable. A natural spring pours from a tap into a stone trough, green with moss. When we stop walking, the only sound is the steady trickle of water. The monastery is shut up tight. There are no monks about.

Two years from now, the last two monks living in this monastery will move to a nursing home. They leave vacant a beautiful, sturdy stone building that has housed monks and nuns for 723 years. Apparently, the resident donkey refused to budge and will live out his years on the terraces.

When I was growing up, Nonno Anni and Nanna Francesca would return from their trips to Italy full of stories, high spirits and shining eyes. Impatient with the adults' conversations, I would sit poised, waiting for the moment when Nanna Francesca would reach into her gaping straw carrybag and extract little presents she had brought back for me. The parcels were wrapped in the decorated paper of various Italian gift shops. I would finger the unfamiliar-smelling 'exotic' packaging and dream of places on the other side of the world that I would have to wait until adulthood to visit. (Though I later developed a reticence about travel to Italy to explore my heritage, I always knew that once I hit my twenties I would travel, just as my parents had. I grew up surrounded by their reminiscences and the items they brought back from Europe, Asia and Russia, when not as many people travelled abroad and places like Russia remained closed.)

Nanna Francesca often brought me an Abruzzi tea towel and a miniature version of a copper *conca*. Other times it was an Italian children's book, a marble jewellery box, an elaborate embroidered bedspread or tablecloths 'for my glory box'. There was one item that I would always seek out — its telltale rectangular packet about the size of a wooden pencil box — the Italian sweet, *torrone*. Sometimes it was the white teeth-cracking version of the Italian nougat; other times it would be my favourite soft, chewy chocolate nut-studded variety. I loved the paper-thin wafer it came sandwiched between, thinner than a communion host. It was like eating sweet paper. Nanna Francesca usually brought back a couple of bars for herself too, indulging the sweet tooth she had passed on to me. (I would often have to tussle with my father to keep him from devouring all my *torrone* too.)

The key ingredients of *torrone* — honey and almonds — have been used in confectionery throughout the Mediterranean since ancient times. Historian Titus Livius wrote of the Romans eating *cupedia*, a sweet made from those ingredients. The Arabs called their version *qubbayt*. According to legend, a shepherd from the area near Benevento had a divine inspiration to mix honey, almonds and milk to create a concoction that would solidify when cold. Nougat became a traditional Christmas treat, offered to visiting friends or tucked into the baskets of shoppers as a thank you for their regular custom throughout the year. Over time, it evolved to become the expected final dish of an Italian Christmas dinner.

In the middle of the valley below Fossa, a handful of box-like warehouses, which were not there the first time I came to Fossa, have cropped up among the farm fields and lovely old stone houses. I have often lamented this unsightly 'sign of our times' blighting the picturesque landscape. Then, as Roger and I are driving past one day, I notice a signboard that says, *Cioccolati.*

I turn to Roger. 'You know, for curiosity's sake we really should take a look.'

He looks at me but his lips do not form the words he is probably thinking. Instead, he swings the Fiat into the carpark. My hand is already on the car door handle. I am imagining how much cheaper it will be buying *torrone* from a wholesaler.

The warehouse entrance is unclear. Roger slides open an unmarked door and we find ourselves in the middle of a huge tiled room that is mostly empty except for a corner piled with boxes of chocolates. A woman rushes over to us, all apologies. They are refurbishing. She shows us blocks of dark and white chocolate wrapped in clear cellophane and we choose a couple but then I mention that what we have really come for is the *torrone*.

'Ahh. *Sì. Un momento.*' She disappears out the back.

I wish Nanna Francesca could have seen this place. I could imagine her filling the straw shopping bag she so often carried on her forearm. In Australia, when her stash of *torrone* ran out she would resort to tins of Quality Street chocolates (I knew all her hiding places). A door slams and the woman returns juggling an armful of *torrone*. There are flavours I have never seen before — chestnut, *limoncello*, *strega* (witch liqueur), saffron — as well as the original plain and chocolate. They cost less than half the usual price.

Roger turns to me. 'Shall we choose three or four?' I stare at him and he laughs.

Buying one of each flavour, my rationale is that I will cut up the bounty into squares for a '*torrone* tasting night' that we will have back in Australia. Of course, I will keep one or two boxes for individual purposes.

That Prickly Pear —
Religione

With Fossa being only an hour and a half from Rome, Roger and I often take a day trip or go for a short stay. The entire valley is swathed in dense fog when we board the bus to L'Aquila at daybreak for the first leg to Rome. It is a knuckle-whitening trip as the bus hurtles through thick fog down *Monte Circolo* and across the valley. The *Lorenzo Natali* bus terminal in L'Aquila is teeming with workers commuting to Rome. We board the bus along with them and several older women armed with empty cloth bags for a shopping excursion. Roger and I disembark in the Roman suburb of Tiburtina and pass through mobs of gypsies to catch a subway train covered in graffiti which pelts through tunnels on a whoosh of fusty air. On one occasion I sit with a nun on one side and a prostitute on the other. The nun's habit is grey. The prostitute wears fluorescent yellow.

At *Colosseo* station, Roger and I emerge from the gloom of the subway into the intensity of a Roman summer morning. The Colosseum looms right in front of us. I think of the Colosseum painted on a vast high-ceilinged wall in the ANFE club in Brisbane. It represents the Italy the migrants left behind and is part of a mural that also shows a boat and Italians coming across to Australia. Nonno Anni arranged for a painter to create this mural for ANFE (short for the *Associazione Nazionale Famiglie degli Emigrati* — or the National Association of Migrant Families). This Italo-Australian welfare organisation cultivates Italian cultural heritage by preserving its history and traditions and providing a place for Italian migrant families to meet and support each other, have Italian meals, play *bocce* or cards, and attend monthly dinner dances. (There was also a 'Miss ANFE' quest for many years, which Nanna Francesca tried to make me enter with no success.)

When Nonno Anni first became a member in 1970, the Brisbane ANFE was destined for closure. Indignant, Nonno Anni argued people needed such a place and set about turning it into the thriving community hub it remains to this day. In 1972, Nonno Anni was voted in as president and was re-elected every year for the next thirty-four years. He was fundamental in fostering the ANFE and building (actual manual labour on the worksite) its current Teneriffe premises in Brisbane, which were opened in 1981 by the lord mayor. Incredibly the club was built a couple of doors down from where Nonno Anni bought his first two houses in the 1950s.

Organising monthly dinner dances, bi-weekly social events and meetings, Italian stalls at festivals, charity work and conducting business are just part of all he does on a volunteer basis. One day he could be escorting Italian dignitaries from Rome to the World Exposition in Brisbane, the next day he could be emptying bins at the ANFE club. No job is too menial and no decision too great for Nonno Anni to take responsibility for. He is a natural leader.

Often when I was staying with my grandparents, I would accompany Nonno Anni to 'the club' as we called it. Nonno Anni may have been the president but he had no qualms about pitching in. He would strap the industrial vacuum cleaner to his back and set about vacuuming the huge expanse of carpet before he disappeared to clean the bathrooms, check the bar stock or kitchen. During the hours it would take him to do this, I would happily occupy myself. I recall being about ten and thinking I might become a famous singer. Nonno Anni let me hop up on the stage and turn the microphone on. I proceeded to clobber his eardrums with a succession of early eighties pop songs all sung somewhat off-key.

Roger loves the monthly dinner dances. He urges me to go and often we are the only ones there under the age of about sixty. Nanna Francesca loved to dance but Nonno Anni refused, saying he had always been too busy working to learn how. As soon as the band strikes up with Italian music, everyone swamps the parquetry dance floor. Roger and I join in but our shuffling is no match for the older Italians. They dance beautifully and know all the steps. If there aren't enough male partners, two women will assume the waltz pose and glide away together. It is lovely to dance with the older men who can lead and swirl me around the dance floor, an art that has been mostly lost in younger generations.

ANFE continues to be a meeting place for Italians, and Australians are starting to become interested too. From his role as the longest-serving president of the ANFE club to assisting Italian migrants when they first settled in Australia, I am proud to say Nonno Anni has been a pivotal figure in Brisbane's Italian community for more than sixty years. Curiously, although he accepted a British Empire Medal in 1977, when he was offered an Italian knighthood he blithely turned it down, scoffing at the idea of a title, and got on with his volunteer work.

When many Italians first arrived in Australia, particularly prior to the sixties, they experienced a sense of isolation and of not belonging. The majority tried their best to learn English and also to mix with Australians and adopt some of the ways of their new country (but not the cooking). Australia has become much more accepting of Italians than it once was, to the point that it is almost inconceivable to think back to the times Italians suffered shunning and overt racism. Sadly, now other 'new' ethinic groups are having their 'turn' at experiencing discrimination. As I stand in Rome looking up at the Colosseum, I wonder whether Nonno Anni was *meant* to end up in Australia because a section of the Italian migrant community there needed a leader to sustain an organisation where they could support each other in a strange land. Perhaps Granny Maddalena was right to give him Hannibal's name.

Rome bombards the senses. I breathe a nauseating combination of fumes, food, river and garbage smells that catches in the back of my throat. The sound of screeching car tyres competes with sirens. Obelisks and fountains stretch to the smoggy sky. Stylish aloof Romans, stray dogs, scarf-wearing gypsies, and tourists are all intent on carving out their bit of space and constantly jostle me. Drama and tragedy and comedy are being played out all at once. The city and its architecture are relentlessly being pushed, knocked and walked over. Rome feels to me like a person who has seen too much, exhausted by time and demands, and almost loved to death, and yet it is so wonderful, the pure *history* of it. To think, Rome was a metropolis of more than a million people when Paris and London were both still villages.

I seek out the *Fontana Trevi* every time I am in Rome. While I sit on the cool white marble at the edge of the water, I am struck by how fresh and light and lovely it is — an oasis in hot and grimy Rome. On this occasion, as Roger and I are wading back through the hordes of people, I overhear a deep male voice with an Australian accent say, 'She'll be right, mate.' I spin around to see a tall broad-shouldered man in his late forties, addressing one of the diminutive pushy Indian merchants who must have almost bumped the Australian's camera out of his hand. I am startled by the pang of homesickness that washes over me.

As we navigate the Spanish Steps, crowded with tourists and terracotta pots of cerise azaleas with the odd sharp branch sticking out to catch on my knee, I ask Roger, 'Are you missing Australia?'

'Are you serious? This is the best trip of my life. I don't want it to end.' He drapes his arm around my shoulders, giving me a squeeze. 'I could live here permanently.'

Roger wants an *espresso* and I don't. I follow him into a *bar* to patiently wait and watch him order, collect and then drink his *espresso*, which on this occasion seems to take longer than usual. There's a bit of a sting in the tail, considering it's something I often wanted to do on our first trip but didn't as he refused to drink coffee. Roger savours the mouthful of *espresso*. The look on my face must say it all for he says he wonders how I sometimes put up with him on that initial trip. *Indeed.*

These days I do not hesitate if I want to see or do something when Roger doesn't. I visit several places on my own, although Roger now usually joins me, eager not to miss any of *Italia*. It is my idea to take a look through the chapels beneath the church of *Santa Maria della Concezione* in Rome, which are decorated with the bones of thousands of Capuchin monks. I am not sure what to expect but I'm interested to take a look. Roger is not so keen. We cross the threshold into a corridor lined with five small grottoes. When I see the very first human bones I am taken aback. There are so many of them. The bones are smooth and have aged to a dull almost bronze colour. I realise I am holding my breath and start breathing again; the air is dry and stale. In one chapel the bone artists have placed piles of skulls to form the backdrop for three fully preserved bodies still clad in their monastic robes. I was not expecting there to be human remains as well as bones or for them to be so close that I can almost touch them. Some monks recline or are strung up as though flying towards me — skin, hair, eyes, nails and teeth are all still intact. Swirling designs of vertebrae and stacked thigh bones form niches from which more robe-wearing skeletons peer out.

It is haunting and sobering, fascinating and stomach-churning all at once. Waves of incredulity and unease wash roughly over me before I adjust to this rare and disquieting sight. Roger recoils and rushes on, leaving me to gaze on my own. I wonder who came up with this bizarre practice of displaying human remains decoratively and contemplate even more gruesome thoughts about how the bones were cleaned and how the bodies were divided up. The chapel floors are covered with earth brought from Jerusalem, and it was in this holy earth that the monks were initially buried. When it became full, the living monks dug up and dismantled the bodies of their long-deceased brothers to make room for new occupants.

Over time, the monks apparently employed different means of preservation. Several corpses in their entirety, including their monastic robes, might be placed sitting or lying in an airtight room with the door locked for one year. Others were immersed in baths of vinegar, arsenic or lime, depending on the period in time it occurred. Some were exhumed almost perfectly dried and preserved.

The bodies of some 4000 monks who died between 1528 and 1870 were used to create the intricate designs that cover entire walls and ceilings of the chapels. Roger silently rejoins me and we stand before a chapel that bears an unsettling resemblance to the Grim Reaper. His face is a real human skull, while the blade of his scythe is created from a column of coccyges. The designs are neat and decorative. A row of femurs creates a border, pelvis bones are a feature, and finger and toe bones make up some of the more intricate details. I am a little alarmed to look up and see a lightshade swathed in bones that look to be from hands and feet swaying slightly just above my head in the snug corridor.

I am intrigued to watch the reactions of people entering the chapels. Most often they gasp and exclaim in initial shock that turns to wonder for some and repulsion for others. All quieten and exit in hushed tones, somewhat stunned and subdued. I think of the monks. Could they ever have foreseen tourists from all different countries shuffling past in awe, fascination and horror? Engraved on one chapel wall are the words:

Quello che voi siete noi eravamo,
Quello che noi siamo voi sarete.
You are what we were.
We are what you will become.

It feels like a statement and a warning. I am reminded of my own mortality. Time passes. Life is fleeting. What is my purpose? Curiously, this bizarre spectacle left by some humble men who gave their lives and remains to a religious order makes more of an impact in its simple frankness on me and my thinking about life and death than all the ostentation and holiness of the Vatican put together.

When I visit the Vatican, I carry with me a personal history of spirituality that, no doubt, slants my perception. Because of my Italian background I was raised a Catholic. I inherited the religion that took me from my baptism in a Gothic-style Brisbane church to my wedding in the same church, twenty-seven years to the very day of my christening. I attended Catholic schools with their heavy wool blazers, canings and dichotomy of good and evil. I was one of those little girls in a white dress and veil, posing for photographs at my holy communion with my hands clasped in prayer, looking 'holier than thou'. At the same age, I was the kid that wore shorts, singlets and rubber thongs, as Brisbane's heat dictated. With fingernails bitten down, I pushed Matchbox cars around in the dirt among the stumps beneath our Queenslander house or had a tea party in my cubbyhouse with my dolls, depending on my mood and my imagination that day.

I never quite felt at ease with the sometimes dour Irish strain of Catholicism I was mostly exposed to in Australia. Being a mischievous child, in confession I would make up as many sins as I could (drawing the line at murder). I would go on for ages until the priest's eyebrows were shooting up towards his receding hairline. The Italian strain of Catholicism was more my speed, where a little rule-breaking seems tolerated as long as you follow the main gist of things, enabling religion to fit more comfortably into everyday life. Someone once said to me that there is an old adage about Catholicism: 'Italians make the rules and the Irish keep them.' Denial and deprivation by choice are not part of the Italian psyche, except maybe for Lent. Nonno Anni chuckled, 'Not eating meat on Friday came about in Italy because at one stage the fishing industry was flagging.'

Being an inquiring teen, it was natural to question not just my religion but also other religions. At school I encountered vigorous debate with several nuns, a priest and some teachers as a result. It was frustrating to face a solid wall of obstinacy from adults when as an adolescent I was prepared to be open-minded. University was refreshing in that I was encouraged to debate, explore, question and contemplate. As Dame Elisabeth Murdoch said with the wisdom of her ninety-nine years at the time, 'I wish I had blind faith. That would be a great comfort. But unfortunately, I haven't. I think I reason a bit too much.'

I did not seek to marry a Catholic, which Roger happens to be, though he grew up without regularly attending Mass or going to Catholic schools as I did. His knowledge came mostly from his religious grandmother, who doted on him. In hindsight, Roger and I agree it has been beneficial to share religious similarity in our backgrounds, though we rarely attend any type of organised religious service, holding more valuable our shared libertarian ethos. I am uncertain whether we come to the Vatican as tourists or pilgrims.

When I cross the threshold into St Peter's Basilica, I am struck by the intricacy, the gold and the opulence. The marble floor is slippery under my shoes as I walk the 200-metre-long nave. Having seen magnificent cathedrals all over Europe, I understand that Saint Peter's is meant to encompass all Catholic churches, which demands it be grand, but even so, the sheer magnitude and splendour verge on excess. Perhaps I am conscious of this due to most Catholic churches in Australia being so much more austere than the Italian ones. I think of the Gothic-style church in Brisbane where I was baptised and married. It is inspired by the Cathedral of Saint Ceciles in Albi, France. (The French cathedral is more ornate, particularly inside.) Constructed in 1914 over the top of the previous stone church, which had been erected in 1877, it is an imposing red-brick structure perched atop a steep escarpment with city and mountain views. While many church buildings leave me cold, especially modern ones, I do feel a certain affinity with this church. I'm not sure if this comes from my having taken significant sacraments there or from memories such as when my grade-one classmates and I were caught playing 'catch and kiss' among the pews while the nuns shrieked.

One Christmas Eve, I attended Mass there with the family as a storm raged overhead. Thunder competed with the pipe organ and hundreds of soaring voices. The rich royal blues and vinous reds of the stained glass windows were lit up with sheet lightning. Howling wind transformed into a spooky moan as it penetrated unknown crevices. The lights went out but dozens of candles illuminated the cavernous church which seats a thousand. As the congregation of voices lifted to sing my favourite carol, 'O Holy Night', the effect was pure magic. And yet for me the same spiritual connection can also happen outside a church. Gazing at a gorgeous sunset over the mountains or listening to a stirring piece of music. Standing on a cliff that is being pounded by the might of a ferocious sea, and tasting the salty spray on your lips. Holding the hand of a loved one giving birth or quietly dying.

I stand in front of the canopied altar in St Peter's, where only the Pope can say Mass. The sophisticated gold, marble and bronze grandeur seems far removed from the humble beginnings and philosophies of most holy men. For me, it does not feel like the sacred place I expected it to. There are too many tourists, too many camera flashes going off. People leaning on altars to pose for photographs do not seem respectful. It is noisy. I have visited modest temples in Asia with more rules, including one with a brusque little sign decreeing, 'No woman with menstruation to enter.' I think of Uluru — the giant sandstone monolith in central Australia — which is a sacred place for Aboriginals, being clambered over by tourists, usually with no knowledge of or regard for indigenous spirituality. It is not right.

More than a dozen religious souvenir shops line the street directly adjacent to the Vatican. I am entranced, taken aback and curious, all at once. Shelves strain under hundreds of statues of Mary, Jesus, angels, nativity scenes, cats — yes, cats — popes, Saint Peter. There is traditional Mary in blue and white, Mary praying, Mary holding her cloak outstretched, Mary with a snake at her feet, pink Mary, Mary covered in glitter, glow-in-the-dark Mary ... I am astounded to find a plastic, gold replica of the Vatican with an electrical cord trailing out the back, identical to the one that sat in my grandparents' lounge room for years. Nanna Francesca bought hers on their trip to Italy in 1975, and here is one exactly the same, thirty years later. Sentimental, I almost buy one. *Almost.*

I look in the shops for a black Madonna. Despite twelve years of Catholic schooling, I had never heard of her. After Pope John Paul II's death, it emerged he had adopted and worshipped the Black Madonna, and my mother mentioned she had a liking for her also. I ask an Italian shop assistant, a woman in her sixties, impeccably dressed with an elegant coiffure, if they have any '*Madonna nera*'. With her high heels catching on the carpet, she leads me down a little hallway to a wall at the rear of the shop. There are just two small portraits of the Black Madonna and Child, painted on wood, with gilt edging. I choose one and seek out Roger in another part of the shop. He is picking out a traditional Mary for his very religious Nan, who is in her late nineties. I take both up to the woman to pay for them. She writes out a docket and hands it back to me, keeping my purchases to nattily package in decorative paper.

'Over *there.*' She gestures towards where a woman in her eighties, who looks as though she could be this woman's mother (they are both sporting the same twin sets, coiffure and noses). The octogenarian sitting behind a glass-topped counter looks half out of it, but when I present the docket, she springs into life, operating the cash register with unexpected dexterity.

The next shop also has a dynastic air. An older man presides over the counter as what look to be his five daughters mill about offering assistance. All the daughters have shining dark, straight hair hanging in even heavy curtains to the middle of their backs. One of them thrusts a large plastic box into my hands. 'For your purchases,' she smiles.

I smile, not having the heart to tell her I won't need it. Roger emerges from another part of the shop. His eyes widen in alarm when he sees me lumbering along with the box.

'What *are* you buying?' No doubt he is envisaging me hauling back gigantic religious statues in our luggage.

'Just this.' I hold out a small statue of Mary that fits snugly in my palm.

Roger laughs. I watch him carry back the bright orange box over the heads of people in the crowded shop. One of the Nativity scenes would have fit perfectly in the box …

Nanna Francesca had the usual Catholic detritus around her house — boxes of rosary beads, holy cards, *ex-voti*, Sacred Heart pictures, the odd crucifix, a glow-in-the-dark Mary, even fridge magnets and, of course, the plug-in plastic miniature Vatican. I have inherited much of this now. I love both the kitsch and art of religious iconology. My family were perhaps fortunate when they migrated to Australia that their religion, Catholicism, was one of the mainstream religions in Australian society. I can appreciate it would be doubly hard to migrate to a country where both your culture and your religion were in the minority.

In pouring rain, the line to get into the Vatican Museum stretches along the gleaming footpath halfway down the street.

Roger and I huddle together under our umbrella. I have been inside before, but this is Roger's first time. On my initial visit to the Vatican Museum when I was on my own, two things had the greatest impact on me. The first was seeing a tiny rock from the moon. I happened upon it lying beneath the glass of a display cabinet. It had been brought back from the first moon landing and presented to the Pope. The rock was charcoal-coloured with a texture I had never seen before. This fascinating small exhibit lay unobtrusively among others in a long, impressive art-filled corridor bathed in golden light falling through tall windows.

The second lasting impression was the Sistine Chapel, infinitely better in reality than in pictures or memory, as I discover when I return. I had forgotten the vibrancy of the colours, the intricacy of each portrait ... Michelangelo's *The Last Judgment* demands your eye, the ceiling steals it, the other walls snatch it, before the *Judgment* commands your gaze again. Completed in 1541, it is Michelangelo's masterpiece. To think he worked for *years* within these confines, sometimes by candlelight or in extreme physical pain from the efforts of his task. Considering the Catholic viewpoint on homosexuality, it is perhaps ironic that one of the jewels in the Vatican crown, the Sistine Chapel, was painted by someone rumoured to be so.

Despite 'No Cameras' signs everywhere, flashes keep going off. Vatican staff sternly advise, 'No photos, please!' (always in English), but most tourists continue to snap away. I don't know why this gets under my skin. The first time I was here, no one dared take a photo. It seemed right not to. It is, after all, a chapel. Wistfully, I wonder whether being a resident of the Vatican means having the privilege to pass through this chapel and the Raphael rooms and along the corridors of art, sculpture and relics after hours. Incredibly, it was only as recently as the eighteenth century that the artworks the popes accumulated for centuries were first 'shared with the masses'.

Roger and I wander Vatican City and I reflect that, overall, it seems to be a competitively masculine place rather than a holy place. This is the domicile of my birth religion, and yet the extravagance and the spectacle of men trying to outdo each other via religion rankles. Outside the Vatican, an elderly gypsy woman sits on the ground begging. She leans against the towering stone wall, which was built with a slight outward angle to prevent anyone from being able to climb inside. I have a splitting headache. I'm not sure if it is due to a lack of coffee or water or too much Vatican. Roger and I go into a *bar* and ask for extra strong coffees. Roger sees a sign for *ciambelle* and although this conjures up memories not of the snake festival but of an awful stale van-bought Roman version we dubbed the 'gas ring', he wants to give the doughnut another go. A waitress brings him a triangular piece of plain cake. We both peer at the plate, baffled.

'The trees that are slow to grow bear the most fruit.'

Molière (Jean Baptiste Poquelin) (1622–1673)
French actor and comic dramatist

Witches' Brew

The aroma of frying eggs and freshly brewed coffee pervades the Fossa house. At breakfast time the house comes to life, dispelling the stillness and quiet of another night in the mountains. I open the French-style doors and step out onto the balcony. I love how in the morning, the village comes to life too. Shutters are flung open, the first load of washing is pegged to the line, and small, sweet chirruping birds swoop up and down the lanes and over the rooftops. An occasional car bumps along the cobblestones on the way to work, cats clamour on our doorstep, and the church bells remind us that time is passing.

Roger and I drive into L'Aquila then go off in separate

directions, having arranged to meet up again in a few hours. I wander up and down among the market stalls, watching the exchanges between people. I see a teenage girl having words with her *nonna* over a top she wants to buy. Of course, the older woman wants her granddaughter to choose something more modest. The *nonna* grabs the top and puts it back. The girl's dark eyes flash fire as she picks it up again. A tussle ensues. It reminds me of myself in my early teens with Nanna Francesca. We were both headstrong. She resented my resistance to Italy. I resented her 'Italianness'. She represented what I was being teased for by some Anglo-Australian kids. If only I had wasted less time resisting and spent more time asking questions. Naturally, as a teenager, I thought I knew best. Sometimes the benefit of hindsight comes when time has run out. I see another *nonna* holding the hand of her young granddaughter as they browse the stalls. Both are dressed smartly. My heart aches remembering Nanna Francesca's hand warm and dry in mine.

The relationship between Nanna Francesca and me was less fiery when I was a little girl. Being her only grandchild for almost a decade, we were close, particularly as she was only forty-seven when I was born. I often stayed over at the Brunswick Street house, every week for many years. In the seventies and eighties, New Farm was not the trendy mecca of cafés, boutiques and apartments that it is now. Leafy streets and wooden houses on stumps contained an eclectic mix of families, the aging, the homeless and a good smattering of migrants — mainly Italians who took advantage of the rich soil that originally gave the inner city suburb its name. Nonno Anni and Nanna Francesca's house on Brunswick Street was a few doors down from the shops clustered at the intersection with Merthyr Road. In those days, the shops consisted of a chemist, a newsagent, a grocery store, a hairdresser, a bakery, a butcher and a deli. The small dimly lit deli smelt strongly of *baccalà*, the salted cod that stood stiff as a board, leaning against the counter. I would tug at Nanna Francesca's hand, desperate to escape the smell, frustrated that she and the shopkeeper kept talking to each other in rapid Italian I could not understand. When I pinched my thumb and forefinger over my nostrils, the shopkeeper thought it was hilarious. Embarrassed, Nanna Francesca jabbed me.

My grandparents' house had a bus stop right outside the front. I thought this was grand. My parents and I lived in steep inner-city Red Hill, where people were reluctant to park cars let alone navigate a bus. At my grandparents' house, as I lay in bed at night too keyed up to sleep, I listened to the lonely sounds of late-night buses sailing by the empty stop. The last thing I saw before I closed my eyes was the hallway light shining through the fretwork above the bedroom door creating speckled patterns on the linoleum floor. Sometimes, after they had gone to bed, through the fretwork I could hear Nonno Anni and Nanna Francesca softly talking to each other about their days.

The first buses of the day, wheezing into the stop out the front, usually woke me around dawn. Soon after, I would hear the bathroom door slam and the water pipes shudder, and I knew that when Nanna Francesca emerged from the bathroom, fully dressed, she would come and get me out of bed. I always slept in my dad's old room. It made me feel close to him. The walls were still the same sky blue. There was a time when he and my uncle shared this room, my grandparents slept across the hall, and my great-grandparents had the third bedroom. At one stage, my great-uncle Vincenzo was living here too, sleeping in a tiny storage room they since converted into the bathroom. The weatherboard house was full. In my child-like mind, yet to learn of the intricacies of adult relationships, with parents and in-laws and siblings, I thought such living arrangements must have been splendid.

With her hair still slightly damp from the shower and smelling of rose-scented talcum powder, Nanna Francesca would haul back the covers that she had piled on top of me the night before. She had a thing about 'getting a chill' and tucked me into bed so tightly that I could barely roll over. For a tiny woman she had tremendous strength. She loved dressing me up in frocks and doing my hair, shushing me if I cried out as the sharp end of an errant bobby pin stuck into my scalp.

'I dearly wished I'd had a daughter,' she would murmur as she helped me into the 'good' green velvet dress that I only wore when going out. It had tiny sleeves trimmed in lace that stood up off my shoulders like little wings. Nanna Francesca was only thirty when her mother died and she frequently told me how much she still missed her mother. Although I was a child, I wish I had shown her more compassion at the time. Little was I to know I would be not much older than she was when she lost her mother when I experienced the same debilitating loss of my own mother. I realised then you cannot fully appreciate such pain unless you have also lost your mother at a young age.

Right after breakfast Nonno Anni would take his hat from where it hung on a gigantic nail beside the back door and head off to work. He had actually 'retired' at age forty-six when he sold his successful fruit shop and milk bar after Ann Street in the city was turned into a one-way thoroughfare, killing business. Yet he never really retired because, as landlord of several blocks of flats throughout New Farm, he always had lawns to mow, a toilet to fix or some repainting to do. And he also had much work to do as the president of ANFE.

Sometimes Nanna Francesca and I would take the bus up to the Village Twin cinemas on Brunswick Street, but on a fine, cooler day, when the sun was pleasantly warm on our backs, we would stroll up the hill past the archbishop's house. Nanna walked so slowly I was frequently tempted to skip ahead until she would call me back in an agitated tone shouting, '*Vieni qua!*' one of the oft-spoken Italian phrases that I understood. I loved going to the movies. (Nanna Francesca called it 'the pictures' even though I pointed out to her that nobody called it that anymore.) She would always buy us a box of Maltesers and each a lemonade in a waxed cardboard cup. I always managed to suck the paper straw closed. The usherette would rip our tickets and lead us to our seats in the dimly lit theatre, her torchlight bobbing on the purple carpet. It felt like entering another magical world with the cinema's 'moon crater' ceiling. The movie would start and I'd forget my surroundings. That is, until Nanna started talking in her loud, heavily accented voice causing people to turn around and look at us in annoyance. (Apparently Granny Maddalena used to do the same with my father.)

Some days Nanna Francesca and I would take the bus into Fortitude Valley. Still on Brunswick Street, we would get off at a stop outside a hotel. I would screw up my nose at the smell of stale beer and urine. Nanna Francesca would make me take her hand because the Valley was very busy with lots of people. She had a firm grip. My thumb was a miniature version of hers, except she did not bite her nails as I did. I loved being in among the bustle of the Valley on a busy weekday. There was no mall back then in the seventies — Brunswick Street was a hectic road that we would cross to reach the shops which lined each side. We would go to Target, Myer, Vic Jensen's and the Italian emporium. The emporium had all manner of things imported from Italy — statues and ornaments, clothing, kitchen implements, books, records, pictures and shoes.

Nanna Francesca bought me Italian leather shoes from the emporium. I sat quietly, staring at the shining pate of the Italian owner as he took off my white shoes, then slid on and buckled up a pair in cream and maroon leather. I obediently walked around on the carpet while he and Nanna Francesca discussed the shoes in Italian. As he wrapped the shoes in tissue paper and boxed them up, the balding man spoke to me in Italian. I had no idea what he was saying. When he realised this, he spoke sharply in Italian to my grandmother. Outside, the busy street was a noisy contrast to the quiet air-conditioned emporium. Nanna was a contrast too. She went from smiling and gracious to frustrated and pestering.

'It's wrong you don't know Italian!' she despaired. 'Your heritage! Why doesn't your father teach you?'

'No one at school speaks it, Nanna. I'm *Australian.*'

'Call me Nonna …' She broke off, her scowl swiftly replaced by a smile as another well-dressed Italian lady approached us.

The two women spoke to one another in brisk Italian while, bored, I drew an imaginary circle on the bitumen footpath with the toe of my white leather shoe.

'Ah, *bella bambina!*' The woman suddenly grabbed my cheeks and pinched them so hard it hurt. I blinked back watery eyes and forced a smile to make Nanna Francesca happy.

'Why do they do that?' I whined, as the woman went into the emporium and Nanna Francesca and I, each of us no longer falsely smiling, walked towards Coles.

'I must get some chuck steak for the pasta gravy tonight.' Nanna was shuffling in her purse. 'Don't let me forget to go to the butcher on the way home.'

I pouted in sulky silence, but I would not let her forget. I heard Nanna Francesca's purse snap shut. It hung over her forearm and had a big gold clasp on it. I loved the crisp snapping noise it made. I usually heard it when I accompanied her from grocer to baker to butcher, or when she retrieved twenty dollars to surreptitiously slide into my hand when my parents came to take me home. My grandparents were unpretentious and lived so simply I did not realise until almost adulthood they were millionaires several times over, an incredible feat of hard work and endurance, considering they arrived in Australia peasants and penniless.

In Coles, Nanna Francesca and I walked past aisles of food, cookware and clothing towards the back of the store where we climbed the stairs to the cafeteria. I got the same thing for lunch every time — a cardboard cup of hot chips followed by a ceramic plate of pikelets. The good thing about Nanna Francesca was that she would let me choose without having to have anything 'good' to eat, like sandwiches. On the way out through Coles, Nanna Francesca was often distracted by something like tea towels, which I found thoroughly boring. Out of duty, I would go through the piles with her. The little square cardboard price tags were held on with a pin, one of which would invariably find its way into my finger.

The 178 bus was often crowded on the way home. If Nanna Francesca and I had to sit sideways instead of front on, I would feel carsick. I was glad to disembark in Merthyr Road, and dutifully reminded Nanna Francesca about the butcher. Inside the butcher shop was like standing inside a fridge and smelt funny. I would hover near the door to get warm blasts of fresh air whenever another customer came in, wishing fervently that Nanna Francesca would hurry up. She would ask me to hold the meat, wrapped in paper, as she bought some bread from the bakery next door. The meat parcel felt cool and pliable and smelt like the butcher shop. I would ask to carry the bread home instead. When we got back to the house, Nanna Francesca would tell me to change out of my good dress, stockings and shoes. I would keep on the white T-shirt she made me wear underneath so I wouldn't 'get a chill', wriggle into a pair of red shorts, and thrust my small broad feet into well-worn rubber thongs. When I ventured out to the kitchen, I would find Nanna with a wooden spoon, moving pieces of sizzling chuck steak around in a pan to make 'the gravy'. I prayed I could kick my ball in the backyard rather than having to help in the kitchen.

Curiously, these memories come back to me now in L'Aquila's markets seeing the demeanour of the *nonna* and her granddaughter. I once read somewhere that what we remember is shaped and shifted by the thousands of individual experiences we have that transform us over time. The person we are when remembering is very different to the person we were who lived through those remembered events. And yet such events shaped me into the person I am right now. I know my formative years in Australia would have been completely different without the influence of my Italian family. I watch the *nonna* and the little girl wander towards the fountain. The older woman lets go of the little girl's hand to rummage among packages in her large straw bag. The *nonna*'s movements are deliberate and unhurried; the little girl is all eagerness and energy. In her pretty dress and buckle-up shoes the little girl dances away towards the water.

'*Vieni qua!*' shouts the *nonna* in an agitated tone, echoing one of Nanna Francesca's oft-spoken Italian phrases to me. '*Vieni qua! Come here.*

Goosebumps rush across my skin. Despite the lands and seas that separate us through race and migration perhaps we are all cut from the same cloth and it is only our distinct journeys that make us unique.

I venture out of the *piazza* into the adjoining streets. Walking around on my own, I lose that buffer zone that a travelling companion gives and the place no longer merely rests on my skin — it penetrates. I walk in among the Aquilani, ducking into a shop here and there, going about my business as they are. When I put in a film to be developed and give my surname, the shopkeeper writes it down without my having to spell it. This is the first time this has ever happened in my life. I am chuffed. It makes me feel like I fit in. Is this what it feels like in Australia if you never have to spell out your surname?

In a tiny dimly lit grocery shop I peer at the different, artistically decorated bottles of *passata*. The shopkeeper engages me in conversation and is amazed that although I am from Australia, my family come from not far from L'Aquila. He is stunned to learn that my family still has 'tomato day' to make the *passata*. He tells me such customs no longer exist in most parts of Italy. When I tell him that some Italians in Australia also make their own wine and bread and sausages his eyeballs threaten to pop their sockets.

Such sentiments are echoed when I speak to an older woman who is a friend of my grandparents. 'You don't still make the *passata* with tomatoes? Oh no! We buy ours. We're modern. That's too much work. *Troppo lavoro.*' Not for the first time I am reminded that many Italian migrants in Australia live with the customs of mid-twentieth-century Italy, and unless their descendants carry these on, such traditions will be lost.

I amble along L'Aquila's quiet residential streets where real life is lived. Almost wherever I walk in L'Aquila there are views in the distance of the encircling mountains, alpine forest or pretty chalet-style houses with steeply pitched roofs. I duck into a *bar* for a *macchiato*, an *espresso* stained with milk, and the *barista* recognises me and says hello. The same happens with the sales girl in a shoe shop I have frequented several times — stares replaced by friendly recognition. I never thought I would contemplate this, but I am starting to mull over whether I could live here. Roger would certainly be more than willing.

When my parents arrived here by train in 1970, the A24 motorway that penetrated the mountains had just opened. There was much gaiety and balloons decorating the *piazza* as the people of L'Aquila celebrated. Progress was somewhat slower in the mountain villages. Relatives conveyed my parents around Fossa and its surrounds on the back of a horsedrawn cart. Sometimes it was a hair-raising ride set at a cracking pace, the thin wooden cartwheels perilously close to the precipitous drop beside the mountainous track.

My parents were the first of our Boccabella family to return to Fossa since Granny Maddalena and her other son, Elia, were the last to migrate to Australia in 1948. The young couple were warmly welcomed by family and villagers alike. My parents talked for years about the thirteen-course Christmas dinner they shared with relatives in Fossa. To her dismay, Mum had been happily patting one of the courses — a white rabbit — the day before.

When I meet up with Roger, I discover he has spent all his time sitting in a *bar* near *Piazza Duomo*. He ordered a glass of *Montepulciano d'Abruzzo* that was served with a tray of several bowls of snacks — chips, puffed rice nibbles, nuts and mini prosciutto and mozzarella sandwiches. (Italians always serve food with alcoholic drinks.) The only thing he has bought was what he originally went into the *bar* to get, a bottle of *Centerba d'Abruzzo*. The inimitable liqueur, made in Sulmona in the Abruzzo, is called 'one hundred herbs' for the ingredients that are picked from the mountains not far from where the snake festival was, around *Monte Maiella* (the peak can be seen from Fossa). The same herbs and method of infusion have been used since Beniamino Toro created *Centerba* in 1817 and handed down from father to son since. I turn the medieval-style straw-covered fifty-centilitre bottle over in my hands. The head of Latin poet Ovid adorns the label (Sulmona being his birthplace). On the neck of the bottle is one of the intimidating brown bears, which roam these mountains.

Roger and I have both had *Centerba* before at my parents' house. It is a potent draught, about seventy per cent proof, and as a digestive it works. A small sip after indulging in some gastronomic feast and the liquid seems to burn straight through, dissipating any feeling of fullness. My father has also used *Centerba* in an Italian dessert to soak layers of cake spread with hazelnut cream.

Strega, meaning 'witch', is another Italian liqueur that 'whacks you about the ears' at eighty per cent proof. Currently, only two people know the original recipe, passed down through generations of the Alberti family. The family has been distilling *Strega* since 1860 in the town of Benevento. Located roughly between Rome and Naples, Benevento is the place where witches from all over the world gathered (and still do at a certain time of year). There is an old legend, very much alive, that this drink was a love potion witches created to forever unite couples that drank it. *Strega* liqueur continues to be tied to the sorcery of its origins. Some modern covens use the liqueur in their rites, burning it in bowls for various purposes.

Created from steam distillation in small stills, with around seventy herbs and spices from Europe, Central America and Asia, the yellow colour of the liqueur comes from the saffron in its recipe. Other ingredients are said to be mint, fennel, cardamom pods, anise seeds, angelica root, sticks of cinnamon, cloves and mace. The rest remain a secret. My great-aunt Caterina came from the village of Casalduni, just north of Benevento. She had eyes that were almost black and a cheeky smile. Her eldest daughter, who was named after Granny Maddalena, told me she was first allowed to try *Strega* when she was six. My cousin said it was strong, but she 'handled it'. When Roger and I first tried the 'witches' brew' at the Fossa house, we found one shot of *Strega* was enough to bestow upon us the throaty voice of a seasoned jazz singer. After taking it straight, we followed the recommendation on the bottle to tone it down with ice. It barely cooled the embers.

Before we leave L'Aquila, Roger and I walk to *Santa Maria di Collemaggio* which sits at the end of a long avenue of trees. The first time I saw it I immediately fell for the fresh lightness

CASSATA ALL'ABRUZZESE
abruzzese-style dessert with centerba

INGREDIENTS
~ 100g *torrone* (Italian nougat)
~ 50g almond *croccante* (brittle)
~ 50g dark chocolate
~ 300g butter softened and cut into pieces
~ 4 egg yolks
~ 200g icing sugar, sifted
~ 50g cocoa powder
~ 400g round sponge cake
~ 200ml *Centerba* liqueur (sweet)*
~ Flaked raw almonds

*Centerba liqueur comes in two types: *toro* — strong (70%);
and *dolce* — sweet (45%). The *dolce* version is not so dry and
best suited for this recipe.

METHOD

Chop separately the *torrone*, *croccante* (both available from Italian delicatessens), and chocolate.

Beat the softened butter until light and fluffy, then beat in the egg yolks one at a time, alternating with the icing sugar.

Divide the creamed butter equally into three bowls. Add the *torrone* to one bowl, *croccante* to the second, and chocolate and cocoa powder to the third. Mix each of the creams thoroughly. Take one heaped tablespoon of each cream and mix in another bowl. Set aside to cover the entire cake with at the end.

Cut the sponge cake into four discs. Drizzle *Centerba* liqueur over each disc.

Spread one disc with *torrone* cream, the second with *croccante* cream and the third disc with chocolate cream. Arrange in layers, putting the fourth disc on top. Cover the whole cake with mixed cream mixture. Leave in the fridge for at least six hours.

Just before serving, place flaked raw almonds in a dry pan and lightly toast over a low-to-medium heat. Allow almonds to cool and sprinkle over the top of the cake.

of L'Aquila's basilica. It is built of marble bricks the colours of cream and pale rose. To the right is the remainder of a belltower that collapsed in 1880. When we cross the long rectangle of grass in the foreground, a monk strolls out of the cathedral. He is wearing a long brown robe tied at the waist with a piece of rope. With just the façade and the monk in view, it could be Pietro del Morrone himself, in the year 1290.

Pietro was a Benedictine monk who for five years lived as a hermit in a cave in the Abruzzo, fasting six days a week while wearing a hair shirt and iron chains. He later instigated the building of this cathedral on a hill just outside L'Aquila called *Colle di Maio* (May Hill), in 1287, after the Madonna appeared to him in a dream asking him to do so. The Vatican had been unable to agree on the next pope when the selfless monk Pietro came to their attention. Devoted to a life of prayer and helping others, it was rumoured the aging Pietro was naïve (and therefore a suitable stooge for those with internal political power in the Vatican). They crowned him Pope Celestine V in 1294, not at the Vatican but at *Santa Maria di Collemaggio* here in L'Aquila, in the presence of kings, cardinals, ambassadors and a crowd of 100,000 people, including the poet Dante Alighieri. (Dante refers to Celestine in his epic poem *Inferno*.)

After just five months in the Vatican, however, Pope Celestine V felt he could do more for the people as a monk and he made history by being the first pontiff to perform the 'great refusal' and abdicate his leadership of the Roman Catholic Church. His successor, Pope Boniface VIII, imprisoned Celestine at *Castello Fumone*. With the aid of his supporters

Celestine escaped, but he was pursued by Boniface, for nine months and recaptured. He died in prison. Many scholars believe he was murdered by Pope Boniface, as a nail-sized hole was found in Celestine's skull.

Celestine's resting place is not in the Vatican but in his beloved *Santa Maria di Collemaggio*. On 28 August every year, his remains are placed at the entrance to the *Collemaggio* for the faithful. It is said that if you pass by him, all your sins for the year are absolved in an instant. Nonno Anni and Nanna Francesca have attended. Nonno Anni told me with a twinkle in his eye that a lot of businessmen make the pilgrimage. Estella Canziani was there with her father on 28 August 1913 and witnessed the cathedral filled with townspeople, friars, soldiers, peasants in costume, chickens in baskets and dogs running in and out, all while the 'lunatics' moaned and clambered at the barred windows of the asylum next door. Aided by a priest, the bishop held up relics including a tibia, a humerus, a clavicle, various jawbones and a thorn said to be from the Crown of Thorns. The ceremony ended with the bishop blessing everyone followed by the firing of guns outside.

When I step inside the cathedral, the sense of history hangs like a fog. I envisage cardinals' robes sweeping across the medieval floor of uneven diamond-shaped stones the colour of rust and cream, and reflect on all those who might have walked along this nave over the centuries — popes, lords, brides, pallbearers, townspeople … I dip my hand in the font; feel the holy water cooling on my forehead. In the Abruzzo it is said that anyone making the sign of the cross on entering a church leaves all sins behind, but if you do so on leaving the church those sins will be retaken. Slipping into one of the wooden pews, I imagine a congregation centuries ago shivering through Sunday Mass on a snowy morning — the cold cavern-like interior offering little warmth. The interior smells like stone and dust, candle smoke and the beeswax used for polishing wood.

Roger and I each deposit a coin and light a candle, our faces lit by rows of burning tapers. The white wax melts rapidly. In Abruzzese folklore it is a good omen if a candle in the church falls when one invokes God or the souls of the dead or during a marriage ceremony. Different religious votives, books and rosary beads cover a wooden table. I have not owned a pair of rosary beads since my pink plastic ones when I made my first holy communion aged seven. I decide to buy some hand-carved wooden beads, placing the requested five euros in the honesty box. As we are leaving, I notice the monk we saw out the front has been lingering, watching us. Up close, I see he is completely bald, his pate shining under the harsh light falling through the open front entry. His skin is not olive like most Italians, but very white with the ruddy complexion of an Englishman. I smile as we pass. He scowls and heads down towards the front of the cathedral.

Roger leans in and jokes in a whisper, 'He's probably gone to check the honesty box.'

Outside the *Collemaggio*, some boys kick a football on the expanse of lawn facing the cathedral. Another group of teenagers huddle in a corner, sitting on each other's laps, flirting and carrying on. The thirteenth-century façade of their local church gleams in the soft light. With its mountain backdrop, it could be the subject of a grand-scale work of art.

I muse to Roger: 'How wonderful would it be to see such sights on a daily basis?'

In front of me, two local boys try to shove each other's heads into the ground.

Footsteps in Fossa

Dusk is just beginning to fall as Roger and I take a *passeggiata* through Fossa. We do not know it, but it is to be our last leisurely walk through the village before the earthquake. The sun has slid behind the castle ruins on top of the mountain, leaving an oyster-coloured sky. There is barely the hint of a breeze. Rich aromas of evening meals cooking hang heavy in the air as we pass several open shuttered windows. The spontaneous football game in the main *piazza* breaks up and teenage boys head home to the supper table. We pass two elderly women strolling arm in arm and exchange greetings. A final few birds swoop overhead and disappear into nests. Nonno Anni told me the birds fly to Africa during Fossa's winter. One year, a friend of his put a little red tag around the leg of a swallow that nested in a tree near his bedroom window. He wanted to see if the birds came back to the same spot after winter. Sure enough, in spring, the bird with the red tag came back to the same tree.

We walk along *via dei Beati*, the narrow street on which my family house sits, past the birthplace of San Bernardino, noticing the house window with its stone-fretwork lintel. We pass the epitaph indicating where San Cesidio was born and the stone inscription near the church that reminds us snow fell on 17, 18, 19 and 20 April 1505. Roger and I double back along the side wall of the church, its bell hanging motionless in the tower. On the opposite wall is a fascist slogan from Mussolini's era. Painted in 1937 and partly inspired by the Italian invasion of Ethiopia in 1936, the slogan says, '*Quello che dobbiamo conquistare c'interessa di piu del gia conquistato*,' meaning something along the lines of: 'We don't look back at what we've conquered but forward to what we will conquer.' Nonno Anni clearly remembers a 'government man' from L'Aquila coming to paint the slogan. The man needed a ladder and, as Nonno Anni's house was close by, my grandfather, then thirteen, leant him one. Along with a crowd of villagers, mostly children, Nonno Anni watched the man use a stencil to mark out the slogan. Nonno Anni told me everyone was terribly impressed by the stencil, as they had never seen something that produced such large neat printing on a wall. The words were painted in black.

'He must have used good paint,' Nonno Anni laughs. 'After nearly seventy years it's barely faded.'

Not so the slogan painted on an unprotected side wall of a
house on the road leading up into Fossa. Exposure to the weather,
harsh storms and sun have almost faded it into non-existence. It
once proudly lauded, '*Noi tiremo dritto*', 'We go straight ahead'
— meaning the progress of Italy. This caused a titter among the
villagers, as the slogan had been painted at a curve in the road,
making it literally impossible to go straight ahead. The other
slogan painted in the village is '*Chi sì ferma è perduto*', 'He who
stops is lost'. This was also on a wall of Nonno Anni's school
classroom. There was a time when nearly every Italian town had
similar slogans painted on its walls. The graffiti is now heritage-
listed to prevent any more of it being painted over and residents
seem to accept this. Nonno Anni says, 'History cannot be
changed. It should be remembered, both the good and the bad.'

Roger and I walk through a tunnel created where houses
arc over the street. Despite the gathering shadows, we spot
several faded religious paintings on the tunnel walls, including
one of the Madonna and child, *Madonna de Amicis*, painted
in the sixteenth century. Out the other side, the lane dips and
the houses start to peter out. Some of these houses have small
gardens. We stand at the edge of the village looking across
green fields, wildflowers, forest, and the road leading up to
the convent. Further along this same stretch of mountainside,
obscured from view by tall woods, are the natural caves *Grotte
di Stiffe*. The caves follow an underground river and contain
stalactites, stalagmites, several small lakes and waterfalls.

Some of the lanes in Fossa become so steep and narrow they
merge into steps. We climb in among houses, the occasional

chicken coop, and past terracotta pots of flowers. The villagers' enthusiasm for flowers can be seen in the mostly red, white and pink geraniums blooming prolifically from window boxes and clusters of pots around front doors. In fact, Fossa has won a national *Commune Fioriti* award for the best floral display in the category for towns with fewer than 3000 residents.

The more doors I pass, the more I begin to notice them. The centuries-old exterior stonewalls of the houses might be the same, but the front doors are often where the character of a house's occupants is reflected. Each door is like a different book cover sitting on a laneway shelf. Behind every door lies a different story. Several have stylised doorknobs or doorknockers in the shapes of lion heads or dragons. The doors of the permanent residents look mostly well kept, usually of beautifully varnished wood, the brass door furniture polished to within an inch of its life. Other doors are crude, weathered natural wood archetypes, or painted a dull mission brown, now marred with cobwebs. These are fastened with long draw bolts, some new, some rusty. Some neglected doors are secured with pieces of wood and unravelling rope. Many doors have cat holes cut into a bottom corner.

Behind one of these doors, two storeys down from my family house, is our *cantina*, or storeroom. Another, down a curving lane, is our stable, or *stalla*. I have with me the key to the padlock of the *stalla* and slide the deadbolt. What looks like a wide door is actually sliced in two. They open inwards, much like French doors. This was where Nonno Anni's donkey, a pig and his mother's chickens were kept. It was also where Nonno

Anni hid his stash of figs. The interior of the *stalla* is dark and dusty and cool. It is now filled mostly with junk and firewood.

'This is the perfect place for storing wine in summer,' Roger says in the semi-darkness. 'The temperature wine should be when it's served at "room temperature".'

He takes photos of the oldest, most weathered doors we pass. I wonder what Nonno Anni might think of the photographs of old doors. Back in Australia it is photos of poppies, not the doors, which draw guffaws from him. Roger and I loved the waving seas of green and red, thinking how romantic and beautiful the wildflowers looked; real storybook stuff.

'*Those* things. Bloody pests.' Nonno Anni almost creases the photograph. 'Do you know they would always pop up in among the crops and we'd have to pull them up by hand? Bloody nuisance.' But when he sees a picture of one of the old doors, Nonno Anni's eyes mist with nostalgia. 'By God, that was the door where the barber lived,' he marvels. 'I remember going there when I was young to get my hair cut. Geez, I never thought I would see something like that again.'

Near the road that runs along the highest boundary of Fossa is a grove of almond trees that belonged to our family. In his youth, one of Nonno Anni's tasks was to tend to the trees and harvest the almonds. A narrow dirt path winds up past the coppice to the foot of the mountain, hundreds of metres directly below the Castle Ocre. Here, a cave opening penetrates the sheer rock. The antediluvian peoples who inhabited this area excavated the cave by hand around 1 BC to create a monument to the ancient Indo-Iranian sun-god Mithra. Priests of this cult were great students of astrology and laid the basis for modern astronomy with the creation of a calendar and the division of the year into four seasons. This Mithraic cave captures the first rays of the rising sun each day. The villagers refer to it as *la Ciciuvetta*, meaning 'the little owl', because, I am told, it is 'wise and watching'. From the vantage point of the cave, *la Ciciuvetta* guards the entire valley. The local Fossa paper, which Nonno Anni receives in Australia each month, bears the same name. Many a time when Roger and I have popped over to Nonno Anni's for a coffee, he has shown us the most recent copy of the *Ciciuvetta* and told us the latest village news.

The original people to occupy the area around Fossa, when it was known as Aveia, were the Vestini. (The territory of Aveia extended between Fossa, San Demetrio, Sant'Eusanio Forconese, Ocre and Bagno.) The history of the Vestini is very mysterious, as there are no surviving documents about them. If it were not for the wars of the nearby Marsi, Paeligni, Marrucini and Frentani tribes to whom the Vestini were allied, nothing would be known about them at all. The first date recorded in their history is the year 430 BC, when they fought against Rome. The Vestini were few in number and favoured living in the mountains protected by the formidable cliffs, abysses, dense woods and rivers that were difficult to cross. Considered a courageous, warlike race, the Vestini were adept at hunting the ferocious animals that roamed these mountains. Their typical weapons were a light crooked javelin and a slingshot used to hit birds. In the unforgiving winter they wore the skins of large brown bears, then abundant in the Apennines. For a time, the Vestini occupied all the land in the current provinces of Penne and L'Aquila.

Since they did not write down their history, their origins, including the etymology of the Vestini name, are unknown. Some historians suggest the name derives from the cult of Vesta — the goddess of family and the hearth. Others claim it originates from the Vestini's position between the Piomba and the Aterno rivers, from the Celtic words *ves* (river) and *tin* (country) meaning 'inhabitants of the river country'.

In the valley directly below Fossa are a series of stone megaliths forming a cemetery dating back to between the ninth and the first century BC. Incredibly, the site, which is reminiscent of Stonehenge, was discovered quite recently, in 1992, during excavations to build one of the warehouses where we bought the chocolates and *torrone*. Construction stopped for archaeologists to examine the site, and so far 570 tombs have been found. A series of flat stones, from half a metre to four metres tall, stands mostly upright in a series of circles and straight lines, arranged like the steps of a staircase in order of height. It is thought the slabs may have some horological or astronomical significance, as they are aligned east to west. The graves inside the circles were for single burials with the bodies also oriented from east to west. In addition to their human contents, the graves contained bronze mirrors, jewellery, pottery, vases, weapons and ornaments. In one grave, archaeologists found a jar decorated with geometrical motifs of metallic flakes. Some of the later burials used the hollowed trunks of trees as coffins. The most significant find was in the chambered tomb '520'. A funereal bed circa second century BC, which is intricately carved from large animal bones, depicts the face of a bearded man (most likely representing Dionysus), along with winged lions, seahorses ridden by cherubs and the faces of a lion and a woman. The delicate carvings in the cream-coloured bone look almost to be sculpted from marble.

Fossa is a tiny speck in the world — it currently has less than a thousand inhabitants — but the village is so steeped in history it can be overwhelming. During high school, I studied both modern and ancient history. While I found some of it interesting, at that age I had perhaps not yet lived enough of life to really appreciate history. History took on a completely new perspective when I could actually go to the place where something had occurred and, even more so, when I could go to a place where my ancestors had lived. Then it became exciting.

I have been very blessed to have as my grandfather Nonno Anni, who is such a charismatic and spontaneous storyteller. He brings history alive. Similarly, as I got older and I listened to Grandpa Bob speak of his experiences in the Australian Army and Air Force in the Second World War, and Nonno Anni talk about being interned in Queensland as a prisoner of war, I was captivated. Perhaps because I was hearing it from people who had actually experienced it, people that I knew and loved.

When it comes to talking about the past, I notice that men often talk about the 'facts' and the 'overall picture'. I find myself asking what they 'thought' or how they 'felt' when something happened, and what the personal repercussions were. Nonno Anni recently told me that when he was twelve, the big stone slabs along the centre aisle of *Santa Maria Assunta* were lifted to reveal an enormous cavern underneath. Holding candles, some of the villagers, including Nonno Anni, tentatively ventured inside the dark cavern. They were horrified to find hundreds upon hundreds of corpses down there. Nonno Anni left it at that, but I couldn't.

'My God, how did you feel when you saw *that?*'

His eyes were alive and wide. 'To be honest, I was spooked. It made the hair on the back of my neck stand up.'

Fossa was not the only village that placed their dead in grottoes beneath the church floor (this ceased with the cholera epidemic of 1860). Estella Canziani writes of a villager in nearby Castel del Monte who was making a hole in his cellar wall next to the church and in the dark came face to face with one of the dead, sitting in a chair with a big hat on. Horrified, he closed the hole in the wall and never opened it again. The villagers also told her that the year before, in 1912, some bricklayers testing the foundations of the church found a cave of skeletons and invited the schoolmistress to see. To get a better look, she lit a piece of paper and threw it inside. The skeletons' clothes caught fire, burning for several days. A hose had to be laid from the public fountain. Afterwards the villagers filled the cave with earth and lime and demonstrated against the schoolmistress. This was nothing like the watered-down history I was taught at school.

Roger and I walk up *via dei Beati* towards the house and I wonder if I am one of the lucky ones or the unlucky. Certainly, my ancestors lived in an idyllic setting — but it could also be harsh. They were peasants living on meagre means. In Australia, through the same hard work and with a little luck, the family did well. I am fortunate to be in one of the first generations to have more choices. My father and uncle were the first males in our family to have a university education; I was the first female. I am privileged to live in an era when, as a woman, I can write. Granny Maddalena and Nanna Francesca had no such choices. Yet, looking at Fossa and the beauty of its surrounds, I feel in some way that I have missed out by not being born here.

Back at the house, I am out on the stoop scraping food onto plates for the village cats when I see Musso Nero grab a red mat from someone's doorstep and drag it into the middle of the street. Musso Nero is the village dog; a stray looked after by everyone in Fossa. Before we knew this Roger and I had nicknamed him Brawn after we saw him several times with a little white Pekinese which we dubbed Brains. I have to laugh now as Musso Nero tussles with the mat and I see Brains watching on. No doubt whose idea it was. A woman comes out to retrieve her mat. We exchange friendly waves and a *buonasera*. She berates the dog as one would a child.

I am cleaning the bathtub when Roger returns from *Piazza Belvedere*. He stands in the doorframe telling me he sat talking with the priest and two men Nonno Anni's age. Both of the older men fondly remember my grandfather. One of the men had migrated to Argentina for twenty years but had now returned to Fossa for good. He reminisced about the first time

328

he had to ring the church bell. When the bell got momentum, the rope lifted him right up off the ground, which 'frightened the life out of him'.

Roger cooks the last of Tonino's homemade sausages for dinner, their piquant aroma filling the house. I place the heavy china plates on one of Nanna Francesca's tablecloths. Crusty bread from the village baker sits on the wooden cutting board, the serrated bread knife lying in wait. Roger pours the wine. Nearly seventy years ago, on the eve of leaving Italy for Australia, Nonno Anni sat in this house and ate a final meal cooked by his mother. He did not know if he would ever return, let alone enjoy his mother's cooking again. I cannot imagine many fifteen-year-olds these days having the backbone to embark on the journey he took.

After Roger has gone to bed, I stand at the window of the darkened living room for a long time looking out over the rooftops of the village. I walk around the quiet house. It is almost like a museum in the history that it holds, yet it is still a working house. Whenever any of us come to stay here, we shelter within its foot-thick stone walls expecting from it the necessities of modern life, sometimes oblivious to the fact that it is a centenarian several times over. I reflect how it is impossible to know what its future holds, especially now the owners of the house live on the other side of the world. I hope it never becomes abandoned and left to ruin or causes a tug of war between future owners. At this moment, I cannot imagine that happening.

Nonno Anni's descendants are blessed with this precious dwelling. It is not merely a place to stay in Italy — it is our family history. A place that I hope can remain functional while being treated with the reverence and respect it has earned. It gets more challenging as the family expands and, in future, there will be generations who never knew those who lived here, who never met Nonno Anni or Granny Maddalena or Nonno Vitale or my great-great-grandfather Demetrio. I hope they can understand the significance of this place, to share the house and look after it, to keep it going. The history these stone walls hold will long outlive any of us. I pray that after I am gone those who will be privileged to hold the key to the door of the Fossa house will be astute custodians of our precious family history. All those who have stepped over the threshold before them may be watching.

> *'Do not follow where the path may lead. Go instead
> where there is no path ... and leave a trail.'*
>
> **Anonymous**

Honour

I open my eyes to darkness. It is the last time I will wake up in
Fossa for some time. Something is not right. I lie still, quietening
my breathing. Something woke me up. It wasn't the shrill eerie
shriek that unsettled me on my first night here. The dark forest
will forever keep secret whatever creature made such a sound.
The noise that penetrated my sleep was more substantial, more
primeval. It starts again, far in the distance, at first a muffled
drone that gets louder and louder. As it comes closer it grows
into a roar that seems to roll right over the roof of the house
with frightening intensity. I suck in my breath. For a moment,
all is still, the air thick with tension, and then it comes again —
slow and muffled at first, then building, building, rolling over

the mountain tops and clattering the terracotta roof tiles. I look over at Roger. *How can he still be sleeping?*

I pad over to the window. My fingertips press lightly against the glass. Dawn is still half an hour away but the first thin grey light is enough to illuminate colossal brooding clouds. Bruised blue-black, they move ominously along the mountain ridge towards the village. The thunder is formidable. I can understand how, in ancient times, people thought the gods must be angry. Having grown up in the subtropics, I am not afraid of storms. There are summer days in Brisbane when the heat builds and builds and can only be broken by whip-cracking lightning, blasts of thunder, winds of high-pitched squeals, hailstones and a deluge. But this rolling thunder in Fossa, the unstoppable slow-roaring march coming closer and closer, makes the hairs on the back of my neck stand on end. Perhaps the time of day is making it more eerie, or the fact that we have to go out into the storm to pack the little Fiat and drive to Rome. I wish I could stay safely in the house but a huge white bird awaits us on the tarmac at *Fiumicino* and we must fly south, far south, to Australia. Another intensifying boom comes thundering towards the village. I watch from behind the thin pane of glass. A sheet of harsh white lightning pierces my eyes. Roger stirs.

It is as though the storm is conspiring to prevent us from leaving Fossa. A wind whips up. The electricity wavers. Roger rushes to cook our last breakfast of eggs. I watch the flickering lights with trepidation as I quickly pack our final few things and make the bed with clean sheets. The building storm is blocking out the rising sun. I don't fancy fumbling around in the dark trying to lock up and ensure the water, electricity and gas are all safely turned off. Just as we go to the front door to carry our suitcases out to the car, it suddenly pours with rain.

Waiting for it to subside a little, I glance back into the darkened rooms of the house. I have mixed feelings about going. Despite all the love and comforts that await me back in Australia, I feel sad to leave this centuries-old house with its whitewashed walls and tile floors. I have never felt alone in this house. I can see the marks left by different family members — things that have been in the house for decades, things brought out from Australia, or bought here in Italy. Marks left by family members, some of whom I was alive to know and some who weren't. What marks have I left apart from poems written on Friday the thirteenth that dangle from the earthquake-proof rod sunk deep into the walls?

The antiquated kitchen which has been the domain of my female ancestors for many generations — the women of the Boccabella and Coletti families — now accommodates the men as well. Nanna Francesca had two sons she rarely let inside her kitchen but each of them has worn a path around the terrazzo floor of the Fossa kitchen, just as Roger has. He has left the kitchen immaculate. In the stormy half darkness, the gleaming white stovetop is the last thing I see as I pull shut the heavy wooden front door. The rain is falling in an almost vertical, heavy curtain.

I put my ear to the door to listen for the double lock to click twice into place as I turn the burnished key. Roger has dashed to the car and is already sitting in the fully packed Fiat, the softly idling engine almost inaudible in the pouring rain. Before I make a run for the car, I half shelter beneath the door lintel to take one last deep breath of the pure mountain air, tinged with ozone from the storm. There is a momentary lull. Suddenly the high-pitched ghostly shriek I heard on my first night penetrates the air. It echoes off the stone village walls. Goosebumps sweep across my arms. I look all around but see nothing. Thunder booms. It does not happen again.

As I slide into the passenger seat, my eyes must be wide. 'Did you hear *that*?'

'What?' In the closed car with the engine running, Roger has not heard it.

'Nothing.' I suppress a small shiver.

It is still too dark and stormy for any of the villagers to be about. Their houses remain tightly closed against the thunder, lightning and rain. It is also too wet for the village cats I have become attached to, even giving them names, and I do not get to say goodbye. In the half dark, I peer at my wristwatch to see it is almost six o'clock. The silver Fiat bumps along the uneven cobblestones as we wind our way through Fossa. Both Roger and I are silent. I peer out, trying to take everything in and retain it. Does not being able to see into the future hinder or protect us? I don't know why but leaving Fossa on this particular occasion I am taking an extra careful last look at the town. To leave amid a raging storm is unsettling, like we are making a getaway under the cover of dire weather and darkness.

Whenever we first arrive in the Abruzzo, I feel the ambience transform. In the same way, the change in atmosphere when we leave is palpable. We shoot out of the last long, dark tunnel onto the other side of the mountains and into clement weather. The landscape returns to the gentle wooded hills and quaint cultivated scenery that Italy is renowned for. I look back. The Abruzzo is hidden by the enormous bleak mountains. A few dark storm clouds circle the peaks like ravens around castle turrets. I feel despondent. Judging by Roger's face as he glances over at me with a cheerless half-smile, he does too. We are happy about where we are going but sad about where we must leave.

By the time Roger and I arrive back in Australia, it is late at night, more than a day later. Jetlagged, I lie in my own bed again with familiar night sounds outside — field crickets, flying foxes feeding in the trees, the hum of distant traffic, along with the far-carrying call of a Powerful Owl, or the closer, strangled cry of an errant plover. As I toss and wait for sleep, part of me is back in Fossa where it is daylight. The village is winding down for *siesta*, a copper pot of pasta is boiling on the stove, cats dart about the cobblestoned lanes and the church bells are tolling until the last chime rings out and slowly … slowly … stops.

After travelling for some time it is wonderful to be back in the bosom of family. We all get together at my parents' house

— over a meal of course. My father lights up his wood-fired barbecue (the brickwork laid by an Italian builder in the eighties) and cooks Australian steaks and some Italian sausages laced with fennel. My mother has made lots of salads: potato with mint, coleslaw, homemade dressings, and a green salad with the flavours delicately balanced — bitter and buttery greens, tiny red and orange pear tomatoes, thinly-sliced raw mushroom, edible nasturtium flowers, herbs such as dill and salad burnet, and walnuts. Roger's mother has baked ANZAC biscuits, florentines and melting moments. I cut up several of the Abruzzese nougats Roger and I have brought back and we have a '*torrone* tasting'. Everyone discusses who likes what best — chocolate, hazelnut, strawberry, *strega*, chestnut or the *limoncello*.

Photographs are passed around, laughter abounds, there is much animated conversation and tussles for the 'floor'. Nonno Anni, with his booming voice, usually wins. I come from a family of raconteurs and the anecdotes flow. Everyone is smiling, sentiments are genuine, moods buoyant. For me, no amount of spectacular scenery can compete with the beauty of being with the close family gathered around the table on this particular night. I realise how much I've missed the overlapping conversations, the wit, the wisdom, and the frequent hugs and kisses. Over the years my parents made sure get-togethers were frequent, with family foremost. When I was a child, I was fortunate that all my grandparents were living, as well as two sets of great-grandparents. Being the first grandchild and first great-grandchild, I was blessed with eight kind elders who doted on me. A treasured photo depicts when, as a three-year-old, I cajoled my great-grandmothers to dance with me, the three of us linking hands. Great-granny Maddalena and Great-grandma Charlotte came from such different heritages, yet now they were linked as family through me.

In the first few months after we return from Italy, Roger and I go through varying reactions to being back. I still can't seem to shake the sense when I'm around Italians I feel more Australian and vice versa. It actually irritates me because I thought this might have been resolved following this particular trip to Fossa. In my heart a powerful tug of war wages between Italy, my ancestors, my Italian blood and Australia, where I was born, where I have lived my entire life, my family has lived for more than a century, to where I am intrinsically connected.

Roger feels dejected and is pining to go back to Italy. He drags himself to work on the crowded train, dreaming of the valley and mountains around Fossa. He keeps his watch on Fossa time. He wants me to cook nothing but Italian and I, the Italian descendant, am the one serving Australian, Asian or other European dishes at least a few nights a week.

By marrying me Roger was entitled to take up Italian citizenship, something he hadn't yet got around to. Now he sets the wheels in motion, despite his parents' qualms. It takes almost two years to come through and on the day Roger

ZIPPOLI
sweet dumplings

INGREDIENTS
~ 1½ cups self-raising flour
~ ½ teaspoon salt
~ ¼ cup white sugar
~ 1 teaspoon soft butter
~ 1 egg
~ 1 cup of milk
~ Finely diced zest of 1 orange
~ 20mL (2 caps) Marsala (*Boronia all'ouvo*)
~ Olive oil, for frying
~ Icing sugar, for dusting

METHOD

Stir together all ingredients except oil and icing sugar,
then mix with beaters until batter is smooth and silky.

Fill a wok or saucepan (a wok works best) one-third full
with olive oil and heat to a medium temperature. Place
a teaspoonful of batter into the oil (no more than six at
a time) and cook until golden brown (like a doughnut).
Top up olive oil as needed.

Serve warm, dusted with icing sugar.

Makes 60 (but they disappear fast).

takes his oath for Italian citizenship at the Consulate of Italy in Brisbane, he can hardly contain his excitement. In one pocket he has one of Nonno Anni's hankies with an 'A' on it — something I treasure but let him borrow for this day — in the other, he has two small white rocks he brought back from Fossa on previous trips. I notice he has polished his shoes for the occasion. He has even memorised the oath in Italian. When I show the Italian consul Roger's watch is always set to Italian time, he shakes his head and says to Roger, 'You've got it bad.' The consulate staff all congratulate Roger and tell him he really deserves to become an Italian citizen, as it is obvious he truly loves Italy.

At home, Roger gazes at our pictures of Fossa, dreaming of when he will return, and talks of buying our own place in the village. He resumes Italian lessons. He learns how to play *scopa* and often asks me to play the card game with him on Sunday afternoons. He finds out Nanna Francesca's recipe for *zippoli*, the doughnut-like dumplings she used to make, and becomes adept at making them for the family.

With Nonno Anni and other older Italian men, he discusses winemaking and pruning techniques for the Isabella grapevines in our backyard. Over the years Roger says he learns more about grape-growing and winemaking from these Italian elders than any book or his winemaking course could provide. At the fruit and vegetable market his is the only Australian name chalked on the blackboard amid all the Italian names, as he stands among the other men waiting for their latest shipment of wine grapes from South Australia to supplement those they grow themselves. I roll my eyes and give Roger a hard time but secretly I adore it.

For much of my life, I thought (and some led me to believe) that I had to renounce any non-Anglo associations, especially the Mediterranean ones, to be 'Australian'. But I have discovered that having a part of Italy in you, a little of '*la dolce vita*' and a little of the '*diavoletto*' (little devil), means it is always with you, shaping you, influencing your life and enriching it. And despite my having mostly Italian blood in my veins, I am well aware that I also have some Irish, German and British ancestry. My migrant ancestors include peasants from Italy, vine dressers from Germany, coal miners from England and labourers from Ireland. It complicates one's cultural and individual identity even further to have several migrant roots thrown into the blend. Added to that, Australia is not an easy country to be 'different' in. Although it is the twenty-first century and there is increasing acceptance of Italian culture, ignorance still exists, left over from a time, not so long ago, when Italian migrants were not always treated well in Australia.

From as young as five or six, I could see this. It hurt when I saw Nonno Anni's Italian accent was made fun of. I watched my father be a 'good sport' when mates or co-workers called him a wog or made some inane comment about Italians. Sometimes shop assistants did not give Nanna Francesca the same service they gave to the Anglo-Australians in the shop. The first time Nonno Anni went into an Australian pub for a beer, the barmaid poured the dregs from a drip tray into a glass and handed it to him. We have all been called 'wogs', 'dagoes' or 'eye-ties' at some stage. No matter how thick-skinned you try to be, it has an effect. It is demoralising when fellow Australians cut you down in a multitude of tiny ways to make it clear that you do not fit in because your name is foreign or you look different, despite being born in Australia too.

When I got married some people actually said to me they were surprised that I didn't 'get rid of' my 'cumbersome Italian surname for something simpler'. Maybe they did not realise that I deliberated over the decision and concluded that I could not give up my birth surname. I had *seen* where my family came from, where my name came from. By keeping my surname, I was honouring my own identity and my family history, something to which Roger lends his wholehearted support. I still receive comments, both negative and positive, about my name. I'm dismayed to realise how much impact a simple arrangement of letters in a name can make. After all, my names, though ethnically different, come from a similar alphabet.

In a colonised country, if you are not a descendant of the original indigenous inhabitants, at some stage your ancestors either sailed or flew across the water to come there. Strangely, there is a tacit, almost competitive element in some white Australians to assert who has been here the longest. To me, only Aboriginal Australians can claim that. Australian writer Patrick White has been quoted as saying, 'Australians will never acquire a national identity until individual Australians acquire identities of their own.' With deep respect for indigenous Australians, I have for some time struggled to determine my cultural — what is termed 'white Australian' — identity.

Birthplace is not a choice one can make, whatever your heritage may be, however far your ancestral land is from the location of your birth. If you try to run from your heritage it will eternally beleaguer you. In the end it is easier to reconcile with it because you can never detach yourself from it, not through name changes or turning your back on language, culture or cooking. It is in your make-up and assimilation cannot touch that. In the same way, one cannot ignore one's birthplace by choosing to adopt all the customs of one's parents or grandparents who may have born elsewhere. After travelling for twenty-nine years throughout the known world in the fourteenth century, Ibn Battuta wrote that he felt compelled to return to the place of his birth, where his skin first touched the earth. It is a delicate balance.

Whenever I return from time overseas in various countries, I am conscious how many different foods Australia's multicultural society gives us access to. Italian cuisine was initially a source of contention for many Anglo-Australians during Italian migration from the 1920s to the 1950s — 'Spaghetti eaters, spaghetti eaters!' — and yet this same food helped foster the acceptance of multiculturalism in the second half of the twentieth century. It also enabled Italian migrants to retain some of their cultural identity and stave off home sickness as they forged a new life in Australia.

Conversely, Nonno Anni told me that when they first saw 'hot dogs' in Australia with, what was to them, an unfamiliar bright red sausage, they thought, 'Bloody hell, they eat dog here.' And it is not just Anglo-Australians that have adjusted to migrant foods; migrants were exposed to foods of migrants from other countries and, like Anglo-Australians, were sometimes wary of these new tastes (when we went to a Chinese restaurant when I was a child Nanna Francesca struggled with the Asian food). There remain those with less adventurous palettes but Australian society as a whole has embraced many migrant foods. I am both excited and proud that in Australia we have cafés and restaurants cooking foods from every continent. To me this is an evolving society and the differing cultures can only enrich each other. As recently as 1970, ninety-nine per cent of Australia's population was of white Anglo-Celtic origin (incredibly the White Australia Policy was not abolished until the mid 1970s). Yet, pleasingly, by 2011 Australia is home to citizens with origins from among 199 different countries, making it one of the most multicultural places on earth.

I find myself back at Nonno Anni's house, drinking a cup of International Roast which has been boiled in an ersatz copper pot on the gas ring. I was once jaded by Nonno Anni's stories. Now I am like a sponge, racing against time to hear as much from him as I can while he can still tell me in *his* way with *his* voice. Pictures of Fossa and Poggio Picenze surround me. Of course they mean so much more to me now. I loved being there and look forward to going back. Roger and Nonno Anni talk of Fossa together like two lovesick teenagers, pining over their 'great love who is far away'.

'Ah, Fossa,' Nonno Anni sighs, cursing old age for preventing him from seeing her.

'So beautiful,' Roger sighs also, and they exchange the glances of two in cahoots.

Again I am relegated to looking on, perturbed. I love that Nonno Anni and Roger share this passion for Italy and, in particular, Fossa, but it almost threatens to usurp my relationship with my grandfather. Nonno Anni has such a captive audience in Roger that he begins directing all his stories to him, and all his eye contact. In turn, Roger jumps in and comments or asks the questions that I have opened my mouth to voice. Naturally I am a little put out; I am the one who writes down Nonno Anni's anecdotes. These are *my* family stories; I feel possessive. It is even more difficult when Roger tries to authoritatively correct something I have heard Nonno Anni describe many times throughout my life. If I double check with Nonno Anni, he confirms Roger was mistaken, but then looks at me incredulous for double checking as though to say, *You should know this by now.* On one hand it is hard not to feel like Roger has appropriated my culture as well as my family stories, and yet on the other, his passion for Italy has been wonderfully positive for me in so many other respects.

Watching Nonno Anni and Roger freely express their feelings for *Italia*, I am struck by the fact they are each clear in their national identity. Roger knows he is Anglo-Australian yet he has made a choice to adopt Italy with a fervour I have never seen him express for his Anglo-Celtic ancestry. Perhaps being so confident in his Australian identity enables him to unreservedly adopt another culture. As for Nonno Anni, he may have lived most of his life, raised his family in, and have great affection for Australia, but he was born in Italy to Italian ancestors and will always know in his heart he is inherently Italian.

Sitting back in his chair, expansively spreading his huge hands on the tabletop, Nonno Anni says, 'I reckon one day you'll be the ones to live six months in Australia, six months in Fossa each year.'

I watch Roger eagerly nodding and wish life could be so simple.

I went to Italy to research a different project and in snatched moments ended up writing about my family folklore and about being half Australian, *mezza Italiana*. I did not plan to write of something so personal I had hidden for so long, but my hand seemed guided, perhaps by my ancestors. With such a responsibility, I wrote with nothing but respect and the most honourable of intentions. Nonno Anni only got to read a few chapters before he died, but his eyes filled with tears of emotion and pride, on his lips a contented smile, for he knew he had finally got through to me. I had come to love and be proud of our heritage as much as he.

He did not live to know of the earthquake ...

Epilogue —
After the Earthquake — Early June 2009

I stand just inside the doorway of the Fossa house and try to calm the surge of emotion that is suddenly making it difficult for me to breathe properly. Through the soles of my shoes I can feel the crunch of smashed crockery and slipperiness of plaster dust. The earthquake has cut power to the house. A shaft of daylight falls through the front door onto the toppled kitchen cabinets, smashed glasses and crockery, and food packets scattered about. The chimney pipe, torn from the wall, lies diagonally across the room. Rain has come in through the ceiling where sections of roof tiles slid off and smashed onto *via dei Beati*. I am conscious of Roger standing behind me, but for a moment I cannot move.

The *Vigili del Fuoco* (fire/emergency) worker who must accompany us inside the unstable house gets out a torch and goes further in, checking first if it is safe for us to follow. The main earthquake happened two months ago, yet in the last couple of days there have been aftershocks registering 3.2 and 4.1 on the Richter scale, and damaged buildings continue to crumble further. (There will end up being more than 10,000 aftershocks.) The main earthquake, which occurred at 3.32am on 6 April 2009, measured 6.3 and was felt as far away as Rome and Naples. The epicentre of the *terremoto* was just three kilometres from Fossa. We are indeed blessed that none of our family members were killed and the house is our only casualty. Many others were not so fortunate. Three hundred and eight people have lost their lives, including five of Fossa's residents, among them a young mother and her three-year-old daughter, one of twins. Around 1500 are injured and more than 15,000 buildings and homes are reduced to rubble, making nearly 70,000 people in the Abruzzo homeless (at last count). Many have moved in with family or into hotel rooms, but the majority (almost 40,000) are living in tents with 161 'tent cities' established in the surrounding area. Fossa itself has been completely evacuated, its inhabitants sheltering in tents pitched on the soccer field in the valley below the village.

Although my uncle managed to get to the house within two weeks of the earthquake happening, the *Fuoco* workers were reluctant to allow him too far inside. Now the house is partly shored up, Roger and I have the opportunity to walk all the way through. I am aware of the sound of the *Fuoco* worker tripping over rubble in the darkness as he moves to open up the wooden shutters. The rooms suddenly brighten, revealing more damage. There are cracks of various sizes in the plasterwork and stone of every single wall and ceiling. Some cracks are superficial, perhaps the width of a pencil; others are serious, leaving gaping holes a fist could fit through. We all have hard hats on (mine damp with another *Fuoco* worker's sweat), although I consider how little protection they would offer should the house implode. I saw the *Fuoco* workers who are guarding the evacuated village grimace when I told them the address of my family's home. A burly worker with forearms like two enormous Christmas hams, muttered, '*Zono rosso.*' Red or danger zone. The worst.

In the bedroom the entire ceiling has fallen in, crashing down onto the beds. My tears fall. The *Fuoco* worker nods and averts his eyes. This is where Nonno Anni and Nanna Francesca once slept. Heavy beams and terracotta tiles lie across where they would have lain. Perhaps this affects me more because I am already grieving. The pain I endure for the recent loss of my mother I carry in my chest, particularly raw as her death occurred not long after Nonno Anni's, and before that Nanna Francesca's. I never knew one could feel an ache so raw that it could go beyond tears, chiselled to a depth that also brings with it clarity. A calm surface belies the currents eddying beneath. The feeling may dull slightly but *stays* with you.

Sunlight penetrates where the roof above the bedroom has gone. Rain has stained the white walls the colour of milk coffee. A mixture of grey dust and plaster the consistency of talcum powder coats everything, as though it has been sieved from the ceiling. The two piles of bricks where I stood to hang sheets on the line outside the window are completely buried in dust and grit. I vaguely hear in the background Roger telling the *Fuoco* worker this house has been in my family for centuries, and the worker responding with amazement. Through the rooms of the house I pick my way over broken furniture, strewn belongings and books, thick dust and chunks of plaster. The holy picture card of San Bernardino, which I tucked behind the light switch, has moved and once again he stares at me. All the while I am breathing the familiar fireplace scent of the Fossa house.

The poems I wrote still hang from the earthquake-proof rod in the wall. The *Fuoco* worker tells me it is good the rod hasn't buckled; it has probably saved the house. I look up at the rod, which was put in so many decades ago, before any current generation's time. My ancestors were preparing for this. It has also helped that Nonno Anni tiled all the floors in the living areas. There is much restoration work to be done and it will be many years before the house is habitable again, as naturally priority will go to the homes of Fossa's inhabitants.

I knew my ancestral home had found a place in my heart, but since the earthquake I have realised just how much it means to me. It seems especially cruel that now I have come to form an attachment to it and am coming back regularly to stay, the earthquake snatches it away, rendering it uninhabitable. And even when or if the house is rebuilt, it will be different. It will never again be the same as when Nonno Anni was alive. When we escorted Nonno Anni on his final journey, the deep, resounding male voices of the Giuseppe Verdi choir filled the vast interior of the cathedral with '*Va, pensiero, sull'ali dorate*', 'Fly, thought, on wings of gold'. Locking the front door behind me I feel like a part of this house in Fossa has died with him.

The façade of the house is covered with scaffolding and bracing. Roger helps me negotiate the short flight of front steps, which are covered in slippery rubble. It is eerie walking around Fossa's deserted streets. We are silent. Many buildings are braced or cordoned off. Most appear damaged. Some entire sides of houses have slidden away to reveal several storeys of furnished rooms like a doll's house. It is disorienting but one of them appears to be Lucina's sister's house where we had lunch. The ledge where Checkpoint used to sit is covered with rubble that we must clamber onto and over to continue on.

Via dei Beati is littered with debris: a bedside table, a shoe, a chair, even a car door wrenched off by falling stones. Five people perished in Fossa. I have seen pictures of a woman and also a couple who died when their house collapsed. Although I did not know them, I cried. They reminded me of Lucina and Fulvio. In Australia, I anxiously gleaned what information I could in the hours and days following the earthquake. Initially, we heard that Speranza, who lived in the house above ours, had been killed but fortunately this was not true. I was told our house had collapsed, then it was okay, of which it was neither. No one could get hold of Placido. Suddenly I found myself in contact with relatives in Europe, America and other parts of Australia — all of us exchanging what information we had to progressively build a better picture of what was happening in the Abruzzo. It highlighted how far and wide many villagers and family members from Fossa had scattered when they emigrated.

Both of Fossa's churches are braced. The older, smaller one, *Santa Maria ad Cryptas*, is actually wrapped many times in thick bands hugging it together. Inside, the 800-year-old frescoed walls painted by hands long gone from this earth are smashed and cracked. The village is very quiet. The belltower of *Santa Maria Assunta* opposite our house has collapsed. The bell which once reverberated through the village sits on the ruins of the campanile. It is so strange to see the top of the belltower gone, reduced to rubble spilling onto the church roof and the narrow street. A belltower is such a strong focus and identity for a small town — for it to be damaged is very dispiriting.

On the periphery of Fossa, where Roger and I once walked up to the convent and the monastery while we ate ice-creams, landslides have covered the road. The *Fuoco* worker, Roger and I pass several enormous boulders that have crashed down from the mountain above, crushing cars and leaving gaping holes in buildings and craters in the bitumen. One of the boulders that toppled down the mountain face is about the same size as the nearby Fiat it almost flattened. I look up to see the path of the landslide. Parts of the centuries-old walls of *Castello d'Ocre* above have also tumbled down the mountain onto the houses. The stone walls of the castle ruins have been drastically reduced in height. History has been lost.

My gaze sweeps over Fossa and the depth of feeling catches me unawares. I cry at the despair and anguish I have seen on the faces of the people directly affected. My heart goes out to them. I know how distressing this would have been for Nonno Anni and it occurs to me that perhaps it is for the best that he is no longer alive to see what has happened. Roger feels such an affinity with Fossa and the Abruzzo he is beside himself.

I am struck by the quietness. No tolling of church bells, no buzz of a *Vespa* or an *Ape*. The houses are empty. A brand new phone book sits uncollected on a doormat. Once-well-kept verges are already beginning to overgrow with grass and poppies, helped along by the spring rain. A large coop I recall being full of chickens and a rooster stands empty. Fossa is a ghost town of valuables and furniture, cars and dying pot plants — abandoned apart from the cats and dogs.

We come to some plates scattered upon the cobblestones and the *Fuoco* worker reaches into his big coat and pulls out several tins of cat food. I eye him curiously. He has piercing blue eyes and a head of thick pale-grey hair. I estimate him to be about forty-five. He is tanned and well built, his face expressive and kind. *Vigili del Fuoco* means 'fire watchers' but the men and women of this fire-and-rescue service do so much more to safeguard people, animals and property in Italy. I ask and he tells me he is from Frosinone (where Roger and I once got caught in a traffic jam on the way to Positano). The scale of the earthquake disaster has summoned emergency workers from all corners of Italy. I watch him tear off the lids of the cat food, emptying the tins onto the plates. He then pulls out some Tetra packs of long-life milk and rips them partially open so they sit like little bowls on the road. The village cats spring from their hiding places, including a mother trying to raise her kittens. My heart melts seeing this tough-looking bloke caring for the animals.

'That is very good of you,' I tell him.

He shrugs. 'We have three cats at home.'

More cats appear, squeezing out of nooks and crannies or jumping down from walls, as well as a couple of little dogs who bolt down the food. There are several spring litters and scrawny, ill-looking kittens mew pitifully. I don't see Brawn or Brains. I had wondered what might happen to all the cats and dogs that once survived on the scraps left outside doorways in the now deserted village. I later discover other locals living in tents on the football field down in the valley come up to Fossa with bags of dry pet food and empty it into mounds in the laneways for the starving animals. These people have lost so much yet they still care.

I thank the *Fuoco* worker profusely for the time he has given us in the empty village.

'*Niente, niente,*' he expostulates, but to me it wasn't 'nothing'.

In the *tendopoli*, or tent city, which has been set up to house Fossa's almost 700 inhabitants, Placido is dwelling in his tiny, white Fiat. Having lived most of his life alone, Placido prefers being solitary and struggles to share a bright blue tent with numerous people. I see the doona lying across the cramped back seat of his car and my eyes fill with tears hidden by my sunglasses. I give him an extra long hug. We take Placido to dinner at a pizzeria in Bazzano (the only place close by that is currently open at night). It is a far cry from the trout restaurant, which sadly has been damaged in the earthquake. We drive over the epicentre of the quake on the road between L'Aquila and Paganica, near the *bar* where we had drinks with Placido all those years ago. The tiled pizzeria echoes with the noise of a television in the corner and dozens of emergency workers, mostly men, in their different uniforms.

Placido finds it hard to talk about the earthquake. I can see that he is traumatised. When it happenend, he stayed in his house until daybreak before assembling with the rest of the town in the football field. He says the shared living is hard. Tents, showers, dining facilities, TV room — all are communal. It has been eight weeks since the main earthquake. The government has promised temporary wooden huts (again some of it communal living) by November — seven months after the quake. I think of the freezing snowy winter. Disturbingly there is no timeframe for when people can return to their houses. Those who lost their homes in the 1997 Umbrian earthquake are still living in temporary housing thirteen years on. Despite media and government reports that the earthquake victims are in favour of the G8 conference being held in L'Aquila, my experience is that most locals would prefer the funds and energies going to better housing and basic facilities for the children.

I find Placido changed; an innocence lost. He is still in shock. Yet there is a slightly harder edge that will stay with him. He does not joke like he used to and is less bashful. When we say goodbye, I hug him tight. He looks tired but like many Abruzzese is calm and strong. It is agonising to drop him off at his 'home', his car. I could just put my head down and cry.

Televison footage and media photos did not prepare me for the awful reality of the things I have seen. The distress and tension are palpable. I am moved and also traumatised. I was so determined to get to the earthquake zone to see Placido and the house I had not factored in the impact it would have. Roger and I are ready to help shift rubble, anything to assist, but the authorities puzzlingly keep all aid at arm's length.

Roger and I are staying at a local farmhouse in nearby *Sant'Eusanio Forconese* with several elderly people who have lost their homes in the earthquake, some of whom knew Nonno Anni. There is no hot water. I am covered in dust from the rubble, but not being able to have a shower is nothing compared to what others are going through. The centre of *Sant'Eusanio* is totally destroyed, the devastation compared to when Second World War bombings ripped through towns.

Surrounded by restless mountains and scarred, empty villages, Roger and I lie in bed in the darkness. Sleep does not come easily after what we've seen and with the threat of more aftershocks during the night. I wonder if these thick walls will hold. Roger and I have been together verging on twenty years and are fortunate to have a relationship that continues to evolve and become even closer. And yet, if it is possible, going through the experience of being in the earthquake zone has bonded us even more strongly. The enormity of life-and-death struggles, the history lost and the might of nature we have witnessed keeps us talking far into the night. I struggle to keep the emotion out of my voice. Roger's voice sounds flat.

Driving around the Abruzzo under blue skies and beautiful sunshine it is curious to see that most of the natural environment seems untouched by the earthquake. It is easy to be tricked into thinking all is well, and then we pass the shocking rubble of the almost-levelled village of Onna where thirty-eight of its 350 residents perished. Roger and I cannot get into Poggio Picenze at all due to the damage (there have been fatalities there too). I am unable to see far enough beyond the barricades to ascertain whether the Urbani *locanda* is damaged. I know that part of the dome and roof has caved in at the church where Granny Maddalena and Nonno Vitale were married.

L'Aquila is the same. We get as far as *Porta Napoli*, the centuries-old gate to the city and find it blocked, several *Alpini* soldiers monitoring who goes in. Roger and I do not try to enter. We could only get into Fossa to see the house after going through the necessary channels, meeting with authorities, filling in forms and surrendering our passports, to finally each be given a plastic clip-on permit allowing us to enter Fossa's *zono rosso*.

I have already seen extensive footage on Italian television of the devastation in Abruzzo's capital. Many of L'Aquila's historic buildings have been damaged. The apse of L'Aquila's largest Renaissance church, the *Basilica di San Bernardino*, is seriously damaged and its campanile has collapsed. Almost the whole dome of the eighteenth-century church in *Piazza Duomo* has fallen down. The third floor of *Forte Spagnolo*, the sixteenth-century castle housing the National Museum of Abruzzo (and the bones of the mammoth) has collapsed. The cupola of the eighteenth-century baroque church of Saint Augustine, rebuilt after it was destroyed in the 1703 earthquake, has collapsed, damaging L'Aquila's state archives.

I was most shocked by the thirteenth-century *Basilica di Santa Maria di Collemaggio* where I bought the rosary beads and we were watched by the surly monk. This beautiful 800-year-old cathedral where Pope Celestine lay has collapsed from the transept near the altar to the back of the church. Almost the entire interior is a pile of rubble. Emergency workers have since removed large-scale artworks and Celestine's bones from the debris.

While most of L'Aquila's medieval structures bear damage, many of its modern buildings which were believed to be earthquake-proof suffered the greatest harm, including L'Aquila hospital's new wing and, devastatingly, the dormitory at the University of L'Aquila which collapsed and killed many young students. Poor building standards or construction materials seem to have further contributed to the large number of victims. According to *Fuoco* workers and other rescuers, some concrete elements of the fallen buildings seem to have been made poorly, possibly with too much sand in the cement, which points to criminal involvement and corrupt building contracts. There is concern about mafia infiltration in the reconstruction, despite government reassurances.

I stand in the deserted middle of what was once one of L'Aquila's busiest roads, where we watched the end of the *Giro* bike race. Beside me is a block of units where the top half has collapsed onto the bottom half. It seems improbable that all the occupants would have survived. Giant hunks of concrete hang from the top of another building, precariously held in place by doubled-over steel reinforcing. A TV sits on the ground beneath a window hanging off its frame. The screen of the box set is still intact. Curtains billow out through broken windows and quality furnishings are subject to the elements. I think of the *barista* who fastidiously kept his *bar* clean, the photography shop where the assistant knew how to spell my surname, the *forno* where we bought a peach custard cake. I remember the joyful faces of the locals at the *Giro*, even the rude couple who snatched at the freebies. The once vibrant regional capital is a ghost town. Eerily, at night lights glow in houses exactly as people left them, the power not having been cut. L'Aquila is altered, sobered, closed-off, traumatised; just like its inhabitants. The colourful daily market in *Piazza Duomo* is now an apparition. The square stands empty except for debris.

To see the faces of the Abruzzese, as familiar to me as Nonno Anni's face, contorted in distress, grief, or simply

blank with shock, tugs at my heart more than any rubble. I see
people touch the top of a coffin, bless themselves and kiss their
fingertips. It reminds me of my own family funerals. There
is anger, sadness and suffering, and yet also the underlying
strength of the Abruzzese that is admired by all Italians. When
a ninety-eight-year-old woman is rescued after almost forty
hours trapped beneath the rubble, she says she passed the time
crocheting. Faced with a wall of TV cameras, she quips, 'You
could have given me a comb to tidy my hair!'

The Fossa youth joke they will open a nightclub called
'*Epicentro*' with a sound system that makes the village shake. A
reporter asks a frail elderly man if he ran away frightened when
the quake hit and the man replies, 'Run? Are you kidding? I can
hardly walk.'

After I leave the earthquake zone, wherever I go throughout
Italy, when I talk to locals about the earthquake, over and over
I am told the Abruzzese will recover as they are considered the
strongest of all Italians. I would add they are also incredibly
down to earth. And yet it should be said that no matter how
strong people are perceived to be, they can only tolerate so
much and shouldn't be expected to show infinite patience.

Almost two years after the earthquake, the houses in Fossa
remain exactly as they were when the quake occurred. Across
the Abruzzo the 70,000 made homeless continue to reside in
temporary housing or hotels. Some must commute more than
200 kilometres daily to reach their jobs; many whose places of
work were damaged remain unemployed. Family pets roam
deserted towns among rubble yet to be cleared for repair work

or rebuilding to begin. Thousands have been prevented by authorities from returning to their homes, even if the damage has been assessed as minimal and the survivors are prepared to privately pay for and organise repairs. Many L'Aquila residents tied their house keys to barricades encircling the city, symbolising they no longer needed keys as the government won't let them go home. The Abruzzese were told they would be allowed back home in 2014. That was revised to 2019 and then 2024. L'Aquila was completely rebuilt after the earthquake in 1703, yet in 2010 there was alarming talk of leaving it to possibly become a latter-day Pompeii.

I speak to people in Fossa a year and a half after the *terremoto* and they tell me they want to return to their old houses. They have been told this will most likely take fifteen years and my heart breaks for the elderly coming to terms with never being able to return. There seems to be general agreement that the initial handling of the emergency was swift and well executed, but as the months and years have rolled on there is much concern regarding 'slowing down' of the reconstruction process to spread the cost, particularly as plans and rules are constantly changing.

Meanwhile, certain villagers take turns going up to the deserted village to feed Fossa's cat population. A year after moving into temporary housing in their 'new village' called San Lorenzo, Fossa's residents opened a *bar*, a food store and, a month later, a church (interestingly in this order, perhaps a telling insight into the Italian psyche). A collapsed bridge in the middle of the valley between Fossa and Poggio Picenze has almost been rebuilt, which means Fossa's children can take the bus to resume school in a neighbouring village. The older villagers fear the younger generations are moving on with their lives and will not want to return to Fossa.

I speak to Nuncio, a villager in his fifties, who regularly updates me with what is really happening to the earthquake survivors (government-run Italian media is not always as objective as it could be). He tells me they will work hard to preserve the history and traditions of Fossa for future generations, because the government will do little. Nuncio has hope, due to the fact that everyone wants to rebuild, even those like my family with houses in Fossa they did not habitually live in. I can see he looks forward to the village being reborn. It is clear it will be mainly up to the villagers to do so and this illustrates the real strength of the Abruzzese spirit. They are fighting for what is just, not only for the return of their lifestyle and homes, but for their traditions and the area where they live in the same way evidence shows people have been defending this particular tract of land since prehistoric times.

In Italy, the Italians of other regions have a phrase to describe the people of the Abruzzo: *forte e gentile* — strong and kind. Traits said to be born of lives spent in tranquil villages that habitually rumble with earthquakes. It creates character that is exceptionally strong, but not hard or indifferent. The Abruzzese have heart and a deep well of hope that enables them to endure.

In my naivety I thought my first trip to Italy may have been the only one, but over the years Roger and I have returned to Italy many times, eventually traversing 'the boot' from top to toe. I continue delving into my family tree, its branches reaching higher and higher. Not for the first time I am astounded at the fortitude and audacity of my grandparents in leaving century upon century of family history and residence in the same place to go to an unknown land with no means to return.

When they first arrived in Australia, life was mostly tough, the climate unforgiving, the opportunities not always as abundant as promised, the racism rife … but they got through, they survived. I admire that they dared to migrate in the first place (not everyone in their position chose to). When life in their new country was hard, they didn't give in; they kept going, carving out an existence for themselves and their future family.

I did not realise until I travelled that the migrants had become a different race to the natives of the birth countries they left behind. This was not a race belonging to any particular country or continent; it was the race of what I would term 'migrancy'. The experiences of the migrants taught them to be stronger, more adaptable and tenacious; calm in times of crisis, unperturbed if something went wrong. Some raised large families, others became millionaires, some just got by, many faced great personal loss at an early age, but they did not 'go back', whether they had a choice to or not. They created new paths, lighting trails to begin again on the other side of the world. Sometimes the extraordinary emerges from what may have appeared ordinary at the time.

It is this strength that made me realise perhaps my cultural identity cannot necessarily be neatly boxed into 'European' or 'Anglo' this or 'Mediterranean' that. I am a descendant of migrants and it occurs to me if that is my cultural identity then so be it. I am honoured to derive from such strong, hardy people, who dreamed and took risks — something many never do in a lifetime — encompassing all their cultures and my birthplace. Whether I am standing in Fossa or Beutelsbach, Lincoln or Brisbane, I sense all those who have been before me, who are immortal because their blood continues to flow through my veins, through my heart. I hope future descendants will have the freedom to be proud of their heritage from an early age and do not spend decades surrendering part of themselves as I did. Forsaking migrant heritage because of racism or other pressures means denying the existence of people who worked hard and made sacrifices. There is an honour in remembering.

Roger comes home one day, lugging a large manually-operated coffee machine.

'What are you doing?' I protest. 'We already have one.' (From Italy, which has done the job for years.)

'This one will make a better cup.' He edges the box down onto the kitchen floor.

Soon the kitchen fills with the scratchy hiss of a grinder converting fresh roasted beans into ground coffee, the whoosh as Roger froths milk. Coffee gurgles into pre-warmed cups and rich caramel aromas pervade the house. On the kitchen walls a large painted tile from Orvieto hangs near a Bavarian plate and a German cooking witch, who guards against food getting burnt (although sometimes she must get distracted). On a shelf sits a collection of coffee pots, teapots and copper kettles that belonged to my mother and my two grandmothers. The pieces range from 1950s England to 1960s Italy to a teapot bought from a Sydney street market in the 1980s. Below them are shelves of cookbooks for different cultures.

I fling one of Nanna Francesca's tablecloths over the table. Roger stirs sugar into his *espresso* with one of the miniature *espressi* spoons we bought in Rome. Paintings we brought back from Europe hang beside local artists. We have little conversations in Italian, reverting to English if we get stuck. Cats lie about or curl on a chair. Roger puts on a CD I bought in L'Aquila. The music wafts out over the backyard where the Hills Hoist stands sentry by the pool, palm trees and the cypresses. A banana tree and an Arabica coffee tree, cultivated from offshoots of Nonno Anni's trees, grow side by side, as do a *Frantoio* olive and a mulberry tree. The grapevine, from which Roger continues to make his homemade wine, thrives.

No longer do I feel cursed by having several cultures in my make-up — I am blessed. Stars glow in both northern and southern night skies. Warm, soft earth feels the same beneath bare feet, whatever colour the skin may be. Night rain falls. A breeze caresses the curve of a face. Language, food, music, traditions, loved ones ... like one of Nanna Francesca's colourfully embroidered antique linens, we all have our uniquely interwoven threads, but the tablecloth is the same.

Postscript

In January, 2011 Brisbane experienced a severe flood inundating more than sixty suburbs including the CBD. Sadly the section of Brunswick Street in New Farm where Nonno Anni and Nanna Francesca's house sits was flooded, destroying what remained stored of a lifetime of their belongings. To lose my grandparents and then have their homes and possessions in both Italy and Australia affected by earthquake and flood is a double blow. Still, the belongings lost are just 'things', not people though it's hard not to feel sentimental about some items. Memories endure. We endure.

ACKNOWLEDGMENTS
gratitudine, baci e abbracci ...

Ringraziamenti sinceri to all my ancestors ... I will honour your memory, always.

Eternal thanks to my parents, Sandy and Remo, for encouraging imagination, a love of reading and an open mind in my childhood. My life is richer for it.

A special thank you to my mother for believing in me and taking the time to read earlier drafts of my writing. *If only you could have held this book in your hands ...*

Grazie mille to my grandparents, Annibale and Francesca, for persevering to instil in me a love of our Italian culture and heritage and for passing on to me precious memories and folklore. *Per avere un altro giorno insieme ...*

Heartfelt thanks and appreciation to my agent, Selwa Anthony, for believing in my writing, seeing this story with the same eyes and guiding me through new territory.

A thousand thanks to Karen Penning, Mary Rennie, Susan Morris-Yates and everyone at ABC Books/HarperCollins who contributed their expertise with genuine enthusiasm.

I am grateful to all who in their unique ways contributed their generosity, support or memories enabling me to bring this story together; thank you: Alvaro Corona, Ginetta and Serafino Lazzaro, Katherine Howell, Luigi Calvisi, Soccorsa 'Nancy' Ambrosini, Vincenzo Solano, Elia Boccabella, Maddalena Cullis, Lina Boccabella, Megan Grenenger, Maria

Pia Girardi, Gladys Rose, Ian Bonaccorso, Carlo Urbani, Maria Luisa Battistini, Frances Mayes and the people of Fossa, Poggio Picenze and L'Aquila (some of whose names have been changed when they appear in this book).

Thank you to the University of Queensland for recognising my research in diasporic writing with a Graduate School Research Travel Award (GSRTA), which partially funded a study trip to Italy.

I acknowledge Estella Canziani (1887–1964), artist, writer and folklorist, whose voice through her books told me of a time in the Abruzzo there is now no one alive to remember.

And … of course, deepest *grazie mille* to Roger. *Tu sei il mio equilibrio.* I couldn't ask for a better husband and best friend … *we two are to ourselves a crowd — Ovid.*